examples and applications

The empirical and applied approach to teaching and learning in Goolsbee, Levitt, and Syverson's *Microeconomics* is shown in this listing of features.

microeconomics

Austan Goolsbee
The University of Chicago Booth School of Business

Steven Levitt
The University of Chicago

Chad Syverson
The University of Chicago Booth School of Business

Worth Publishers

Senior Vice President, Editorial and Production: Catherine Woods
Publisher: Charles Linsmeier
Senior Acquisitions Editor: Sarah Dorger
Media and Supplements Editors: Jaclyn Ferry, Lukia Kliossis
Developmental Editors: Jane Tufts, Bruce Kaplan
Consulting Faculty Editor: Linda Ghent
Assistant Editor: Mary Melis
Executive Marketing Manager: Scott Guile
Marketing Assistant: Julie Tompkins
Director of Market Research and Development: Steven Rigolosi
Assistant Market Development Manager: Kerri Russini
Art Director: Babs Reingold
Senior Designer: Kevin Kall
Cover Designer, Interior Designer: Amanda Kavanagh
Photo Editor: Ted Szczepanski
Director of Development for Print and Digital Products: Tracey Kuehn
Associate Managing Editor: Lisa Kinne
Project Editor: Robert Errera
Production Manager: Barbara Seixas
Composition: TSI Graphics
Printing and Binding: RR Donnelley

ISBN-13: 978-1-4641-0688-0
ISBN-10: 1-4641-0688-6

Printed in the United States of America

First printing 2012

Worth Publishers
41 Madison Avenue
New York, NY 10010
www.worthpublishers.com

about the authors

This breakthrough text revitalizes the intermediate microeconomics course by focusing on the tools people need to make better decisions in business and in their lives. The authors make the core concepts underlying the field real and relevant, answering the question, "How could you actually use this for something?" with the latest empirical work and memorable, meaningful examples.

The Authors

Austan Goolsbee is the Robert P. Gwinn Professor of Economics at the University of Chicago Booth School of Business. He earned a bachelor's and a master's degree from Yale University and a PhD in economics from the Massachusetts Institute of Technology. Goolsbee's work focuses on the new economy, government policy, taxes, and technology. He was appointed chairman of the Council of Economic Advisers in 2010, returning to the University of Chicago in August 2011. Goolsbee serves as a member of the U.S. Census Advisory Committee and as a research fellow for the American Bar Foundation.

Steven Levitt is the William B. Ogden Distinguished Service Professor of Economics at the University of Chicago, where he directs the Becker Center on Chicago Price Theory. He earned a bachelor's degree from Harvard University and his PhD from Massachusetts Institute of Technology. He has taught at the University of Chicago since 1997. In 2004, Levitt was awarded the John Bates Clark Medal, and in 2006, he was named one of *Time* magazine's "100 People Who Shape Our World." He co-authored *Freakonomics* and *SuperFreakonomics*, and he is also the co-author of the popular *Freakonomics* blog.

Chad Syverson is Professor of Economics at the University of Chicago Booth School of Business. His research spans several topics, with a particular focus on the interactions of firm structure, market structure, and productivity. His work has earned multiple National Science Foundation awards. He serves on the editorial boards of several economics and business journals and is a research associate of the National Bureau of Economic Research. He earned bachelor's degrees in economics and mechanical engineering from the University of North Dakota and a PhD in economics from the University of Maryland. Syverson joined the Chicago faculty in 2001.

brief contents

This volume contains chapters 2–5 only of _Microeconomics_ by Goolsbee, Levitt, and Syverson.

contents

contents

contents

contents

contents

Using *Microeconomics*

Intermediate microeconomics is the course that decides majors and introduces the tools that are fundamental to effective decision making in business, government, and everyday life. *Microeconomics* bridges the gap between the theory and practice of microeconomics. In a course that is too often overwhelmingly theoretical, *Microeconomics* provides an empirical dimension that will make the course immediately relevant and useful to students. *Microeconomics* provides examples that offer unusual perspective on the seemingly ordinary. With carefully crafted features, the text moves students from understanding the basics of economic principles to applying the powerful and revelatory tools of economic analysis. See below and the pages following for examples of these features, as well as readers' reactions to them.

theory and data

Theory and Data discussions summarize research and provide an empirical dimension, reveal how economic theory relates to real-world data.

Golfers' Backward-Bending Labor Supply Curves

Tiger Woods is perhaps the most recognizable face in professional golf. He's won 71 PGA tour events and picked up 14 Majors. He's lent his name to campaigns for Nike and Titleist—and taken home a cool $40 million and $20 million, respectively, for the work. But it's not just his athletic skill that separates him from the average American laborer: He's probably one of the few people facing wages on the backward-bending portion of his labor supply curve. In other words, as his wages increase, he actually decreases the number of tournaments in which he plays.

PGA rules allow each golfer to elect which and how many events to play in, meaning the athlete considers the labor–leisure tradeoff separately for each tournament event. With tournament payoffs in the millions of dollars for just four rounds of golf, you probably think it a no-brainer to play. Indeed, for most golfers, it is. Generally, around 100 players sign up for any given event. This doesn't even include the over 1,000 hopefuls who play in brutal qualifying rounds, vying for just 25 spots on the PGA Tour.

Given the opportunity, these hopefuls would gladly play every tournament, but as economists Otis Gilley and Marc Chopin discovered, players like Tiger Woods don't.* In a 2000 paper, Gilley and Chopin looked at how low- and middle-income PGA players in the 1990s responded to increases in their wages and compared this result to the effects of wage increases on high-income players. Whereas low-level players entered more events as their event winnings increased, golfers at the top of their game decreased their tournament play as their wages increased. Top golfers were actually operating on the backward-bending portion of their labor supply curve! In particular, for every $1,000 increase in expected per-event winnings, the number of tournaments entered in a season by high-income players decreases by 0.05 to 0.1. For these select players, the income effect dominated the substitution effect, and faced with the leisure–labor tradeoff, they elected to consume more leisure.

Workers in other fields—including many economists—often spend their leisure time on the golf course. But for a professional golfer, a day on the green is work, not leisure. So just what does a PGA player do on his day off? Gilley and Chopin found that married golfers took more days off than did single golfers. Drawing on their own experiences as family men, the two hard-working economists concluded that golfers must be taking off work to spend more quality time with their wives and kids. The example of Tiger Woods, however, shows that the predictions of economic theory don't always hold up in the real world.

* Otis W. Gilley and Marc C. Chopin, "Professional Golf: Labor or Leisure." *Managerial Finance* 26, no. 7 (2000): 33–45.

> "Students often complain about the abstractness of course material. Theory and Data examples will convince students of the relevance of the subject matter and show students how theory translates into the real world."
>
> —*Marie Rekkas, Simon Fraser University*

> "[T]he authors have done an exceptional job in general of finding current and interesting research related to the topics discussed in the chapters."
>
> —*Paul Hettler, California University of Pennsylvania*

(see page 5-28)

Goolsbee Levitt Syverson

application

The cost of the black-liquor loophole

A recent example of an (accidental) subsidy gone awry is the so-called black-liquor loophole in the law that gave companies tax credits for using alternative fuels. The tax credit is given to businesses that combine alternative fuels with traditional fossil fuels used in their operations, with the idea of encouraging companies to reduce their fossil fuel use in doing so.

It turns out that there is a chemical by-product of paper making called "black liquor" that paper companies have traditionally recycled to use as fuel in their plants. The government determined that this chemical qualified as an alternative fuel under the definition in the law. However, the paper companies couldn't qualify for the tax credit unless they *combined* the alternative fuel with a fossil fuel. So they started adding a bit of diesel fuel—a fossil fuel they weren't using at all before—to the black liquor before burning it. This led to two results. First, paper companies used more diesel than they did before, even though the point of the tax credit was to encourage movement away from use of fossil fuels. Second, paper companies got paid (in the form of tax credits) to burn the black liquor they were already using without payment. They got paid a lot too: This tax credit, originally projected to cost the government $61 million, ended up costing an estimated $6 to $8 *billion* in tax credits in 2009, almost all of it going to paper companies.

How does our analysis in this section explain what happened? The tax credit became, in practice, a diesel subsidy for the paper industry. By tying the credit to the use of blended fuels, it lowered the effective price of diesel that the paper companies faced. Before, when they had to pay the market price, their quantity demanded for diesel to fuel their plants was zero—they had a plentiful and cheap alternative in the black liquor. But now every gallon of diesel they bought came with a big tax credit attached—meaning they faced a downward-shifted supply curve for diesel. The quantity of diesel they demanded at these lower supply prices became positive.

As a result of this policy, the paper companies and the diesel sellers are better off because of the subsidy. (The former very much so in this case.) But the costs are large. First, there is deadweight loss: An industry that wasn't using diesel before because it had a superior alternative now demands it, even though the industry values it at less than the cost of supplying it. Second, the government has to pay the subsidy. And as noted above, that's a really big number. So big, in fact, that Congress closed the loophole in 2010 because they decided that we couldn't afford it. ∎

(see page 3-44)

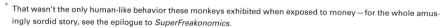

freakonomics

Even Animals Like Sales

If you think the laws of economics only apply to humans, think again. Monkeys, and even rats, behave in ways that would make you think they've taken intermediate micro.

Some of the most intensive testing of the economic behavior of animals was carried out by Yale economist Keith Chen and his co-authors on a group of Capuchin monkeys. As a first step, Chen introduced the monkeys to the concept of money. He gave them "money" in the form of metal washers that they could exchange for various types of foods including Jell-O, grapes, and Marshmallow Fluff (Capuchin monkeys *love* sweet foods).

Just Like Us?

Courtesy M. Keith Chen

After about six exasperating months, these monkeys finally figured out that the washers had value. Chen observed that individual monkeys tended to have stable preferences: Some liked grapes the best, others were fans of Jell-O. How did he learn this? He would give a particular monkey a coin and then offer that monkey a choice between a bowl of three Jell-O cubes and a bowl of six grapes and see which one the monkey chose.

Next, Chen did what any good economist would do: He subjected the monkeys to price changes! Instead of getting three Jell-O cubes for one washer, he would offer the monkey, say, the choice between a single Jell-O cube per washer and a bowl of six grapes per washer. Thus, the relative price of Jell-O became three times as high. The monkeys responded exactly the way economic theory would predict, shifting their consumption away from the goods whose prices had risen.[*]

Perhaps it is not that surprising that monkeys, one of our closest relatives in the animal kingdom, would be sophisticated consumers. But there is no way rats understand supply and demand, is there? It seems they do. Economists Raymond Battalio and John Kagel equipped rats' cages with two levers, each of which dispensed a different beverage.[†] One of these levers gave the rat a refreshing burst of root beer. Rats, it turns out, love root beer. The other lever released quinine water. Quinine is a bitter-tasting substance initially used to treat malaria, and now used primarily to give vodka tonics their distinctive flavor. Rats are far less fond of quinine than they are of root beer, and they made that quite clear to the researchers by pressing the root beer lever far more often. Battalio and Kagel, like Chen, then explored changes in "prices" (how much liquid came out per press of the lever) and in the rats' budget constraint (how many times they could press the levers each day). Like monkeys (and humans), the rats consumed less of a drink when its relative price increased. Even more interesting is that when the rats were made very poor (i.e., they got very few lever presses each day), they shifted their consumption away from root beer toward quinine water. The researchers found that root beer is a luxury good for rats, and quinine water is an inferior good! Wonder what rats would make of a vodka tonic. . . .

[*] That wasn't the only human-like behavior these monkeys exhibited when exposed to money—for the whole amusingly sordid story, see the epilogue to *SuperFreakonomics*.

[†] A description of the work by Battalio and Kagel may be found in: Tim Harford, *The Logic of Life: The Rational Economics of an Irrational World* (New York: Random House, 2008), pp. 18–21.

> "I find these [Freakonomics essays] very useful as they illustrate the universality of the tools of economic analysis. They show students that the tools and skills they acquire in economic courses are not confined to the area of economics only, but can be applied to many other situations and areas."
>
> —*Tibor Besedes,*
> *Georgia Institute of Technology*

(see page 5-14)

Figure It Out exercises walk through the process of applying economic tools and analysis to explore a problem and develop solutions. Figure It Out exercises provide a model for the end-of-chapter exercises often assigned by instructors.

2.1 figure it out

Suppose that the demand and supply curves for a monthly cell phone plan with unlimited texts can be represented by

$$Q^D = 50 - 0.5P$$
$$Q^S = -25 + P$$

The current price of these plans in the market is $40 per month. Is this market in equilibrium? Would you expect the price to rise or fall? If so, by how much? Explain.

Solution:

There are two ways to solve the first question about whether the price will rise or fall. The first is to calculate the quantity demanded and quantity supplied at the current market price of $40 to see how they compare:

$$Q^D = 50 - 0.5P = 50 - 0.5(40) = 50 - 20 = 30$$
$$Q^S = -25 + P = -25 + 40 = 15$$

Because quantity demanded is greater than quantity supplied, we can tell that there is excess demand (a shortage) in the market. Many people are trying to get texting plans, but are finding them sold out because few suppliers want to sell at that price. Prices will rise to equalize quantity supplied and quantity demanded, moving the market to equilibrium.

Alternatively, we could start by solving for the market equilibrium price:

$$Q^D = Q^S$$
$$50 - 0.5P = -25 + P$$
$$1.5P = 75$$
$$P = \$50$$

The current market price, $40, is below the market equilibrium price of $50. (This is why there is excess demand in the market.) Therefore, we would expect the price to rise by $10. When the market reaches equilibrium at a price of $50, all buyers can find sellers and all sellers can find buyers. The price will then remain at $50 unless the market changes and the demand curve or supply curve shifts.

(see page 2-17)

"This feature is extremely important in my opinion. I would definitely use it in class and assign similar problems for homework."
—Nara Mijid,
Central Connecticut State University

"Love the Figure It Out! I think that this is a great addition to the text. The problems are also not so easy that the students [wouldn't] need help on them."
—Jennifer VanGilder,
Ursinus University

Make the Grade points out possible pitfalls students may encounter as they develop as economic practitioners and helps them negotiate the finer points of micro theory.

make the grade

Does quantity supplied equal quantity demanded in equilibrium?

Solving for the market equilibrium as we just did is one of the most common exam questions in intermediate microeconomics classes. The basic idea is always the same: Take the equations for the demand curve and the supply curve, solve for the equilibrium price, and then plug that equilibrium price back into either the supply curve or the demand curve (it does not matter which) to determine the equilibrium quantity. It is simple, but it is easy to make math errors under the time pressure of an exam, especially if the demand and supply curves take on more complicated forms than the basic examples we deal with here.

A simple trick will ensure that you have the right answer, and it only takes a few seconds. Take the equilibrium price that you obtain and plug it into both the demand and supply curves. If you don't get the same answer when you substitute the equilibrium price into the supply and demand equations, you know you made a math error along the way because the quantity demanded must equal the quantity supplied in equilibrium.

(see page 2-15)

Supply and Demand

The pursuit of gold has driven people to extremes for centuries. Much of the initial exploration of the Americas was funded with the hope of acquiring gold. Centuries later, the discovery of gold at Sutter's Mill in Coloma, California, in 1848 triggered a gold rush that led 300,000 men, women, and children to migrate to California, turning San Francisco from a sleepy hamlet to a thriving city.

In recent years, the search for gold has taken on a decidedly modern flavor. It might surprise you to know that as many as 400,000 Chinese workers currently spend their days mining for gold. But they aren't panning for gold in a stream or working in a gold mine. Rather, they are seated in front of computer screens, logged onto online games like *World of Warcraft,* using virtual picks and axes to mine virtual gold that they sell on eBay to players willing to pay real money for the virtual gold that serves as the game's currency.

Whether the gold is real or virtual, the economic forces at work that determine its price and how much of it is "mined" are the same. In this chapter, we explore these forces, the two most powerful forces in economics: supply and demand.

Armed with an understanding of supply and demand, we can begin to tackle some of the fundamental questions in economics: How do consumers and producers interact in the market for a good or service to determine how much is sold and at what price? What happens to the market if tastes change, new technologies are invented, the government intervenes, or any one of a wide range of other forces changes?

This chapter outlines the basics of the supply and demand model. We first introduce the concept of the demand curve, which embodies consumers' desires for goods, and then move on to the supply curve, which embodies producers' willingness to make those goods available. We explain why these concepts are so useful in describing and analyzing markets, especially when we combine them to understand the concept of market equilibrium. We then analyze how equilibrium prices and quantities are influenced by the variety of forces that affect markets: consumer tastes, input prices, overall economic activity, new goods that can be substituted for an existing good, innovations that make a product easier to produce, and so on. Finally, we dig deeper and look at how quantities demanded and supplied respond to price changes, and discuss how this responsiveness affects market equilibrium.

2.1 Markets and Models

Modern economies are amazingly complex. Producers from all over the world offer a nearly unlimited number and variety of goods and services from which consumers can choose. A large supermarket will have more than 100 different kinds of cold cereal on the shelf. There are thousands of degree-granting colleges and universities. On any given day, millions of items are on sale on Amazon or eBay. With over 6 billion people in the world, each of them with different tastes and incomes, and 10s of millions of businesses that supply goods and services to these people, how do consumers decide what products, and how much of each, to buy? And how do producers know what products to produce? And who decides at what price the products sell?

Answering these questions might seem like a hopelessly complex task. Indeed, if we tried to tackle them all at once, it *would* be hopeless. Instead, we follow the economist's standard approach to complexity: Simplify the problem until it becomes manageable.

The supply and demand model represents the economist's best attempt to capture many of the key elements of real-world markets in a simple enough way to be easily analyzed. We start exploring that model by first defining what we mean by a market, and then discussing the model's most important assumptions. As you will see, the simplifying assumptions underlying the model are fairly strong. While actual markets don't often conform to all of these assumptions, the supply and demand model has proven to be remarkably useful for thinking about how an economy functions. We'll see the broad usefulness of the supply and demand model once we assemble it and put it to work.

What Is a Market?

The idea of a market is central to economics. What do we mean when we use the term "market"? In the strictest sense, a market is defined by the specific product being bought and sold (e.g., oranges or gold), a particular location (a mall, a city, or maybe the Internet), and a point in time (January 2012, maybe, or even 8:13 P.M. on January 4, 2012). In principle, the buyers in a market should be able to find the sellers in that market, and vice versa, although it might take some work (what economists call "search costs") to make that connection.

In practice, the kinds of markets we talk about tend to be much more broadly defined than these examples. They might be broader in terms of the product (e.g., fruit or groceries rather than oranges), the location (often we consider all of North America or even the world as the geographic market), or the time period (the year 2012 rather than a specific day). These broader markets often have more general interest and more data to analyze, but as we will see, defining markets this broadly makes the assumptions of the supply and demand model less likely to hold. Thus, we face a tradeoff between studying small, less consequential markets that closely match the underlying assumptions and broader, more important markets that do not match our assumptions well.

Now that we have defined a market, we are ready to tackle the key assumptions underlying the supply and demand model.

Key Assumptions of the Supply and Demand Model

There are four basic assumptions that underpin our development of the supply and demand model. Table 2.1 summarizes these assumptions. You will notice that the assumptions of the supply and demand model are in many cases very unrealistic, and few of the markets you participate in satisfy all these assumptions. It turns out, however, that a strength of this model is that when some (or even most) of the specific assumptions of the model fail, it still manages to provide a good description of how markets work in the real world. No model is perfect, but the supply and demand model has survived the test of time and is the workhorse of economics because of its flexibility and broad applicability. Developing a deep understanding of the basic supply and demand model is one of the most important tools you can have as an economist, even if the model does not perfectly fit every market. Plus, economics isn't completely wedded to the most stringent form of the model. Much of the rest of this book, and the field of economics more generally, are devoted to examining how changing the model's assumptions influences its predictions about market outcomes.

supply
The combined amount of a good that all producers in a market are willing to sell.

demand
The combined amount of a good that all consumers are willing to buy.

1. **We restrict our focus to supply and demand in a single market.** The first simplifying assumption we make is that rather than trying to tackle all markets at once, we look at how **supply** (the combined amount of a good that all producers in a market are willing to sell) and **demand** (the combined amount of a good that all consumers are willing to buy) interact in just one market to determine how much of a good or service is sold and at what price it is sold. In focusing on one market, we won't ignore other markets completely—indeed, the interaction between the markets for different kinds of products is fundamental to supply and demand. (We'll focus extensively on these interactions in Chapter 14.) For now, however, we only worry about other

Table 2.1	**The Four Key Assumptions Underlying the Supply and Demand Model**
1.	We focus on supply and demand in a single market.
2.	All goods sold in the market are identical.
3.	All goods sold in the market sell for the same price, and everyone has the same information.
4.	There are many producers and consumers in the market.

markets to the extent that they influence the market we're studying. In particular, we ignore the possibility that changes in the market we're studying might have spillover effects on other markets.

2. **All goods bought and sold in the market are identical.** We assume that all the goods bought and sold in the market are homogeneous, meaning that a consumer is just as happy with any one unit of the good (e.g., an ounce of gold or a tomato) as any other unit.[1] If we use the supply and demand model to analyze the market for "cars," it is only really a crude approximation to automobile markets in the real world. There are many different types of cars in reality, and consumers do not view them as identical. Most consumers would not be as happy with a Kia as they would be with a Ferrari sold at the same price. In the strictest sense, cars of the same make and model might not even be considered a single market. For instance, if a consumer wants only a silver Toyota Prius, then the market relevant to her is the market for silver Toyota Prii. To simplify our analyses, we often ignore such detail and treat groups of goods as though they were identical.

commodities
Products traded in markets in which consumers view different varieties of the good as essentially interchangeable.

The kinds of products that best reflect this assumption are **commodities,** which are traded in markets where consumers view different varieties of the good as essentially interchangeable. Goods such as wheat, soybeans, crude oil, nails, gold, or #2 pencils are commodities. Custom-made jewelry, the different offerings on a restaurant's menu, and wedding dresses are unlikely to be commodities; the consumer typically cares a lot about specific varieties of these goods.

3. **All goods sold in the market sell for the same price and everyone has the same information about prices, the quality of the goods being sold, and so on.** This assumption is a natural extension of the identical-goods assumption above, but it also implies that there are no special deals for particular buyers and no quantity discounts. In addition, everyone knows what everyone else is paying.

4. **There are many buyers and sellers in the market.** This assumption means that no particular consumer or producer has a noticeable impact on anything that occurs in the market and on the price level in particular. This assumption tends to be more easily justified for consumers than for producers. Think about your own consumption of bananas, for instance. If you were to stop eating bananas altogether, your decision would have almost no impact on the banana market as a whole. Likewise, if you thought you were potassium-deprived and increased your banana consumption fourfold, your effect on the market quantity and price of bananas would still be negligible. On the producer side, however, most bananas (and many other products) are produced by a few big companies. It is more likely that decisions by these firms about how much to produce or what markets to enter will substantially affect market prices and quantities. We're going to ignore that possibility for now and stick with the case of many sellers. Starting in Chapter 9, we analyze what happens in markets with one or a few sellers.

Having made these assumptions, let's see how they help us understand how markets work, looking first at demand and then at supply.

---

[1] Throughout this book, we often use the word "good" to mean both tangible goods, like trucks, computers, jewelry, and so on, as well as services, like haircuts, dog walking, financial planning, and so on. In this usage, anything a consumer values—tangible or not, concrete or abstract—is a good.

2.2 Demand

Pike Place Market, one of the best known public markets in the world, spans several blocks in the northwest corner of downtown Seattle. It has operated continually since 1907, and on any given day hosts hundreds of vendors selling everything from fish and meat to produce and flowers to crafts and antiques. The market sees approximately 10 million visitors per year.

Factors That Influence Demand

Tomatoes are a popular item for shoppers at farmers' markets like Pike Place Market. All sorts of factors influence how many tomatoes consumers purchase at the market. Let's discuss the most important.

Price   The price of tomatoes is probably the most important consideration. Few consumers would pay $40 per pound for tomatoes. At $1 a pound, however, there would be many interested customers.

The Number of Consumers   All else equal, the more people there are in a market, the greater the quantity of the good desired. If there are a lot of people visiting the market on a given day, a relatively large amount of tomatoes will be sought for purchase.

Consumer Income or Wealth   As a consumer becomes richer, he will buy more of most goods. Tomatoes (and clothes and cars and jewelry and porterhouse steaks) probably fall in that category for most people. Sometimes, however, when a consumer becomes richer, he buys less of a good. For example, he might buy a car and stop taking public transportation and might stay in nice hotels instead of youth hostels. The consumption of these goods still responds to income or wealth, but in a different direction.

Consumer Tastes   A change in consumer preferences or tastes for tomatoes (given the consumer's income and tomato prices) will change the amount of tomatoes the consumer wants to purchase. Taste changes can be driven by all sorts of forces. For example, news about the health benefits of eating tomatoes would make many consumers want to eat more of them. On the other hand, news about salmonella being found in some tomato crops will make consumers reluctant to purchase them. For other products, taste changes might arise due to a really popular advertising campaign, fads, changes in demographics, and so on.

Prices of Other Goods   Produce vendors at Pike Place Market sell other goods such as onions and peppers that consumers can use to make their salads or top their burgers. Goods that can be used in place of another good are called **substitutes.** When the price of a substitute good falls, consumers will want to buy more of it and less of the initial good. The lower the prices of onions and peppers relative to the price of tomatoes, the fewer tomatoes consumers will want to buy. We can also think of tomatoes in some other market (say, at another location, like a consumer's neighborhood grocery store) as substitutes for tomatoes at Pike Place Market. If grocery store tomatoes become cheaper, shoppers at Pike Place are going to want to buy fewer tomatoes there.

> **substitute**
> A good that can be used in place of another good.

Vendors at Pike Place Market also sell goods that consumers like to use with tomatoes. Goods that are often purchased and used in combination with a certain

complement
A good that is purchased and used in combination with another good.

good are called **complements.** When the price of a complement falls, consumers will want to buy more of it and more of the initial good. There are some goods that people like to consume with tomatoes—basil, for instance, or mozzarella cheese or lettuce. If basil prices fall, consumers are likely to want to buy *more* tomatoes as a result.

The prices of substitutes and complements both affect how much of a good consumers want to buy, but they have opposite effects. A price decrease in a good's substitute will cause consumers to want less of the good; a price decrease in a good's complement will cause consumers to want more of the good.

Demand Curves

In economics, "demand" is a catch-all word that captures the many different factors that influence the willingness of consumers to purchase a good. With so many factors influencing demand, it is difficult to wrap our minds around what would happen if all those various factors changed at the same time. We simplify the problem by considering what happens to the amount consumers demand when only a good's price changes, while everything else that determines consumer demand stays the same. (Later in the chapter, we look at how changes in all the other factors that influence demand affect the quantity of a good consumers demand.)

Graphical Representation of the Demand Curve   The result of this simplifying assumption is a **demand curve.** Figure 2.1 depicts a demand curve for tomatoes at the Pike Place Market. The curve shows how the quantity of tomatoes that consumers want varies with the price of tomatoes. Price is on the vertical axis and quantity demanded is on the horizontal axis. This demand curve shows that when the price of tomatoes is $5 per pound, no tomatoes are desired. At a price of $4 per pound, consumers are willing to buy 200 pounds of tomatoes. At prices of $3, $2, and $1, the quantities of tomatoes demanded rise to 400, 600, and 800 pounds, respectively.

demand curve
The relationship between the quantity of a good that consumers demand and the good's price, holding all other factors constant.

The point about demand curves holding all factors other than price constant is so important that it is worth saying it again: A demand curve is drawn with the as-

---

Figure 2.1   Demand for Tomatoes

The demand curve D_1 for tomatoes at Pike Place Market shows how the quantity of tomatoes demanded varies with the price. As the price of tomatoes decreases, consumers demand greater quantities of tomatoes, creating a downward-sloping demand curve. At a price of $5 per pound, consumers demand no tomatoes; at $4, $3, $2, and $1, consumers are willing to purchase 200, 400, 600, and 800 pounds of tomatoes, respectively.

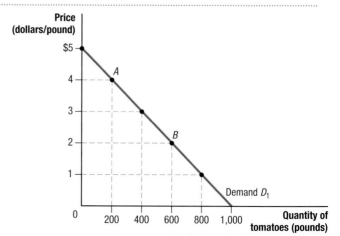

sumption that there is no change in *any* of the other factors—such as consumers' incomes, tastes, or the prices of other goods—that might also affect how much of a good consumers buy. This means the demand curve in Figure 2.1 embodies the results of the following thought experiment (demand curves for other goods reflect similar thought experiments specific to their own contexts). We show up at Pike Place market some weekend and observe both the price of tomatoes and the total amount that consumers buy. Imagine that we have magical powers that allow us to go back in time. We use those powers to replace the price tags on tomatoes at the market, lowering their price by $1 per pound. Then we let the weekend happen all over again—the same weather, the same visitors to the market, the same set of items on display, and so on; the only difference is that tomatoes are $1 per pound cheaper. We then count up the total amount of tomatoes consumers buy at this new price. We continue using our magic powers to keep reversing time over and over, adjusting tomato prices up and down and by a different amount each time. When we connect all of the price and quantity combinations we have collected in this way, we have a demand curve.

The demand curve in Figure 2.1 exhibits a fundamental characteristic of demand curves: They slope downward.[2] This is another way of saying that, all else equal, the lower the price of a good, the more of it consumers will buy.

Mathematical Representation of the Demand Curve   The demand curve in Figure 2.1 can also be represented mathematically by the equation

$$Q = 1{,}000 - 200P$$

where Q is the quantity demanded (in pounds) and P is the price (in dollars per pound). This equation implies that every $1 per pound increase in price leads to a 200-pound decline in the quantity of tomatoes demanded.

Because of the odd condition in economics of plotting price on the vertical axis and quantity on the horizontal axis, and because it is easier to work with in certain contexts, economists often write demand curve equations in the form of the price as a function of quantity. This approach results in an **inverse demand curve.** The inverse demand curve simply rearranges the demand curve to put price in terms of quantity rather than the other way around.

We can find the inverse demand curve by solving for P:

$$Q = 1{,}000 - 200P$$

$$200P + Q = 1{,}000$$

$$200P = 1{,}000 - Q$$

$$P = 5 - 0.005Q$$

One thing this inverse demand curve makes clear is that no consumer will be willing to buy tomatoes at a price greater than $5 per pound, because the vertical intercept of the inverse demand curve (i.e., the price when the quantity demanded Q equals zero) is $5 per pound. This level is also called the **demand choke price.**

> **inverse demand curve**
> A demand curve written in the form of price as a function of quantity demanded.

> **demand choke price**
> The price at which no consumer is willing to buy a good and quantity demanded is zero; the vertical intercept of the inverse demand curve.

---

[2] An interesting but unusual exception to this is a Giffen good, which has an upward-sloping demand curve. We will discuss such goods in Chapter 5. Demand curves for regular (non-Giffen) goods can also sometimes be flat, as we discuss in the next section. We explore the deeper reasoning behind why demand curves usually slope down in Chapters 4 and 5.

Shifts in Demand Curves

A given demand curve such as D_1 in Figure 2.1 illustrates how the quantity demanded of a good changes as its price, and only its price, changes. When one of the other (nonprice) factors that affect demand changes, the change can affect the quantity of tomatoes consumers want to buy at every price. For example, if there is an outbreak of salmonella poisoning, and public health officials believe that tomatoes may be the source of the outbreak, consumers' tastes will change. They will want fewer tomatoes at any given price than they did before and the demand curve will shift down and to the left to D_2, as shown in Figure 2.2. Mathematically, the demand curve D_2 corresponds to $Q = 500 - 200P$.

Similarly, if scientists discover that tomatoes help prevent cancer, consumers who wanted to buy 200 pounds of tomatoes at $4 per pound may now want to buy 300 pounds at $4. Those who wanted to buy 600 pounds at $2 per pound will now want to buy 700 pounds, and so on. Because consumers demand a higher quantity of tomatoes at any given price, the whole demand curve for tomatoes will shift out to the right from D_1 to D_3, illustrated in Figure 2.2. Mathematically, the new demand curve D_3 is described by the equation $Q = 1,100 - 200P$. Note that we are shifting the demand curves in the simplest way—sliding them over with the same slope. In real markets, this doesn't need to be true. The new curve can change steepness too, if demand becomes more or less sensitive to price.

The changes in the quantity demanded at every price that occur when any nonprice factor changes illustrate an essential distinction. When a good's price changes but nothing else does, this change creates a movement *along* a fixed demand curve. Changes in any of the other factors that influence demand create *shifts* in the demand curve. To clarify this distinction, economists distinguish **changes in quantity demanded,** which happen when a change in a good's price creates movement along a given demand curve (e.g., the move from point A to point B in Figure 2.1), from **changes in demand,** which happen when a good's entire demand curve shifts (e.g., the shifts from D_1 to D_2 and D_3 in Figure 2.2).

Quantity demanded is a single number, expressed in units of the good: 400 pounds of tomatoes, 30 cars, or 20 movie downloads, for example. Different

change in quantity demanded
A movement *along* the demand curve that occurs as a result of a change in the good's price.

change in demand
A shift of the entire demand curve caused by a change in a determinant of demand other than the good's own price.

Figure 2.2 Shifts in the Demand Curve

The demand curve D_1 shifts with a change in any nonprice factor that affects demand. If tomatoes are suspected to be a source of salmonella, consumers will demand fewer tomatoes at any given price and the demand for tomatoes will shift inward, from D_1 to D_2. In contrast, if tomatoes are found to have cancer-fighting properties, the demand for tomatoes will shift outward, from D_1 to D_3.

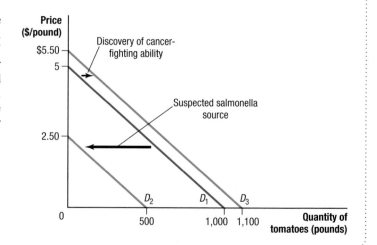

prices imply different quantities demanded; the combination of all such price–quantity combinations is represented by the demand curve. Shifts in consumers' desired quantities caused by changes in any (or all) other factors move this entire combination of prices and quantities demanded—that is, they shift the demand curve.[3]

We motivated the shifts from D_1 to D_2 and D_3 in Figure 2.2 as changes in consumer tastes. But similar pictures occur for a change in any other nonprice factor that affects consumers' quantity demanded. The increase in demand reflected by the shift to D_3 would also occur if beautiful weather leads to higher attendance at the market. Of course, had the weather been cold and rainy, the number of customers at the market would fall, and the demand curve would have shifted inward to, perhaps, D_2.

Why Is Price Treated Differently from the Other Factors That Affect Demand?

Why do prices get special treatment relative to the other determinants of demand? After all, nothing prevents us from putting, say, income on the vertical axis in Figure 2.1 instead of price.

There are at least three reasons why economists focus on the effects of a change in a good's price. First, price is typically one of the most important factors that influence demand. Second, prices can usually be changed frequently and easily. Therefore, when we contemplate how markets respond to changes or "shocks," price fluctuations are likely to be a common response. Third, and most important, of all the factors that influence demand, price is the only one that also exerts a large, direct influence on the other side of the market—on the quantity of the good that producers are willing to supply. Price therefore serves as the critical element that ties together demand and supply. Let's turn to that other side of the market now.

2.3 Supply

We have one half of the demand and supply model assembled. In this section, we present the supply half. By supply we mean the combined amount of a good that all producers in a market are willing to sell.

Factors That Influence Supply

Just as there are many factors that determine demand, so too with supply. Let's discuss these again in the context of our Pike Place Market tomatoes example.

Price   Just as it does with demand, price plays an important role in supply decisions. If farmers expect to be able to sell tomatoes at $40 a pound at Pike Place Market, the market will be loaded with them. The farmers will grow more tomatoes and choose to sell them at Pike Place rather than other outlets. If they expect the price to be only $1 per pound, there will be a much smaller quantity available for sale.

---

[3] Economists often draw demand curves as straight lines, and we do so as well throughout much of this book. This is really just for convenience. As their name suggests, demand curves in reality can be, and probably quite often are, *curves*. Also, when we use the word "shift," this includes not only parallel shifts of the demand curve as shown in Figure 2.2, but also rotations (which change the steepness or slope of a demand curve). We'll later discuss in further detail what economic forces affect the slopes of demand curves.

theory and data

Changes in Taste and the Demand for Cigarettes

If you were a cigarette company executive in 1960, you had to feel optimistic. Between 1940 and 1957, the share of Americans over the age of 25 who smoked had risen from 38% to 46%. Affluent people were more likely to smoke than the poor, so with people getting richer over time, the demand for cigarettes was likely to skyrocket.

But, things didn't turn out as the executives planned. Today, only about 20% of the adult population smokes. Moreover, among those who currently do smoke, the number of cigarettes smoked per day is smaller than it was for the average smoker 50 years ago.

Why has the demand for cigarettes shrunk so much? One factor that no doubt has contributed to the decline is a rising price. In 1960 a pack of cigarettes cost around 30 cents. Adjusting for inflation, that's equivalent to $2.20 in 2010 dollars. But the average price for a pack of cigarettes today is $4.80, more than twice as high. Much of that price increase is the result of heavy taxation—taxes that now account for more than half of the price of cigarettes. Price changes are unlikely to be the whole story, however. Based on economists' measurements of smokers' sensitivity to price changes, a price increase of this size only explains about half of the drop in quantity demanded. Looking at changes in who smokes further reinforces the idea that price increases are not the whole story: Currently, fewer than 15% of Americans with college degrees smoke, compared to more than 25% of people with less education. That is the reverse of the pattern in the 1950s. In general, we expect high-income people to be *less* sensitive to price changes than the poor, so it is unlikely that rising prices would lead cigarette consumption to shift sharply toward those with low education. Clearly, something else happened.

One major "something" was the realization on the part of consumers that smoking is dangerous. The 1964 Surgeon General's Report, considered one of the top news stories that year, broadly disseminated information on the link between lung cancer and cigarette smoking that had been steadily growing in the academic community. In 1970 the addition of the ubiquitous Surgeon General's Warning to all cigarette packages sold in the United States furthered the spread of this information. Knowledge of the health risks associated with smoking led the demand curve for cigarettes to shift inward. What does it mean for a demand curve to shift inward? It means that *holding price constant,* the quantity demanded is lower.

Prevalence of Smoking by Education Category in the United States, Age 25 and Older, 1940–2000

Prior to the mid-1960s, smoking prevalence was high across all educational groups, ranging from approximately 40 to 45% of the population. After the Surgeon General's Warning in 1964, the percentage of smokers declined more among the highly educated than among those with a high school education or below. In 2000 approximately 30% of people with a high school education or below smoked, while only around 15% of people with more than a college degree were smokers.

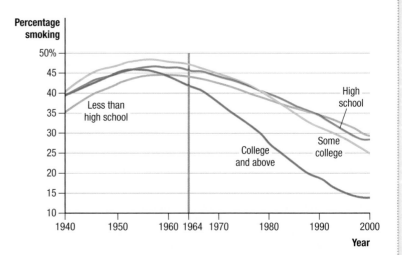

Thus, the observed decline in demand for cigarettes reflects both movements along the demand curve (the rising price) and shifts in the demand curve (awareness that smoking is dangerous), as shown in the figure. Economist Damien de Walque studied whether these types of shifts in the demand curve are also related to the fact that the highly educated smoked more in the 1950s, but smoke much less today.[*] There is a growing body of evidence suggesting that more education pays off not just in the labor market, but in many other activities as well. (The benefits are especially great when you study economics—well, at least that's what economists will tell you.) People with more education have better access to information and are better prepared to properly interpret the information they receive, so it makes sense that the highly educated would react more to information about the risks of smoking than would the less educated. That is exactly what de Walque found in his study.

[*] Damien de Walque, "Education, Information, and Smoking Decisions: Evidence from Smoking Histories in the United States, 1940–2000," *Journal of Human Resources* 45, no. 3 (2010): 682–717.

Suppliers' Costs of Production   Suppliers' production costs will change when input prices and production technology change. There are many inputs a supplier must use to produce tomatoes and bring them to market, including land, tomato seeds, fertilizer, harvesting equipment, booth rental prices at markets like Pike Place, and the gasoline needed to ship tomatoes to markets, to name just a few. If the prices of these inputs change, the suppliers' costs will change and will influence the quantity of tomatoes supplied to the market.

Similarly, changes in **production technology,** the processes used to make, distribute, and sell a good such as tomatoes, will change the costs of production. The more efficient these processes are, the lower the costs to sellers of providing tomatoes for sale. Lower costs will raise sellers' willingness to supply tomatoes.

production technology
The processes used to make, distribute, and sell a good.

The Number of Sellers   More farmers bringing tomatoes to Pike Place will raise the available supply.

Sellers' Outside Options   Farmers who are busy selling tomatoes at Pike Place Market aren't selling some other product or selling tomatoes at some other place. A change in farmers' prospects for doing business in markets for other goods or in other markets for tomatoes can affect their willingness to supply tomatoes at Pike Place Market. These prospects depend on factors such as the prices of other goods the farmers might be growing and selling (radishes, peppers, or green beans) or tomato prices at markets other than Pike Place.

Supply Curves

Just as we introduced demand curves as a way to think in a more focused way about demand, we can do the same thing for supply. Supply curves, like demand curves, capture the idea that factors that influence supply can be divided into two sets: price and everything else. Supply curves isolate the relationship between price and quantity supplied.

Graphical Representation of the Supply Curve   Figure 2.3 depicts a supply curve for tomatoes at the Pike Place Market. The vertical axis reflects the price of the good, and the horizontal axis is the quantity supplied. The curve indicates that, for

---

Figure 2.3 : Supply of Tomatoes

The supply curve S_1 for tomatoes at Pike Place Market shows how the quantity of tomatoes supplied varies with the price. As the price of tomatoes increases, producers supply greater quantities of tomatoes, creating an upward-sloping supply curve. At a price of $1 per pound, producers supply no tomatoes; at $2, $3, $4, and $5, respectively, producers supply 200, 400, 600, and 800 pounds of tomatoes.

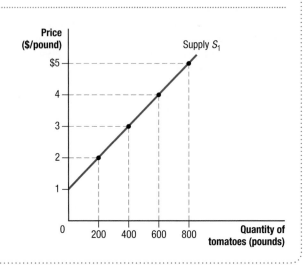

---

example, if the price of tomatoes is $2 per pound, 200 pounds of tomatoes will be offered for sale. If the price is $5 per pound, the quantity supplied will be 800 pounds.

The **supply curve** in the figure slopes upward: Holding everything else equal, producers are willing to supply more of a good as price rises.[4] The simple intuition behind the upward slope of most supply curves is that, given their costs of production and other nonprice factors, firms want to supply a greater quantity to the market when prices are high. For example, many firms experience increasing costs of production as their output rises. When this is the case, they need to earn a higher price in the market in order to induce them to produce more output.

Mathematical Representation of the Supply Curve   The supply curve in Figure 2.3 is expressed mathematically as

$$Q = 200P - 200$$

where Q is the quantity supplied (in pounds of tomatoes) and P is the price in dollars per pound. This indicates that holding everything else constant, for every dollar increase in price, the quantity supplied of tomatoes increases by 200 pounds.

Just as it is common to write demand curves as inverse demand curves (price as a function of quantity demanded), economists often use **inverse supply curves** as well:

$$Q = 200P - 200$$
$$200P = Q + 200$$
$$P = 0.005Q + 1$$

The inverse supply curve makes clear that no firm will be willing to supply tomatoes at a price of $1 per pound (or less), because the vertical intercept of the supply is $1 per pound (i.e., the price at which the quantity supplied Q equals zero). This is often called the **supply choke price.**

supply curve
The relationship between the quantity supplied of a good and the good's price, holding all other factors constant.

inverse supply curve
A supply curve written in the form of price as a function of quantity supplied.

supply choke price
The price at which no firm is willing to produce a good and quantity supplied is zero; the vertical intercept of the inverse supply curve.

---

[4] We typically expect that supply curves slope upward, although in some cases (especially in the long run), they may be horizontal, and in others they might be perfectly vertical. We will discuss these special cases later.

Shifts in the Supply Curve

A given supply curve such as S_1 in Figure 2.3 illustrates how the quantity supplied of a good changes as its price, and only its price, changes.

When one of the other (nonprice) factors that affect supply changes, the change affects the quantity of tomatoes that suppliers want to sell at every price. For example, if someone invents a machine that can harvest tomatoes faster and at lower cost, producers who wanted to produce 600 pounds of tomatoes at $4 per pound will now be willing to supply 800 pounds of tomatoes at $4. Those who were willing to supply 200 pounds at $2 will now be willing to supply 400 at $2, and so on. Because producers supply more tomatoes at every price, the whole supply curve will shift out to the right from S_1 to S_2, as shown in Figure 2.4. The way we've drawn it, that additional quantity is the 200 pounds at any price, though there's nothing that says all supply shifts must exhibit this pattern.[5] Mathematically, the supply curve S_2 is described by the equation $Q = 200P$.

Similarly, if there is a drought, it will cost producers more to irrigate their fields. They will want to supply fewer tomatoes at any given price than they did before and the supply will shift up and to the left, to S_3. Mathematically, the supply curve S_3 corresponds to $Q = 200P - 600$.

Analogous to demand curves, the changes in a good's price when everything else stays constant lead to **changes in quantity supplied,** movements *along* a supply curve. Changes in any other factors that influence supply change the quantity supplied at any given price and create *shifts* in the supply, which is called a **change in supply.**

Quantity supplied is a single number, such as 600 pounds of tomatoes, 100 iPads, or 40 haircuts, and different prices imply different quantities supplied. Supply curves show all possible price–quantity combinations producers would supply. Changes in any (or all) other factors move the entire combination of prices and quantities supplied—that is, they shift the supply curve.

change in quantity supplied
A movement *along* the supply curve that occurs as a result of a change in the good's price.

change in supply
A shift of the entire supply curve caused by a change in a determinant of supply other than the good's own price.

Figure 2.4   Shifts in the Supply Curve

The supply curve S_1 shifts when any nonprice factor that affects supply changes. If a faster harvesting method is developed, the supply of tomatoes will shift outward, from S_1 to S_2. In contrast, if there is a drought, the supply of tomatoes will shift inward, from S_1 to S_3.

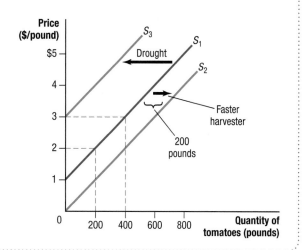

---

[5] Note that, just like demand curves, there's no requirement that supply curves be linear. We just draw them as such for simplicity.

Why Is Price Also Treated Differently for Supply?

Supply curves isolate the effect of prices on supply just as demand curves isolate price effects on demand. We mentioned one of the big reasons for this focus on price in the demand curve is that price is the only factor that has a direct influence on both demand and supply. Price is the critical element that ties together the two sides of a market. Price's roles in both the demand and supply sides of a market mean that prices can adjust freely to make the quantity demanded by consumers equal to the quantity supplied by producers. When this happens, we have a market in which everyone who wants to buy at the current price can do so, and everyone who wants to sell at the current market price can do so as well.

As we see in the next section, we can also use the supply and demand model to predict how changes in nonprice factors affect market outcomes. To get to the point where we *can* do that, however, we need to identify an initial market price and quantity sold. Treating price as special allows us to do that.

2.4 Market Equilibrium

The true power of the demand and supply model emerges when we combine demand and supply curves. Both relate quantities and prices, so we can draw them on the same graph, with price on the vertical axis and quantity on the horizontal axis. Figure 2.5 overlays the original demand and supply curves for tomatoes at Seattle's Pike Place Market. As a reminder, expressed as equations, the demand curve is $Q = 1{,}000 - 200P$ (with an equivalent inverse demand curve $P = 5 - 0.005Q$), and the supply curve is $Q = 200P - 200$ (with an inverse supply curve of $P = 1 + 0.005Q$).

market equilibrium
The point at which the quantity demanded by consumers exactly equals the quantity supplied by producers.

equilibrium price
The only price at which quantity supplied equals quantity demanded.

The point where the supply and demand curves cross is the **market equilibrium.** The equilibrium is labeled as point E on Figure 2.5, and the price and quantity associated with this point are labeled P_e and Q_e. The **equilibrium price** P_e is the *only* price at which quantity supplied equals quantity demanded.

The Mathematics of Equilibrium

So what is the market equilibrium for our Pike Place tomatoes example? We can read off Figure 2.5 that the equilibrium price P_e is $3 per pound, and the equilibrium quantity Q_e is 400 pounds. But we can also determine these mathematically by using the equations for the demand and supply curves. Quantity demanded is given by $Q^D = 1{,}000 - 100P$ (we've added the superscript "D" to quantity just to remind us that equation is the demand curve), and quantity supplied is $Q^S = 200P - 200$ (again, we've added a superscript). We know that at market equilibrium, quantity demanded equals quantity supplied; that is, $Q_e = Q^D = Q^S$. Using the equations above, we have

$$Q^D = Q^S$$

$$1{,}000 - 200P = 200P - 200$$

$$1{,}200 = 400P$$

$$P_e = 3$$

At a price P of $3 per pound, quantity demanded Q^D equals quantity supplied Q^S, and so the equilibrium price P_e is $3, as we see in Figure 2.5. To find the equilibrium quantity Q_e, we plug this value of P_e back into the equation for *either* the demand

Figure 2.5 ┊ Market Equilibrium

The intersection of the supply curve S_1 and the demand curve D_1 at point E represents the market equilibrium. The equilibrium price and quantity of tomatoes are $3 per pound and 400 pounds, respectively.

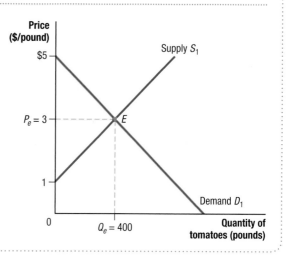

or supply curve, because both quantity demanded and supplied will be the same at the equilibrium price:

$$Q_e = 1{,}000 - 200P_e = 1{,}000 - 200(3) = 1{,}000 - 600 = 400$$

We just solved for the equilibrium price and quantity by using the fact that the quantity demanded equals the quantity supplied in equilibrium, and substituting the demand and supply curve equations into this equality. We could have obtained the same answer by instead using the fact that the price given by the *inverse* demand and supply curves is the same at the market equilibrium quantity. That is,

$$5 - 0.005Q_e = 1 + 0.005Q_e$$

Solving this equation gives $Q_e = 400$ pounds, just as before. Plugging $Q_e = 400$ back into either the inverse demand or supply equation indicates that the market price P_e is $3 per pound, as expected.

make the grade

Does quantity supplied equal quantity demanded in equilibrium?

Solving for the market equilibrium as we just did is one of the most common exam questions in intermediate microeconomics classes. The basic idea is always the same: Take the equations for the demand curve and the supply curve, solve for the equilibrium price, and then plug that equilibrium price back into either the supply curve or the demand curve (it does not matter which) to determine the equilibrium quantity. It is simple, but it is easy to make math errors under the time pressure of an exam, especially if the demand and supply curves take on more complicated forms than the basic examples we deal with here.

A simple trick will ensure that you have the right answer, and it only takes a few seconds. Take the equilibrium price that you obtain and plug it into *both* the demand and supply curves. If you don't get the same answer when you substitute the equilibrium price into the supply and demand equations, you know you made a math error along the way because the quantity demanded must equal the quantity supplied in equilibrium.

Why Markets Move toward Equilibrium

When a market is in equilibrium, the quantity demanded by consumers and the quantity supplied by producers are equal at the current market price. To see why equilibrium is a stable situation, let's look at what happens when price is at a non-equilibrium level. If the current price is higher than the equilibrium price, there will be excess supply. If the price is lower, there will be excess demand.

surplus
The amount by which quantity supplied exceeds quantity demanded when market price is higher than the equilibrium price.

Excess Supply   Suppose the price in a market were higher than the equilibrium price, say, at P_{high} instead of P_e, as shown in Figure 2.6a. At that price, the quantity supplied, Q^S_{high}, is greater than the quantity demanded, Q^D_{high}. Producers come out of the woodwork wanting to sell at this high price, but not all producers can find willing buyers at that price. The excess quantity for sale equals $Q^S_{high} - Q^D_{high}$, the horizontal distance between the supply and demand curves at P_{high}. This excess quantity supplied is known as a **surplus.** To eliminate this surplus, producers need to attract more buyers, and to do this, sellers must lower their prices. As price falls, quantity demanded rises and quantity supplied falls until the market reaches equilibrium at point E.

shortage
The amount by which quantity demanded exceeds quantity supplied when market price is lower than the equilibrium price.

Excess Demand   The opposite situation exists in Figure 2.6b. At price P_{low}, consumers demand more of the good (Q^D_{low}) than producers are willing to supply (Q^S_{low}). Buyers want a lot of tomatoes if they are this cheap, but not many producers will deliver them at such a low price. At the low price, the quantity demanded Q^D_{low} is greater than the quantity supplied Q^S_{low}, and a **shortage** exists. To eliminate

---

Figure 2.6 | **Why P_e Is the Equilibrium Price**

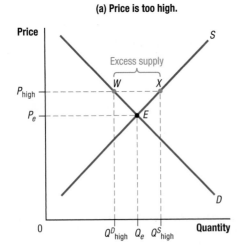

(a) Price is too high.

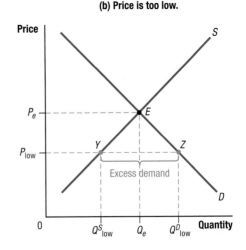

(b) Price is too low.

(a) At the price P_{high} above the equilibrium price P_e, producers supply the quantity Q^S_{high}, while consumers demand only Q^D_{high}. This results in a surplus of the good, as represented by the distance between points W and X. Over time, price will fall and the market will move toward equilibrium at point E.

(b) At the price P_{low} below the equilibrium price P_e, producers supply the quantity Q^S_{low}, while consumers demand Q^D_{low}. This results in a shortage for the good, as represented by the distance between points Y and Z. Over time, price will rise and the market will move toward equilibrium at point E.

this shortage, buyers who cannot find the good available for sale will bid up the price and enterprising producers will be more than willing to raise their prices. As price rises, quantity demanded falls and quantity supplied rises until the market equals equilibrium at point E.[6]

Adjusting to Equilibrium   It is important to note that in the real world an equilibrium can be mysterious. In our stylized model, we're acting as if all the producers and consumers gather in one spot and report to a sort of auctioneer how much they want to produce or consume at each price. The auctioneer combines all this information, computes and announces the market-clearing price, and only then do all the sellers and buyers make their deals at the announced market-clearing price. But few markets work this way in the real world. Real markets must rely on what the great eighteenth-century Scottish economist Adam Smith called the "invisible hand." Producers independently decide how much to produce of their products given what price they expect to be able to sell them at, and consumers show up at stores, gas stations, or Web sites to buy the good. Sometimes producers might supply too much or too little in the short run, but through the market, these mistakes tend to be corrected. Economists typically assume that the market reaches equilibrium one way or another, without being too specific about the process.

2.1 figure it out

Suppose that the demand and supply curves for a monthly cell phone plan with unlimited texts can be represented by

$$Q^D = 50 - 0.5P$$
$$Q^S = -25 + P$$

The current price of these plans in the market is $40 per month. Is this market in equilibrium? Would you expect the price to rise or fall? If so, by how much? Explain.

Solution:

There are two ways to solve the first question about whether the price will rise or fall. The first is to calculate the quantity demanded and quantity supplied at the current market price of $40 to see how they compare:

$$Q^D = 50 - 0.5P = 50 - 0.5(40) = 50 - 20 = 30$$
$$Q^S = -25 + P = -25 + 40 = 15$$

Because quantity demanded is greater than quantity supplied, we can tell that there is excess demand (a shortage) in the market. Many people are trying to get texting plans, but are finding them sold out because few suppliers want to sell at that price. Prices will rise to equalize quantity supplied and quantity demanded, moving the market to equilibrium.

---

[6] Prices can sometimes remain at levels other than their equilibrium value for extended periods of time, especially if there are policy-based interventions in the market, such as price ceilings (maximum prices allowed by law) or price floors (minimum prices prescribed by law). We discuss these sorts of situations in Chapter 3.

Alternatively, we could start by solving for the market equilibrium price:

$$Q^D = Q^S$$
$$50 - 0.5P = -25 + P$$
$$1.5P = 75$$
$$P = \$50$$

The current market price, $40, is below the market equilibrium price of $50. (This is why there is excess demand in the market.) Therefore, we would expect the price to rise by $10. When the market reaches equilibrium at a price of $50, all buyers can find sellers and all sellers can find buyers. The price will then remain at $50 unless the market changes and the demand curve or supply curve shifts.

2.5 Changes in Market Equilibrium When Only One Curve Shifts

As we have learned, demand and supply curves hold constant everything else besides price that might affect quantities demanded and supplied. Therefore, the market equilibrium depicted in Figure 2.5 will hold only as long as none of these other factors change. If any other factor changes, there will be a new market equilibrium because either the demand or supply curve will have shifted. We explore how those shifts affect the equilibrium price and quantity in this section.

Demand Shifts

Suppose the demand for tomatoes falls when, as in our example above, a news story reports that tomatoes are suspected of being the source of a salmonella outbreak. The resulting change in consumer tastes causes the demand curve to shift in (i.e., to the left), as Figure 2.7 shows, from D_1 to D_2.

How does the market equilibrium change after this demand shift? The equilibrium price and quantity both fall. The equilibrium quantity falls from Q_1 to Q_2, and the

---

Figure 2.7   Effects of a Fall in the Demand for Tomatoes

After a salmonella outbreak, the demand for tomatoes decreases, causing a leftward shift of the demand curve from D_1 to D_2. This fall in demand results in a new equilibrium point E_2 lower than the initial equilibrium point E_1. The equilibrium quantity falls from Q_1 (400 pounds) to Q_2 (150 pounds), and the equilibrium price falls from P_1 ($3) to P_2 ($1.75).

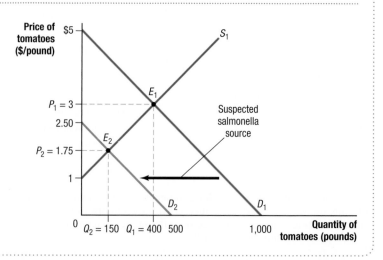

equilibrium price drops from P_1 to P_2. The reason for these movements is that if prices stayed at P_1 after the fall in demand, tomato farmers would be supplying a much greater quantity than consumers were demanding. The market price must fall to get farmers to rein in their quantity supplied until it matches the new, lower level of demand.

We can solve for the new equilibrium price and quantity using the same approach we used earlier, but using the equation for the new demand curve D_2, which is $Q = 500 - 200P$. (The supply curve stays the same.)

$$Q^D = Q^S$$

$$500 - 200P_2 = 200P_2 - 200$$

$$400P_2 = 700$$

$$P_2 = 1.75$$

So, the new equilibrium price is $1.75 per pound, as compared to $3 per pound from before the demand shift. Plugging this into the new demand curve (or the supply curve) gives the new equilibrium quantity:

$$Q_2 = 500 - 200(1.75) = 150$$

The new equilibrium quantity is 150 pounds, less than half of what it was before the negative demand shift.

We could have just as easily worked through an example in which demand increases and the demand curve shifts out. Perhaps tastes change and people want to drink their vegetables by downing several cans of tomato juice a day or incomes rise

2.2 figure it out

Draw a supply and demand diagram of the market for paperback books in a small coastal town.

a. Suppose that a hurricane knocks out electrical power for an extended period of time. Unable to watch television or use a computer, people must resort to reading books for entertainment. What will happen to the equilibrium price and quantity of paperback books?

b. Does this change reflect a change in demand or a change in quantity demanded?

Solution:

a. Books are a substitute good for television shows and computer entertainment. Because there is no power for televisions or computers (effectively raising the price of these substitutes), the demand for books will rise, and the demand curve will shift out to the right. As the figure shows, this shift will result in a higher equilibrium price and quantity of books purchased.

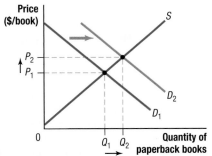

b. Because the hurricane changes the availability (and therefore the effective price) of substitute goods, this shifts the amount of books demanded at any given price. This is a change in the demand for paperback books.

freakonomics

The Price of Fame: President Obama and the Paparazzi

Being president of the United States has its perks—you are the most powerful person in the world, people wait on you hand and foot, and you get to live in a pretty nice house rent-free. But being the president also has its downsides. For instance, every step you and your family take is in the public spotlight. Media coverage of the Obama family has been intense, even by White House standards. The president was particularly troubled by the toll on his daughters Sasha and Malia, so he asked his staff to come up with some solutions to the paparazzi problem.

Their solution shows that someone in the Obama administration knows some economics. White House staff recognized that the number of paparazzi photos represents a market equilibrium. Because of the public's strong demand for pictures of the Obama family, media outlets are willing to fork over large sums of money for high-quality photos. At those prices, many photographers are willing to devote a lot of time to stalking the First Family and supply the market with a huge number of photographs. A hypothetical initial equilibrium in the market for photographs of the Obama family is illustrated in Figure A.

The White House provided the media with this photo of Malia and Sasha Obama leaving for their first day of school in 2010.

The Obama-Biden Transition Project

Figure A

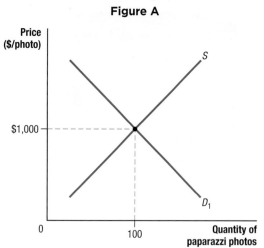

One way to reduce the number of paparazzi taking photos to supply the equilibrium quantity would be to decrease the demand for the photos and shift the demand curve inward. If that were to happen, both the price and quantity of paparazzi photos would decline. How could the White House reduce the demand for paparazzi photos? One thing we know from economics is that if two goods are substitutes, the demand for one good will fall if the price for the other good decreases because consumers will shift away from buying the first good and toward buying the second, cheaper good. So the administration needed a substitute for paparazzi pictures. The answer? Staged photos taken by White House photographers, given to media outlets for free.

Each White House–approved picture of Sasha and Malia hunting for Easter eggs or of the First Dog Bo running around the lawn lowered the demand for paparazzi photos, leading to a decrease in the price unauthorized paparazzi photos could command. As a result, fewer paparazzi spent their days milling around the White House lawn, and the number of unauthorized photos being published decreased, as shown in Figure B. Perhaps most important to President and Mrs. Obama, it meant that Sasha and Malia could go to their first day of school like normal kids—or, at least, like normal kids who happen to have several secret servicemen, the D.C. police, and the White House photographer with them.

After seeing the initial success of this photo project, the administration ventured into the world of social media and created Facebook and Flickr accounts with photo albums depicting everything from staff meetings in the Oval Office to the president instigating a snowball fight on the White House lawn. Up next for the White House presidential photo project? Given the current budget deficit, perhaps they should consider selling the pictures—just as long as they keep the price below the market equilibrium price!

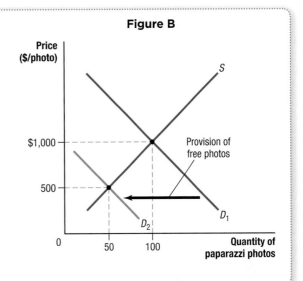

Figure B

or substitute produce items become more expensive. In the face of a stable supply curve, this increase in demand would shift the curve up to the right and cause both the equilibrium price and quantity to rise. At the initial (pre-shift) market price, the post-shift quantity demanded would outstrip sellers' willingness to supply. The price would have to rise, causing a movement along the supply curve until the quantities supplied and demanded are equal.

Shifts in Curves versus Movement along a Curve   This analysis highlights the importance of distinguishing between shifts in a demand or supply curve and movements along those curves. This distinction can sometimes seem confusing, but understanding it is critical to much of the analysis that follows in this book. We saw in Figure 2.7 what happens to a market when there is a change in consumers' tastes that make them view a product more negatively. That change in tastes made consumers want to buy less of the product at any given price—that is, caused an inward *shift* in the demand curve. Remember, anything that changes how much consumers want to buy of a good at any particular price must shift the demand curve. At the same time, this change in tastes had no effect on how much producers wish to sell at any given price. It doesn't affect their costs of producing or their outside options. So, supply does not change, and the supply curve doesn't shift. However, the *quantity supplied* does change. It falls in response to the reduced demand. This change in quantity supplied is a movement *along* the supply curve. The only reason that the quantity supplied falls in this example is because the shift in the demand curve has made the equilibrium price lower, and at a lower price, suppliers produce less of the good. Therefore, a *shift* in the demand curve causes a movement *along* the supply curve to the new equilibrium.

Supply Shifts

Now let's think about what happens when the supply curve shifts, but the demand curve does not. Figure 2.8 shows the case in which the supply of tomatoes rises, shifting the supply curve out from S_1 to S_2. This shift implies that, at any given price, farmers are willing to sell a larger quantity of tomatoes than before. Such a shift would result from a reduction in farmers' input costs—for example, if fertilizer prices fell. The logic of why a cost reduction increases quantity supplied at any given

Figure 2.8   Effects of an Increase in the Supply of Tomatoes

With cheaper fertilizer, farmers supply more to-matoes at every given price and the supply curve shifts outward from S_1 to S_2. The equilibrium quantity increases from Q_1 (400 pounds) at E_1 to Q_2 (600 pounds) at E_2, while the equilibrium price falls from P_1 ($3/pound) to P_2 ($2/pound).

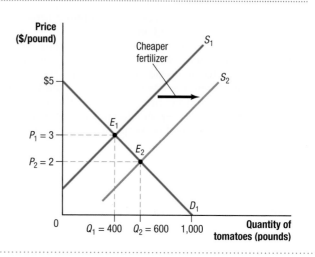

price is straightforward: If the farmers can make an average profit of (say) $1 per pound when the price is $3 per pound, then a $1 decrease in cost (which increases their profit) will lead farmers to offer more for sale. Note, however, that this cost change has no direct impact on the demand curve. Holding price fixed, consumers are no more or less willing to buy tomatoes than they were before.

Figure 2.8 shows how the equilibrium changes. The supply curve has shifted from its original position S_1 (given by the equation $Q = 200P - 200$) to S_2 (given by the equation $Q = 200P + 200$). If the price stayed at the original equilibrium price P_1 after the supply shift, the amount of tomatoes that sellers would be willing to supply would exceed consumers' quantity demanded. Therefore, the equilibrium price must fall, as seen in the figure. This drop in price causes an increase in quantity demanded along the demand curve. The price drops until the quantity demanded once again equals the quantity supplied. The new equilibrium price is P_2, and the new equilibrium quantity is Q_2.

We can solve for the new equilibrium price and quantity using the equations for the original demand curve and the new supply curve:

$$Q^D = Q^S$$

$$1,000 - 200P_2 = 200P_2 + 200$$

$$400P_2 = 800$$

$$P_2 = 2$$

The cost drop and the resulting increase in supply lead to a fall in the equilibrium price from $3 to $2 per pound. This is intuitive: Lower farmers' costs end up being reflected in lower market prices. We can plug this price into either the demand or new supply equation to find the new equilibrium quantity:

$$Q_2 = 1,000 - 200(2) = 600$$

$$Q_2 = 200(2) + 200 = 600$$

The equilibrium quantity of tomatoes increases from 400 to 600 pounds in response to the increase in supply and the fall in the equilibrium price.

2.3 figure it out

Suppose that the supply of lemonade is represented by $Q^S = 40P$, where Q is measured in pints and P is measured in cents per pint.

a. If the demand for lemonade is $Q^D = 5{,}000 - 10P$, what are the current equilibrium price and quantity?

b. Suppose that a severe frost in Florida raises the price of lemons and thus the cost of making lemonade. In response to the increase in cost, producers reduce the quantity supplied of lemonade by 400 pints at every price. What is the new equation for the supply of lemonade?

c. After the frost, what will be the equilibrium price and quantity of lemonade?

Solution:

a. To solve for the equilibrium price, we need to equate the quantity demanded and quantity supplied:

$$Q^D = Q^S$$
$$5{,}000 - 10P = 40P$$
$$50P = 5{,}000$$
$$P = 100 \text{ cents}$$

To solve for the equilibrium quantity, we want to substitute the equilibrium price into either the demand curve or the supply curve (or both!):

$$Q^D = 5{,}000 - 10(100) = 5{,}000 - 1{,}000 = 4{,}000 \text{ pints}$$
$$Q^S = 40(100) = 4{,}000 \text{ pints}$$

b. If the quantity supplied of lemonade falls by 400 pints at every price, then the supply curve is shifting left (in a parallel fashion) by a quantity of 400 at each price:

$$Q^S_2 = Q^S - 400 = 40P - 400$$

The new supply curve can be represented by $Q^S_2 = 40P - 400$.

c. To solve for the new equilibrium, we would set $Q^D = Q^S_2$:

$$Q^D = Q^S_2$$
$$5{,}000 - 10P_2 = 40P_2 - 400$$
$$50P_2 = 5{,}400$$
$$P_2 = 108 \text{ cents}$$

Solving for equilibrium quantity can be done by substituting the equilibrium price into either the demand or supply equation:

$$Q^D = 5{,}000 - 10(108) = 5{,}000 - 1{,}080 = 3{,}920 \text{ pints}$$
$$Q^S = 40(108) - 400 = 4{,}320 - 400 = 3{,}920 \text{ pints}$$

As we would expect (see Table 2.2 on the next page), the equilibrium price rises and the equilibrium quantity falls.

| **Table 2.2** | Effect of Shifts in Demand and Supply Curves in Isolation |

| | | **IMPACT ON EQUILIBRIUM** | |
Curve that Shifts	**Direction of Shift**	**Price**	**Quantity**
Demand Curve	Out (increase in *D*)	↑	↑
	In (decrease in *D*)	↓	↓
Supply Curve	Out (increase in *S*)	↓	↑
	In (decrease in *S*)	↑	↓

Again, we could go through the same steps for a decrease in supply. The supply curve would shift up to the left. This decline in supply would increase the equilibrium price and decrease the equilibrium quantity.

Summary of Effects

Table 2.2 summarizes the changes in equilibrium price and quantity that result when either the demand or supply curve shifts while the other curve remains in the same position. When the demand curve shifts, price and quantity move in the same direction. An increase in demand leads consumers to want to purchase more of the good than producers are willing to supply at the old equilibrium price. This will tend to drive prices up, which in turn induces producers to supply more of the good. The producers' response is captured by movement along the supply curve.

When the supply curve shifts, price and quantity move in opposite directions. If supply increases, the supply curve shifts out, and producers want to sell more of the good at the old equilibrium price than consumers want to buy. This will force prices down, giving consumers an incentive to buy more of the good. Similarly, if supply shifts in, the equilibrium price has to rise to reduce the quantity demanded. These movements along the demand curve involve price and quantity changes in opposite directions because demand curves are downward-sloping.

 application

Supply shifts and the video game crash of 1983

People love video games. About two-thirds of households in the United States have at least one game-playing member. Sales of video game consoles and software were around $15.5 billion in the United States in 2010. To put that number in perspective, it is almost 50% more than 2010's total domestic box office haul of $10.5 billion, and about the same size as the total combined U.S. sales of McDonald's and Burger King restaurants that year.

Seeing these numbers, you'd never know that in the industry's early days, there was a point when many people declared video games a passing fad and a business in which it was impossible to make a profit. Why did they say this? The problem wasn't demand. Early video games, from *Pong* to *Space Invaders* and consoles like the Atari 2600, were a huge hit and cultural touchstones. The problem was supply—way too much of it. In 1983 a set of factors combined to lead to a massive supply shift for the industry in North America that ended up crippling it for years.

Two primary factors led to the supply shift. Home video consoles, led by the Atari 2600 but also including popular machines from Mattel and Coleco, had taken off in the early 1980s. At this early point in the industry, console producers hadn't yet learned the best way to handle licensing arrangements with third-party games producers. As a result, just about anyone could write a game title for a console if they wanted to. And just about everyone did. Even Quaker Oats had a video games division! The pet food company Purina contracted with a software developer to create a game that would publicize its Chuck Wagon brand dog food. (The game, *Chase the Chuck Wagon*, involved a dog chasing a chuck wagon through a maze.) In essence, there was a gold rush: Too many producers, each hoping to capture just a part of the fast-growing market, all entered at the same time, leading to a much larger total supply than any producer expected individually beforehand. The same phenomenon occurred in console production as well. Several companies made clones of Atari's market-leading console, and others produced their own machines and lines of games.

The leading console makers didn't help themselves any with their own game-production decisions either. The most infamous failures were Atari's self-produced games *Pac-Man* and *E.T. the Extra-Terrestrial*. Atari management expected unprecedented sales for both, due to the extreme popularity of the arcade version of the former and the movie tied to the latter. In fact, Atari produced 12 million copies of *Pac-Man* even though there were only 10 million consoles in existence at the time, presuming that not only would just about every owner of a console buy the game, but also millions of others would buy a console just to play the game. Both were rushed through production to take advantage of the holiday shopping seasons. The games were a mess, and quantity supplied well exceeded quantity demanded even at the depressed prices in the market.

The sudden rush of producers to put product on the market created an outward shift in the supply curve—producers' behavior made clear that they were willing to produce more at any given price in early 1983 than they were just a couple years earlier, in early 1981. And while the demand for home video games had been trending upward as the technology diffused through households, the rush to produce new titles and consoles probably didn't have much of an effect on the demand curve. (In fact, because of the poor quality of the new games, it may have even shifted the demand curve inward.) It's reasonable to assume, then, that the demand curve was unmoved by the producer gold rush. The supply and demand model predicts the consequences of this supply shift on the market. A shift out in the supply curve in the face of constant demand will lead to an increase in quantity and a drop in prices, as shown in Figure 2.9. (These days, video game companies take more care in rolling out new games.)

Figure 2.9   Effects of an Increase in the Supply of Video Games

In 1983 a sudden increase in the number of video game producers shifted the supply curve from S_{1981} to S_{1983}. At the equilibrium, the price of video games dropped from P_1 ($35) to P_2 ($5), while the quantity increased from Q_1 to Q_2.

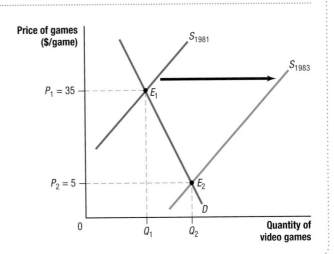

That's exactly what happened in the video game industry. Price changes, in particular, were precipitous. Games that had been selling a year earlier at list prices of $35–$50 were being sold for $5 or even $1. Console prices fell by double-digit percentages as well. With games going at these rates, quantities increased somewhat, but nowhere near enough to make them profitable for their producers. Dozens of firms—console and games makers alike—went out of business. Atari, which until then had been a cash cow, was sold by its parent Warner Communications and never recovered. The carnage was so total that some retailers, figuring the market was hopeless, refused to stock games anymore. It essentially wiped out producers from the market for three to four years, an eternity in this fast-moving industry where technological races are seemingly never-ending. Things finally turned around when a company known as Nintendo managed to convince retailers that its all-new 8-bit Nintendo Entertainment System would revitalize the morbid industry. ■

2.4 figure it out

Last month, you noticed the price of asparagus rising, and you also noted that there was less asparagus being sold than in the month prior. What inferences can you draw about the behavior of the supply and demand for asparagus?

Solution:

We need to work backwards to determine what could have happened to either supply or demand to lead to the change described in this question. Let's start with the change in price. The equilibrium price of asparagus is *rising*. This must mean one of two things: Either the demand for asparagus rose or the supply of asparagus fell. (If you have trouble seeing this, draw a couple of quick figures.)

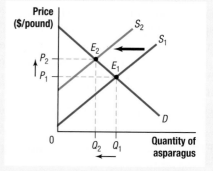

We also know that the equilibrium quantity of asparagus fell. A drop in the equilibrium quantity can only have two causes: either a decrease in the demand for asparagus or a fall in the supply of asparagus. (Again, you may want to draw these out to see such results.)

Which shift leads to both a rise in equilibrium price and a fall in equilibrium quantity? It must be a decrease in the supply of asparagus, as shown in the figure.

What Determines the Size of Price and Quantity Changes?

Thus far, the analysis in the chapter (summarized in Table 2.2) tells us about the *direction* in which equilibrium price and quantity move when demand and supply curves shift. But we don't know the size of these changes. In this section, we discuss the factors that determine how large the price and quantity changes are.

make the grade

Did the curve shift, or was it just a movement along the curve?

A common type of exam question on demand and supply will involve one or more "shocks" to a market—changes in factors that influence demand or supply. Your job will be to sort out how those shocks affect demand and supply, and by extension, the equilibrium price and quantity in the market. Generally, the trickiest part of questions like these is figuring out whether changes in price and quantity are the result of moving along a given demand or supply curve, or whether the curves are shifting.

If you follow a few simple steps, this type of question need not be too difficult.

1. **Figure out what the shock is in any particular problem.** It is the change that causes a shift in either the supply curve, the demand curve, or both. There is a nearly infinite variety of shocks. A pandemic could wipe out a large number of consumers, a new invention might make it cheaper to make a good, a different good that consumers like better might be introduced, or inclement weather may damage or kill off a large portion of a certain crop.

   Importantly, though, a change in either the price or the quantity of the good *in the market being studied* cannot be the shock. The changes in price and quantity in this market are the *result* of the shock, not the shock itself. Be careful, however: Changes in prices or quantities in some *other* market can serve as a shock to this market. If the price of chunky peanut butter falls, for example, that could be a shock to the market for grape jelly or the market for creamy peanut butter.

2. **Determine whether the shock shifts the demand or supply curve.**

   a. *To figure out whether a shock shifts the demand curve and how it shifts it,* ask yourself the following question: If the price of this good didn't change, would consumers want to buy more, less, or the same amount of the good after the shock? If consumers want more of the good at the same price after the shock, then the shock increases the quantity demanded at every price and shifts the demand curve out (to the right). If consumers want less of the good at the same price after the shock, then the shock decreases demand and the demand curve shifts in. If consumers want the same amount of the good at the same price, then the demand curve doesn't move at all, and it's probably a supply shock.

   Let's go back to the grape jelly example. Our shock was a decline in the price of peanut butter. Do consumers want more or less grape jelly (holding the price constant) when peanut butter gets cheaper? The answer to this question is probably "more." Cheap peanut butter means consumers will buy more peanut butter, and since people tend to eat peanut butter and jelly together, consumers will probably want more jelly even if the price of jelly stays the same. Therefore, the decline in peanut butter's price shifts the demand for grape jelly out.

   b. *To figure out whether a shock shifts the supply curve and how it shifts it,* ask yourself the following question: If the price of this good didn't change, would suppliers want to produce more, less, or the same amount of the good after the shock? In the jelly example, a change in the price of peanut butter doesn't affect the costs of making jelly—it's not an input into jelly production. So it's not a supply shock. An increase in the price of grapes, however, would be a supply shock in the market for grape jelly.

3. **Draw the market's supply and demand curves before and after the shocks.** In the jelly example, we would draw the original demand and supply curves, and then add the new demand curve (to the right of the initial demand curve) that results from the increase in the demand for jelly because of lower peanut butter prices. From this, it's easy to execute the final step, interpreting what impact the shock has on equilibrium price and quantity. For grape jelly, the increase in demand will result in a higher equilibrium price and quantity for jelly because the demand shift creates movement up and to the right along the jelly supply curve.

Practice in following this recipe will make manipulating supply and demand curves second nature.

Size of the Shift   One obvious and direct influence on the sizes of the equilibrium price and quantity changes is the size of the demand or supply curve shift itself. The larger the shift, the larger the change in equilibrium price or quantity.

Slopes of the Curves   Even for a fixed-size demand or supply curve shift, the magnitudes of the resulting equilibrium price and quantity changes can vary. Specifically, the *relative* sizes of the price and quantity changes depend on the steepness of the demand and supply curves. If the demand curve shifts, then the slope of the supply curve determines whether the shift leads to a relatively large equilibrium price change and a relatively small equilibrium quantity change, or vice versa. If the supply curve shifts, it's the slope of the demand curve that matters.

Figure 2.10 demonstrates this. Panels a and b show the same shift in the demand curve, from D_1 to D_2. In panel a, the supply curve is relatively flat, while in

---

Figure 2.10 | **Size of Equilibrium Price and Quantity Changes, and the Slopes of the Supply and Demand Curves**

(a) Demand curve shift with flatter supply curve

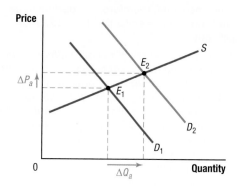

(c) Supply curve shift with flatter demand curve

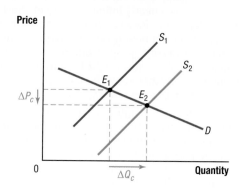

(b) Demand curve shift with steeper supply curve

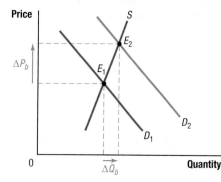

(d) Supply curve shift with steeper demand curve

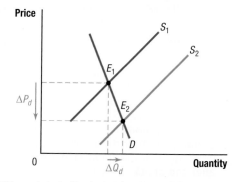

(a) With a relatively flat supply curve, a shift in demand from D_1 to D_2 will result in a relatively small increase in equilibrium price ΔP_a and a relatively large increase in equilibrium quantity ΔQ_a.
(b) With a relatively steep supply curve, a shift in demand from D_1 to D_2 will result in a relatively large increase in equilibrium price ΔP_b and a relatively small increase in equilibrium quantity ΔQ_b.

(c) With a relatively flat demand curve, a shift in supply from S_1 to S_2 will result in a relatively small decrease in equilibrium price ΔP_c and a relatively large increase in equilibrium quantity ΔQ_c.
(d) With a relatively steep demand curve, a shift in supply from S_1 to S_2 will result in a relatively large decrease in equilibrium price ΔP_d and a relatively small increase in equilibrium quantity ΔQ_d.

panel b, it's relatively steep. When the demand curve shifts, if the supply curve is flat, the change in the equilibrium quantity (ΔQ_a) will be relatively large but the change in price (ΔP_a) will be small. When the supply curve is steep (panel b), the price change (ΔP_b) is large and the quantity change (ΔQ_b) small. Similarly, panels c and d show the same supply curve shift, but with differently sloped demand curves. The same results hold for shifts in the supply curve—flatter (steeper) demand curves result in larger (smaller) changes in quantity relative to price changes.

This analysis raises an obvious question: What affects the slope of demand and supply curves? We discuss the economic forces that determine the steepness or flatness of demand or supply curves next.

application

The supply curve of housing and housing prices: A tale of two cities

From panels a and b of Figure 2.10, we can see that, when the demand curve shifts, the slope of the supply curve determines the relative size of the change in equilibrium price and quantity. Data for housing prices provide a good application of this idea. Specifically, we can look at how urban housing prices respond to an increase in the demand for housing caused by population growth.

Consider housing in the cities of New York City and Houston. New York is incredibly dense. Because the metropolitan area is so built up, it is expensive for developers to build additional housing. As a result, developers' costs rise so quickly with the amount of housing they build, the quantity of housing supplied doesn't respond much to price differences. There's only so much the developers can do. This means the supply curve of housing in New York is steep—the quantity supplied isn't very responsive to changes in price. Equivalently, it would take a very large increase in housing prices to induce housing suppliers to be willing to increase the quantity of housing they build. (We'll talk more in the next section about the factors that determine the price sensitivity of quantity supplied and quantity demanded.)

New York City.

Iofoto/Dreamstime.com

Houston, on the other hand, is much less dense. It is surrounded by farm and ranch land, and there is still a lot of space to expand within the metro area. This means developers can build new housing without driving up their unit costs very much; they can just buy another farm and build housing on it if the price is right. For this reason, the quantity of housing supplied in Houston is quite responsive to changes in housing prices. That is, the housing supply curve in Houston is fairly flat.

Houston, Texas.

Comstock/Thinkstock

Theory predicts that in response to an outward shift in the demand for housing in the two cities, New York (with its steep supply curve) should see a relatively large increase in the equilibrium price and very little change in the equilibrium quantity of housing. Houston, on the other hand, with the flatter supply curve, should see a relatively small increase in price and a large increase in quantity for an equal-size shift in demand.

So, let's look at some data. Look first at Figure 2.11, which shows how the populations of the New York and Houston metro areas changed from 1977 to 2009. (The figure shows the population index for each metro area, giving the city's population

Figure 2.11   Population Indices for New York and Houston, 1977–2009

Between 1977 and 2009, the population in New York grew by about 15%, while the population in Houston more than doubled.

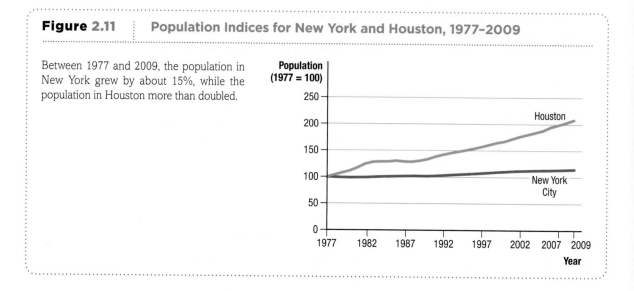

as a percentage of its 1977 value.) Population in both cities rose over these 32 years. New York metro area's population grew about 15%, while Houston's population saw a far greater rise, more than doubling.

We can think of these population influxes as being tied to outward shifts in the demand curve for housing in each city. Again, the prediction of the supply and demand model is that the equilibrium price response to a given-sized shift in demand should be larger in New York, where the supply curve of housing is steep (like that in Figure 2.10b), than in Houston, with its flatter supply curve (as in Figure 2.10a).

Looking at Figure 2.12, it's clear this prediction holds. The figure depicts a housing price index for both the New York and Houston metro areas, showing the price of housing in the cities (again, as an index based on their 1977 values). Despite having a considerably smaller increase in population, New York saw a tenfold rise

Figure 2.12   Housing Price Indices for New York and Houston, 1977–2009

From 1977 to 2009, housing prices in New York rose at a much faster rate than those in Houston.

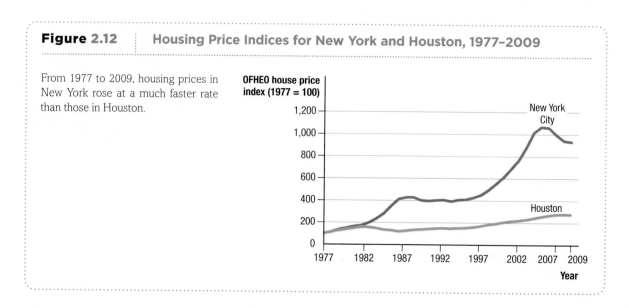

in average housing prices over the past 30 years. House prices went up in Houston too, as you would expect in a city that more than doubles in population, but by only a fraction of the increase seen in New York. In comparing these two cities, we see a clear pattern that the price effects of demand shifts in a market depend on the shape of the supply curve. ■

2.6 Changes in Market Equilibrium When Both Curves Shift

Sometimes, we are faced with situations in which supply and demand curves move simultaneously. For example, Figure 2.13 combines two shifts: decreases (inward shifts) in both supply and demand. Let's return to the tomato market at Pike Place Market and suppose that there is a big increase in oil prices. This increase drives up the cost of production because harvesting and distribution costs rise for sellers. Increased oil prices also decrease the demand for tomatoes. Because driving to the market gets more expensive for consumers, there are fewer people buying at any given price. The original equilibrium occurred at the intersection of D_1 and S_1, point E_1. The new equilibrium is at point E_2, the intersection of D_2 and S_2.

In this particular case, the simultaneous inward shifts in supply and demand have led to a substantial reduction in the equilibrium quantity and a slight increase in price. The reduction in quantity should be intuitive. The inward shift in the demand curve means that consumers want to buy less at any given price. The inward shift in the supply curve means that at any given price, producers want to supply less. Because both producers and consumers want less quantity, equilibrium quantity falls unambiguously, from Q_1 to Q_2.

The effect on equilibrium price is not as clear, however. An inward shift in demand with a fixed supply curve will tend to reduce prices, but an inward shift in supply with a fixed demand curve will tend to raise prices. Because both curves are moving simultaneously, it is unclear which effect will dominate, and therefore whether equilibrium price rises or falls. We have drawn the curves in Figure 2.13 so

Figure 2.13   Example of a Simultaneous Shift in Demand and Supply

An inward shift of both the supply and demand curves results in a new equilibrium point E_2 at the intersection between S_2 and D_2. At E_2, the price has increased slightly from P_1 to P_2, and the quantity has decreased from Q_1 to Q_2.

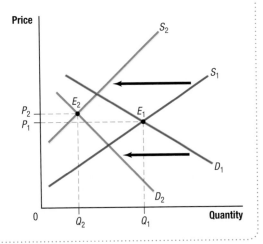

that equilibrium price rises slightly, from P_1 to P_2. But had the supply and demand curves shifted by different amounts (or had they been flatter or steeper), the dual inward shift might have led to a decrease in the equilibrium price, or no change in the price at all.

As a general rule, when both curves shift at the same time, we will know with certainty the direction of change of either the equilibrium price or quantity, but never both. This result can be seen by a closer inspection of Table 2.2. If the demand and supply curve shifts are both pushing price in the same direction, which would be the case if (1) the demand curve shifted out and the supply curve shifted in or (2) the demand curve shifted in and the supply curve shifted out, then the same shifts 1 or 2 will push quantities in opposite directions. Likewise, if the shifts in both curves serve to move quantity in the same direction—either (3) demand and supply both shift out or (4) demand and supply both shift in—the shifts 3 and 4 have opposing effects on equilibrium prices. The example we just looked at in Figure 2.13 involved a case of form 4.

This ambiguity is also apparent in the example in Figure 2.14. The directions of the shifts in the demand and supply curves are the same in each panel of the figure: Supply shifts inward from S_1 to S_2, and demand shifts outward from D_1 to D_2. Both of these shifts will lead to higher prices, and this is reflected in the change in the equilibrium (from point E_1 to E_2). But as can be seen, whether the equilibrium quantity rises, falls, or stays the same depends on the relative size of the shifts and the slopes of the curves. The figure's three panels show examples of each possible case. When examining a situation in which both supply and demand shift, you might find it helpful to draw each shift in isolation first, note the changes in equilibrium quantity and price implied by each shift, and then combine these pieces of information to obtain your answer.

Figure 2.14   **When Both Curves Shift, the Direction of Either Price or Quantity Will Be Ambiguous**

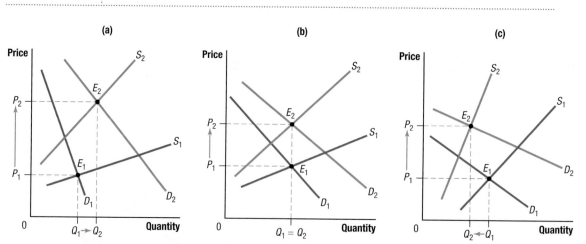

(a) In all three panels, there is an outward shift in demand (D_1 to D_2) and an inward shift in supply (S_1 to S_2). Here, both equilibrium price (P_1 to P_2) and quantity (Q_1 to Q_2) increase as a result.

(b) Equilibrium price increases from P_1 to P_2, while equilibrium quantity stays the same ($Q_1 = Q_2$).

(c) Equilibrium price increases from P_1 to P_2, while equilibrium quantity decreases from Q_1 to Q_2.

2.7 Elasticity

Mathematically, the slopes of demand and supply curves relate changes in price to changes in quantity demanded or quantity supplied. Steeper curves mean that price changes are correlated with relatively small quantity changes. When demand curves are steep, this implies that consumers are not very price-sensitive and won't change their quantity demanded much in response to price changes. Similarly, steep supply curves mean that producers' quantities supplied are not particularly sensitive to price changes. Flatter demand or supply curves, on the other hand, imply that price changes are associated with large quantity changes. Markets with flat demand curves have consumers whose quantities demanded change a lot as price varies. Markets with flat supply curves will see big movements in quantity supplied as prices change.

The concept of elasticity expresses the responsiveness of one value to changes in another (and here specifically, the responsiveness of quantities to prices). An **elasticity** relates the percentage change in one value to the percentage change in another. So, for example, when we talk about the sensitivity of consumers' quantity demanded to price, we refer to the **price elasticity of demand:** the percentage change in quantity demanded resulting from a given percentage change in price.

elasticity
The ratio of the percentage change in one value to the percentage change in another.

price elasticity of demand
The percentage change in quantity demanded resulting from a 1% change in price.

Slope and Elasticity Are Not the Same

You might be thinking that the price elasticity of demand sounds a lot like the slope of the demand curve: how much quantity demanded changes when price does. While elasticity and slope are certainly related, they're not the same.

The slope relates a change in one level (prices) to another level (quantity). The demand curve we introduced in the tomato example was $Q = 1,000 - 200P$. The slope of this demand curve is -200; that is, quantity demanded falls by 200 pounds for every dollar per pound increase in price.

There are two big problems with just using the slopes of demand and supply curves to measure price responsiveness. First, slopes depend completely on the units of measurement we choose. Suppose we measured tomato prices P in cents per pound rather than dollars. Now the demand curve would be $Q = 1,000 - 2P$, because the quantity of tomatoes demanded would fall by 2 pounds for every 1 cent increase in price. But the fact that the coefficient on P is now 2 instead of 200 doesn't mean that consumers are 1/100th as price-sensitive as before. Nothing has changed about consumers' price responsiveness in this market: The quantity demanded still falls by 200 pounds for each $1 increase in price. The change in the slope simply reflects a change in the units of P. The second problem with slopes is that you can't compare them across different products. Suppose we were studying consumers' grocery shopping patterns, and wanted to compare consumers' price sensitivity for tomatoes in the market at Pike Place Market to their price sensitivity for celery hearts, for instance. Does the fact that consumers demand 100 fewer celery hearts for every 10 cent per celery heart increase in price mean that consumers are more or less price elastic in the celery market than in the tomato market? The slope of the celery demand curve implied by these numbers is -100 (if we measure quantity demanded in hearts and price in cents per celery heart). How could we ever compare this slope to the -200 slope for tomatoes?

Using elasticities to express responsiveness avoids these tricky issues, because everything is expressed in relative percentage changes. That eliminates the units problem (a 10% change is a 10% change regardless of what units the thing changing is measured in) and makes magnitudes comparable across markets.

The Price Elasticities of Demand and Supply

The price elasticity of demand is the ratio of the percentage change in quantity demanded to an associated percentage change in price. Mathematically, its formula is

Price elasticity of demand = (% change in quantity demanded)/(% change in price)

The price elasticity of supply is exactly analogous:

Price elasticity of supply = (% change in quantity supplied)/(% change in price)

To keep the equations simpler from now on, we'll use some shorthand notation. E^D will denote the price elasticity of demand, E^S the price elasticity of supply, $\%\Delta Q^D$ and $\%\Delta Q^S$ the percentage change in quantities demanded and supplied, respectively, and $\%\Delta P$ the percentage change in price. In this shorthand, the two equations above become

$$E^D = \frac{\%\Delta Q^D}{\%\Delta P} \text{ and}$$

$$E^S = \frac{\%\Delta Q^S}{\%\Delta P}$$

So, for example, if the quantity demanded of a good falls by 10% in response to a 4% price increase, the good's price elasticity of demand is $E^D = -10\%/4\% = -2.5$. There are a couple of things to note about this example. First, because demand curves slope downward, the price elasticity of demand is always negative (or more precisely, always nonpositive; in special cases that we will discuss below, it can be zero). Second, because it is a ratio, a price elasticity can also be thought of as the percentage change in quantity demanded for a 1% increase in price. That is, for this good, a 1% increase in price leads to a −2.5% change in quantity demanded.

The price elasticity of supply works exactly the same way. If producers' quantity supplied increases by 25% in response to a 50% increase in price, for example, the price elasticity of supply is $E^S = 25\%/50\% = 0.5$. The price elasticity of supply is always positive (or again more precisely, always nonnegative) because quantity supplied increases when a good's price rises. And just as with demand elasticities, supply elasticities can be thought of as the percentage change in quantity in response to a 1% increase in price.

Price Elasticities and Price Responsiveness

Now that we've defined elasticities, let's use them to think about how responsive quantities demanded and supplied are to price changes.

When demand (supply) is very price-sensitive, a small change in price will lead to large changes in quantities demanded (supplied). That means the numerator of the elasticity expression, the percentage change in quantity, will be very large in magnitude compared to the percentage change in price in the denominator. For price elasticity of demand, the change in quantity will have the opposite sign as the price change, and the elasticity will be negative. But its magnitude (its absolute value) will be large if consumers are very responsive to price changes.

Examples of markets with large-magnitude price elasticities of demand would be those where consumers have a lot of ability to substitute away from or toward the good in question. (We also saw above how substitute products can lead to shifts in the demand curve. Substitutes are therefore an example of a force that can rotate demand curves as they shift.) The demand for apples at the grocery store is probably fairly price-responsive because consumers have an array of other fruits they could buy instead if apple prices are high; if apple prices are low, they will buy apples instead of other fruits. The price elasticity of demand for apples might be something like −4: for every 1% increase in price, consumers' quantity demanded would fall 4%.

Markets with less price-responsive demand have elasticities that are small in magnitude. The demand for candy at the circus (certainly for the parents of small children) probably has a fairly small price elasticity of demand. In this case, the price elasticity of demand might be something like −0.3: for every 1% increase in price, quantity demanded would fall by 0.3%. (If you prefer, you could also express this as saying for every 10% price increase, quantity demanded would drop by 3%.)

Markets with large price elasticities of supply—where the quantity supplied is sensitive to price differences—would be those where it was easy for suppliers to vary their amount of production as price changes. Perhaps they have a cost structure that allows them to make as many units as they'd like without driving up their per-unit costs too much. In the market for software, for example, if a program is wildly popular and drawing a high price, it's fairly easy for the game's producer to print more DVDs or make additional copies available for download. So, the elasticity of supply might be quite large in this market, something like 12 (a 1% increase in price leads to a 12% increase in quantity supplied).

Markets with low price elasticities of supply have quantities supplied that are fairly unresponsive to price changes. This would occur in markets where it is costly for producers to vary their production levels, or it is difficult for producers to enter or exit the market. The supply curve for tickets to the Super Bowl might have a very low price elasticity of supply because there are only so many seats in the stadium. If the ticket price rises today, the stadium owners can't really put in additional seats. The supply elasticity in this market might be close to zero. It's probably slightly positive, however, because the owners could open some obstructed-view seats or make other temporary seating arrangements.

 **application**

Demand elasticities and the availability of substitutes

We discussed how the availability of substitutes can affect the price elasticity of demand. When consumers can easily switch to other products or markets, they will be more responsive to changes in price of a particular good. This means that, for any small rise in price, there will be a large decline in quantity demanded and the price elasticity of demand will be relatively large (in absolute value).

Economists Glenn and Sara Ellison found an extreme example of the effect of substitution possibilities and extreme demand elasticities to match.[7] They look at the markets for different CPUs and memory chips on a price search engine Web site. The Web site collects price quotes for well-defined chips and chipsets from hardware suppliers and then groups the quotes together (ranked by price) with links to the corresponding suppliers. While Ellison and Ellison show that suppliers make heroic efforts to frustrate the search engine, it still makes it extremely easy to compare multiple suppliers' prices for certain products. Because the product in this case is so standardized, little distinguishes one chip from another. As a result, consumers are able and willing to respond strongly to any price differences across the suppliers of the chips.

[7] Glenn Ellison and Sara Ellison, "Search, Obfuscation, and Price Elasticities on the Internet." *Econometrica* 77, no. 2 (2009): 427–452.

This easy ability for consumers to substitute across suppliers means the demand curve for any given supplier's CPUs and memory chips is extremely elastic. If a supplier's price is even a slight bit higher than that of its competitors, consumers can easily buy from someone else. Ellison and Ellison, using data collected from the Web site, estimated the price elasticity of demand for any single chip is on the order of –25. In other words, if the supplier raises its price just 1% higher than that of its competitors (which works out to a dollar or two for the chips listed on the Web site), it can expect sales to fall by 25%! This is a huge price response, and it's due to the many substitution possibilities the search engine makes available to consumers. Thus, the availability of substitutes is one of the key determinants of the price elasticity of demand. ■

Elasticities and Time Horizons   Often, a key factor determining the flexibility consumers and producers have to respond to price differences, and therefore the price elasticity of their quantities demanded and supplied, is the time horizon.

In the short run, consumers are often limited in their ability to change their consumption patterns, but given more time, they can make adjustments that give them greater flexibility. The classic example of this is in the market for gasoline. If there is a sudden price spike, many consumers are essentially stuck having to consume roughly the same quantity of gas as they did before the price spike. After all, they have the same car, the same commute, and the same schedule as before. Maybe they can double up on a few trips, or carpool more often, but their ability to respond to prices is limited. For this reason, the short-run price elasticity of gasoline demand is relatively low; empirical estimates by economists that specialize in the market suggest it is around –0.2. That is, for a 1% change in the price of gas, the quantity demanded changes by only –0.2% in the opposite direction as the price changes. Over longer horizons, however, individuals have greater scope to adjust their consumption. If the gas spike is permanent, or at least persistent, they can set up a permanent ride-sharing arrangement, buy a more efficient car, or even shorten their commute by moving closer to where they work. The long-run price elasticity of demand for gasoline is therefore much larger in magnitude; empirical studies typically find it is something like –0.8. This means that in the long run, consumers can make four times the quantity adjustment to price changes they can make in the short run.

The same logic holds for producers and supply elasticities. The longer the horizon, the more scope they have to adjust output to price changes. Manufacturers already producing at capacity might not be able to increase their output much in the short run if prices increase, even though they would like to. If prices stay high, however, they can hire more workers, build larger factories, and new firms can set up their own production operations and enter the market.

For these reasons, the price elasticities of demand and supply for most products are larger in magnitude (i.e., more negative for demand and more positive for supply) in the long run than in the short run. As we see in the next section, larger-magnitude elasticities imply flatter demand and supply curves. As a result, long-run demand and supply curves tend to be flatter than their short-run versions.

Terms for Elasticities by Magnitude   Economists have special terms for elasticities of particular magnitudes. Elasticities with magnitudes (absolute values) greater than 1 are referred to as **elastic.** In the above examples, apples have elastic demand and software has elastic supply. Elasticities with magnitudes less than 1 are referred to as **inelastic.** The demand for circus candy and the supply of previous wine vintages are inelastic. If the price elasticity of demand is exactly –1, or the price

elastic
A price elasticity with an absolute value greater than 1.

inelastic
A price elasticity with an absolute value less than 1.

elasticity of supply is exactly 1, this is referred to as **unit elastic.** If price elasticities are zero—that is, there is no response in quantity to price changes, the associated goods are called **perfectly inelastic.** Finally, if price elasticities are infinite in magnitude ($-\infty$ for demand, $+\infty$ for supply)—the quantity demanded or supplied changes infinitely in response to any price change—this is referred to as **perfectly elastic.**

Elasticities and Linear Demand and Supply Curves

As we discussed above, economists often use linear (straight-line) demand and supply curves, mostly for the sake of convenience. Because they are so common, it's worth discussing how elasticities are related to linear curves. Even more importantly, drawing this connection shows exactly how curves' slopes and elasticities, the two measures of price responsiveness we've been using, are related but still different.

We can rewrite the elasticity formula in a way that makes it easier to see the relationship between elasticity and the slope of a demand or supply curve. A percentage change in quantity ($\%\Delta Q$) is the change in quantity (ΔQ) divided by the original quantity level Q. That is, $\%\Delta Q = \Delta Q /Q$. Similarly, the percentage change in price is $\%\Delta P = \Delta P/P$. Substituting these into the elasticity expression from above, we have

$$E = \frac{\%\Delta Q}{\%\Delta P} = \frac{\Delta Q/Q}{\Delta P/P}$$

where E is a demand or supply elasticity, depending on whether Q denotes quantity demanded or supplied.

Rearranging terms yields

$$E = \frac{\Delta Q/Q}{\Delta P/P} = \frac{\Delta Q}{\Delta P} \cdot \frac{P}{Q}$$

or

$$E = \frac{1}{\text{slope}} \cdot \frac{P}{Q}$$

Elasticity of a Linear Demand Curve   Suppose we're dealing with the demand curve in Figure 2.15. Its slope is -2, but its elasticity varies as we move along it,

Figure 2.15   Elasticity of a Linear Demand Curve

The ratio between price and quantity (P/Q) and the magnitude of the elasticity of a demand curve decrease as we move down the curve. At point A, $Q = 0$, $P/Q = \infty$, and the price elasticity of demand is $-\infty$. Between points A and B, the demand curve is elastic with a price elasticity of demand less than -1. At point B, the demand curve is unit elastic, or the price elasticity of demand equals -1. Between points B and C, the demand curve is inelastic with a price elasticity of demand greater than -1. At point C, $P = 0$, $P/Q = 0$, and the price elasticity of demand equals zero.

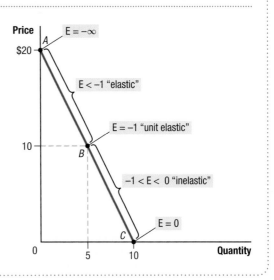

because P/Q does. Think first about the point A, where it intercepts the vertical axis. At $Q = 0$, P/Q is infinite because P is positive ($20) and Q is zero. This, combined with the fact that the curve's (constant) slope is negative, means the price elasticity of demand is $-\infty$ at this point. The logic behind this is that consumers don't demand any units of the good at A when its price is $20, but if price falls at all, their quantity demanded will become positive, if still small. Even though this change in quantity demanded is small in numbers of units of the good, the *percentage* change in consumption is infinite, because it's rising from zero.

As we move down along the demand curve, the P/Q ratio falls, reducing the magnitude of the price elasticity of demand. (Remember, the slope isn't changing, so that part of the elasticity stays the same.) It will remain elastic—that is, have a magnitude larger than 1—for some distance. Eventually, the absolute value of the elasticity will fall to 1, and at that point the demand curve is unit elastic. For the curve in Figure 2.15, this happens to be when $P = 10$ and $Q = 5$, because $E^D = -(1/2) \times (10/5) = -1$. This is labeled point B in the figure.[8] As we continue down and to the right along the demand curve, the magnitude of the elasticity will fall further and demand will become inelastic. At the point where the demand curve hits the horizontal axis (point C in the figure), price is zero, so $P/Q = 0$, and the price elasticity of demand is zero.

To recap, the price elasticity of demand of changes from $-\infty$ to zero as we move down and to the right along a linear demand curve.

Elasticity of a Linear Supply Curve A somewhat similar effect is seen as we move along a linear supply curve, like the one in Figure 2.16. Again, because the slope of the curve is constant, the changes in elasticity along the curve are driven by the price-to-quantity ratio. At point A, where the supply curve intercepts the vertical axis, $Q = 0$ and P/Q is infinite. The price elasticity of supply is $+\infty$ at this point. The same logic holds as with the demand curve: For the smallest increase in price,

---

Figure 2.16 | **Elasticity of a Linear Supply Curve**

The ratio between price and quantity (P/Q) and the magnitude of the elasticity of a supply curve decrease as we move up the curve. At point A, $Q = 0$, $P/Q = \infty$, and the price elasticity of supply is ∞. From B to C to D, the decrease in P/Q is reflected in the decrease of the slopes of the rays from these points to the origin. Unlike the demand curve, the price elasticity of supply will never reach zero because the supply curve never intercepts the quantity axis.

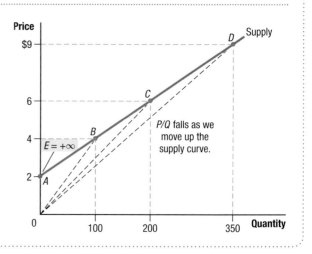

[8] For a linear demand curve that intersects both the price and quantity axes, the point where the demand curve is unit-elastic is always the midpoint. The curve's slope equals the price where it crosses the vertical axis (call this P_Y) divided by the quantity where it crosses the horizontal axis (call this Q_X), so 1 over the slope equals $-Q_X/P_Y$. The price-to-quantity ratio at the midpoint equals $(P_Y/2)/(Q_X/2)$, or simply P_Y/Q_X. The elasticity, which is the product of these two ratios, must therefore equal -1.

the quantity supplied rises from zero to a positive number, an infinite percentage change in quantity supplied.

As we move up along the supply curve, the P/Q ratio falls. While it's probably obvious to you that it must fall from infinity, you might wonder whether it keeps falling, because both P and Q are rising. It turns out that, yes, it must keep falling. The way to see this is to recognize that the P/Q ratio at any point on the supply curve equals the slope of a ray from the origin to that point. (The rise of the ray is the price P, and its run is the quantity Q. Because slope is rise over run, the ray's slope is P/Q.) We've drawn some examples of such rays for different locations on the supply curve in Figure 2.16. It's clear from the figure that as we move up and to the right along the supply curve, the slopes of these rays from the origin continue to fall.

Unlike with the demand curve, however, the P/Q ratio never falls to zero because the supply curve will never intercept the horizontal axis. Therefore, the price elasticity of supply won't drop to zero. In fact, while the P/Q ratio is always falling as we move up along the supply curve, you can see from the figure that it will never drop below the slope of the supply curve itself. Some linear supply curves like the one in Figure 2.16 intercept the vertical axis at a positive price, indicating that the price has to be at least as high as the intercept for producers to be willing to supply any positive quantity. Because the price elasticity of supply equals $(1/\text{slope}) \times (P/Q)$, such supply curves approach becoming unit elastic at high prices and quantities supplied, but never quite get there. Also, because P/Q never falls to zero, the only way a supply curve can have an elasticity of zero is if its inverse slope is zero—that is, if it is vertical. We discuss cases like this below.

2.5 figure it out

The demand for gym memberships in a small rural community is $Q = 360 - 2P$, where Q is the number of monthly members and P is the monthly membership rate.

a. Calculate the price elasticity of demand for gym memberships when the price is $50 per month.

b. Calculate the price elasticity of demand for gym memberships when the price is $100 per month.

c. Based on your answers to (a) and (b), what can you tell about the relationship between price and the price elasticity of demand along a linear demand curve?

Solution:

a. The price elasticity of demand is calculated as

$$E = \frac{\Delta Q/Q}{\Delta P/P} = \frac{\Delta Q}{\Delta P} \cdot \frac{P}{Q}$$

Let's first calculate the slope of the demand curve. The easiest way to do this is to rearrange the equation in terms of P to find the inverse demand curve:

$$Q = 360 - 2P$$
$$2P = 360 - Q$$
$$P = 180 - 0.5Q$$

We can see that the slope of this demand curve is –0.5. We know this because every time Q rises by 1, P falls by 0.5.

So, we know the slope and the price. To compute the elasticity, we need to know the quantity demanded at a price of $50. To find this, we plug $50 into the demand equation for P:

$$Q = 360 - 2P = 360 - 2(50) = 360 - 100 = 260$$

Now, we are ready to compute the elasticity:

$$E = \frac{1}{-0.5} \cdot \frac{50}{260} = \frac{50}{-130} = -0.385$$

b. When the price is $100 per month, the quantity demanded is

$$Q = 360 - 2P = 360 - 2(100) = 360 - 200 = 160$$

Plugging into the elasticity formula, we get

$$E = \frac{1}{-0.5} \cdot \frac{100}{160} = \frac{100}{-80} = -1.25$$

c. From (a) and (b), we can see that as the price rises along a linear demand curve, demand moves from being inelastic (0.385 < 1) to elastic (1.25 > 1).

Perfectly Inelastic and Perfectly Elastic Demand and Supply

The formula relating elasticities to slopes also sheds some light on what demand and supply curves look like in two special but often discussed cases: perfectly inelastic and perfectly elastic demand and supply.

Perfect Inelasticity   We discussed above that when the price elasticity is zero, demand and supply are said to be perfectly inelastic. When would this be the case? We just saw that this will be true for any linear demand at the point where it intercepts the horizontal (quantity) axis. But what would a demand curve look like that is perfectly inelastic everywhere? A linear demand curve with a slope of $-\infty$ would drive the price elasticity of demand to zero due to the inverse relationship between elasticity and slope. Because a curve with an infinite slope is vertical, a perfectly inelastic demand curve is vertical. An example of such a curve is shown in Figure 2.17a. This makes intuitive sense: A vertical demand curve indicates that the quantity demanded by consumers is completely unchanged regardless of the price. Any percentage change in price will induce a 0% change in quantity demanded. In other words, the price elasticity of demand is zero.

While perfectly inelastic demand curves are uncommon (after all, there are almost always possibilities for consumers and producers to substitute toward or away from a good as prices hit either extreme of zero or infinity), we might see some approximations to this case. For example, diabetics might have very inelastic demand for insulin. Their demand curve will be almost vertical.

The same logic holds for supply: A vertical supply curve indicates perfectly inelastic supply and no response of quantity supplied to price differences. The supply of tickets for a particular concert or sporting event might also be close to perfectly inelastic, with a near-vertical supply curve, due to capacity constraints of the arena.

One implication of perfect inelasticity is that any shift in the market's demand or supply curve will result in a change only in the market equilibrium price, not the

Figure 2.17 : **Perfectly Inelastic and Perfectly Elastic Demand Curves**

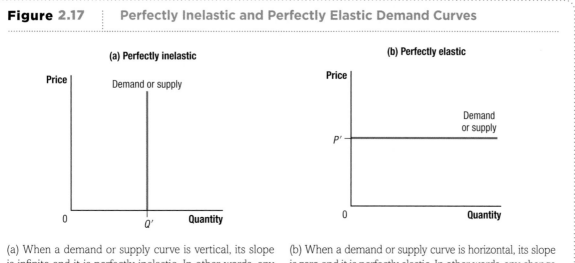

(a) When a demand or supply curve is vertical, its slope is infinite and it is perfectly inelastic. In other words, any change in price will result in a 0% change in quantity demanded or supplied.

(b) When a demand or supply curve is horizontal, its slope is zero and it is perfectly elastic. In other words, any change in price will result in an infinitely large change in quantity demanded or supplied.

quantity. That's because there is absolutely no scope for quantity to change in the movement along a perfectly inelastic demand curve from the old to the new equilibrium. Likewise, for perfectly inelastic supply, if there is a demand curve shift, all equilibrium movement is in price, not quantity.

Perfect Elasticity   When demand or supply is perfectly elastic, on the other hand, the price elasticity is infinite. This will be the case for linear demand or supply curves that have slopes of zero—those that are horizontal. An example of such a curve is shown in Figure 2.17b. This shape makes intuitive sense, too. As flat demand or supply curves imply large quantity responses to price differences, *perfectly* flat curves imply infinitely large quantity changes to price differences. If price is just above a horizontal demand curve, the quantity demanded will be zero. But if price fell just a bit, to below the demand curve, the quantity demanded would be infinite. Similarly, a small price change from above to below a horizontal supply curve would shift producers' quantity supplied from infinite to zero.

When might we see perfectly elastic demand or supply curves? Small producers of commodity goods probably face demand curves for their products that are approximately horizontal. (We'll discuss this more in Chapter 8.) For instance, a small corn farmer can probably sell as many bushels of corn as she wants at the fixed price offered by the local grain elevator. While the elevator couldn't really handle an infinite amount of corn, it has the capacity to buy much more corn than the farmer could ever practically sell. So from the farmer's perspective, the quantity demanded at the offered price can grow as large as would ever matter for her. At the same time, if the farmer decided that the elevator's price was too low and insisted that she be paid more than the going rate, the elevator would likely refuse to buy any corn from the farmer. Effectively, then, it is as if the farmer faces an infinite quantity demanded for her corn at the going price (or below it, if for some reason she's willing to sell for less) but zero quantity demanded of her corn above that price. In other words, she faces a flat demand curve at the going market price.

Supply curves are close to perfectly elastic in competitive industries in which producers all have roughly the same costs, and entry and exit is very easy. (We'll also discuss this point more in Chapter 8.) These conditions mean that competition will drive prices toward the (common) level of costs, and differences in quantities supplied will be soaked up by the entry and exit of firms from the industry. Because of the strictures of competition in the market, no firm will be able to sell at a price above costs, and obviously no firm will be willing to supply at a price below costs. Therefore, the industry's supply curve is essentially flat at the producers' cost level.

As opposed to the perfectly inelastic case, shifts in supply in a market with perfectly elastic demand will only move equilibrium quantity, not price. There's no way for the equilibrium price to change when the demand curve is flat. Similarly, for markets with perfectly elastic supply, demand curve shifts move only equilibrium quantities and not prices.

2.8 The Price Elasticity of Demand, Expenditures, and Revenue

There's an interesting and useful relationship between consumers' expenditures on a good and the price elasticity of demand. Namely, expenditures rise with prices if demand is inelastic, but decrease with prices if demand is inelastic. If demand is unit elastic, a change in price has no impact on expenditures. This same relationship holds between firm revenue and the price elasticity of demand.

To see why this is the case, recognize that expenditures and revenue are the products of price and quantity:

$$\text{Total expenditure} = \text{Total revenue} = P \cdot Q$$

Now think about how expenditure will change when price rises. (In the rest of this section, we examine what happens to expenditure when price changes, but we could instead focus on how prices change revenue and get the same result.) Obviously, the direct impact of the price increase will tend to raise expenditures. However, the higher price will also reduce quantity demanded, which tends to reduce expenditures. Which of these opposing effects is stronger depends on the price elasticity of demand.

We can be more specific. The percentage change in a product of two numbers is approximately equal to the sum of the percentage changes in the product's components. That means the percentage change in total expenditure due to a price change equals the percentage change in price plus the percentage change in quantity demanded that results. Of course, since price and quantity demanded move in opposite directions, when one of these changes is positive, the other change will be negative. For example, suppose that price rises. If the percentage increase in price is larger than the percentage drop in quantity demanded, expenditures will increase as a result of the price hike. Expenditures will decrease if the opposite holds true and the percentage drop in quantity demanded is larger than the price change.

To see this more explicitly, remember the formula for the price elasticity of demand:

$$E^D = \frac{\%\Delta Q^D}{\%\Delta P}$$

If demand is inelastic (the elasticity is smaller than 1 in absolute value, or between −1 and zero if you prefer), then the percentage drop in quantity (the numerator) will be smaller than the percentage increase in price (the denominator). This means the direct effect of price outweighs the quantity effect, and expenditures rise. If demand is elastic (the elasticity is greater than 1 in absolute value) on the other hand, then the percentage drop in quantity (the numerator) will be larger than the percentage increase in price (the denominator). In this case, the indirect effect of the price increase is larger than the direct effect, and total expenditures fall. For unit elastic demand (an elasticity of −1), the percentage increase in price exactly equals the percentage decrease in quantity demanded, so expenditure doesn't change.

For a downward-sloping linear demand curve like the one shown in Figure 2.15 this property means that total expenditures will follow a particular pattern as we move along the demand curve. Let's start at the curve's intercept with the horizontal axis, point C. There, price is zero, so implied expenditure is also zero. Easy enough. Now let's start increasing the price, so we're moving up and to the left along the demand curve. As we know from our previous discussion, along the portion of the demand curve closest to the horizontal intercept, the demand is inelastic. Therefore, the percentage increase in price from moving up the demand curve is larger than the percentage decrease in quantity demanded, meaning expenditures must rise. As we keep increasing price and moving up the demand curve, demand will continue to be inelastic and expenditures will continue to rise until point B, where demand becomes unit elastic. At that point, we know that expenditures will not change when price increases. However, as we keep increasing price and moving further up the demand curve, demand becomes price elastic. This means that the percentage drop in quantity demanded is larger than the percentage increase in price, and expenditure starts to fall. This drop in expenditures continues as we keep raising price and moving up the demand curve. Eventually, we reach point A. There, quantity falls to zero and therefore so do implied expenditures.

If we plot these changes in expenditure along the demand curve versus the price, we get Figure 2.18. When price is zero at point C, so are expenditures (we've labeled

---

Figure 2.18   Expenditures along a Linear Demand Curve

At point C, price and expenditures are zero along the demand curve. Between points C and B, the demand curve is inelastic, and expenditures increase with the increase in price along the demand curve. Point B is the maximum expenditures point; at B, the demand curve is unit elastic, and expenditures neither rise nor fall. Between points B and A, the demand curve is elastic, and expenditures decrease with the increase in price along the demand curve.

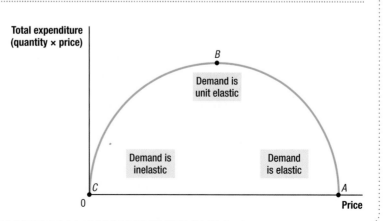

the expenditure plot with points on the demand curve in Figure 2.15 to which they correspond). As price rises through the inelastic part of the demand curve, so do expenditures. When price hits the level at *B*, demand is unit elastic and expenditures are neither rising nor falling. At higher price levels, expenditure falls as price rises until finally hitting zero again at point *A*. Notice how expenditure is maximized at point *B*, where demand is unit elastic. This is because at lower prices demand is inelastic and expenditures rise with price, but at higher prices demand is elastic and expenditures fall in price.

2.9 Other Elasticities

We've been focusing on price elasticities to this point, and with good reason: They are a key determinant of demand and supply behavior and play an important role in helping us understand how markets work. However, they are not the only elasticities that matter in demand and supply analysis. Remember how we divided up all the factors that affected demand or supply into two categories: price and everything else? Well, each of those other factors that went into "everything else" has an influence on demand or supply that can be measured with an elasticity.

The most commonly used of these elasticities measure the impact of two other factors on quantity demanded. These are the income elasticity of demand and the cross-price elasticity of demand.

Income Elasticity of Demand

income elasticity of demand
The percentage change in quantity demanded associated with a 1% change in consumer income.

The **income elasticity of demand** is the ratio of the percentage change in quantity demanded to the corresponding percentage change in consumer income (*I*):

$$E^D_{\ I} = \frac{\%\Delta Q^D}{\%\Delta I} = \frac{\Delta Q^D}{\Delta I} \cdot \frac{I}{Q^D}$$

(Equivalently, it is the percentage change in quantity demanded associated with a 1% increase in consumer income.)

Income elasticities describe how responsive demand is to income changes. Goods are sometimes categorized by the sign and size of their income elasticity. Goods that have an income elasticity that is negative, meaning consumers demand a lower quantity of the good when their income rises, are called **inferior goods.** This name isn't a comment on their inherent quality; it just describes how their consumption changes with people's incomes. (Note, however, that low-quality versions of many product categories are inferior goods by the economic definition.) Examples of likely inferior goods are bus tickets, youth hostels, and hot dogs.

inferior good
A good for which quantity demanded decreases when income rises.

Goods with positive income elasticities (consumers' quantity demanded rises with their income) are called **normal goods.** As the name indicates, most goods fit into this category.

normal good
A good for which quantity demanded rises when income rises.

The subcategory of normal goods with income elasticities above 1 is sometimes called **luxury goods.** Having an income elasticity that is greater than 1 means the quantity demanded of these products rises at a faster rate than income. As a consequence, the share of a consumer's budget that is spent on a luxury good becomes larger as the consumer's income rises. (To keep a good's share of the budget constant, quantity consumed would have to rise at the same rate as income. Because luxury goods' quantities rise faster, their share increases with income.) Yachts, butlers, and fine art are all luxury goods.

luxury good
A good with an income elasticity greater than 1.

We will dig deeper into the relationship between incomes and consumer demand in Chapters 4 and 5.

Cross-Price Elasticity of Demand

The **cross-price elasticity of demand** is the ratio of the percentage change in one good's quantity demanded (say, good X) to the percentage change in price of *another* good Y:

$$E^D_{XY} = \frac{\%\Delta Q^D_X}{\%\Delta P_Y} = \frac{\Delta Q^D_X}{\Delta P_Y} \cdot \frac{P_Y}{Q^D_X}$$

(To avoid confusion, sometimes the price elasticities we discussed above, which are concerned with the percentage change in quantity demanded to the percentage change in the price of the *same* good, are referred to as **own-price elasticities of demand.**)

When a good has a positive cross-price elasticity with another good, that means consumers demand a higher quantity of it when the other good's price rises. In other words, the good is a substitute for the other good: Consumers switch to the good when the other one becomes more expensive. Many pairs of goods are substitutes for one another—different brands of cereal, meals at restaurants versus dinners at home, colleges, and so on. Economist Aviv Nevo measured the substitutability of different cereals. He found that Froot Loops, for example, is a substitute for other kids' cereals, like Frosted Flakes and Cap'n Crunch ($E^D_{XY} = 0.131$ and 0.149, respectively). However, it is much less of a substitute for the more adult Shredded Wheat, which had a cross-price elasticity of only 0.020.[9]

When a good has a negative cross-price elasticity with another good, consumers demand less of it when the other good's price increases. This indicates that the goods are complements. Complements tend to be goods that are consumed together. If either of the goods within each pair were to become more expensive, consumers would buy not just less of that good itself, but of the other good in the pair as well. Milk and cookies are complements, as are tennis rackets and tennis balls, and computers and software.

cross-price elasticity of demand
The percentage change in the quantity demanded of one good associated with a 1% change in the price of another good.

own-price elasticities of demand
The percentage change in quantity demanded for a good resulting from a percentage change in the price of that good.

2.6 figure it out

Suppose that the price elasticity of demand for cereal is -0.75 and the cross-price elasticity of demand between cereal and the price of milk is -0.9. If the price of milk rises by 10%, what would have to happen to the price of cereal to exactly offset the rise in the price of milk and leave the quantity of cereal demanded unchanged?

Solution:

The first step will be to see what happens to the quantity of cereal demanded when the price of milk rises by 10%. We can use the cross-price elasticity to help us with this. The cross-price elasticity for cereal with respect to the price of milk is equal to $\frac{\%\Delta Q_{\text{cereal}}}{\%\Delta P_{\text{milk}}} = -0.9$. Using the equation, we know that the denominator is 10 since the price of milk rose by 10%, so we get

$$\frac{\%\Delta Q_{\text{cereal}}}{\%\Delta P_{\text{milk}}} = \frac{\%\Delta Q_{\text{cereal}}}{10} = -0.9$$

$$\%\Delta Q_{\text{cereal}} = -9$$

Thus, when the price of milk rises by 10%, the quantity demanded of cereal falls by 9%.

---

[9] Aviv Nevo, "Measuring Market Power in the Ready-to-Eat Cereal Industry," *Econometrica* 69, no. 2 (2001): 307–342.

Now, we must consider how to offset this decline in the quantity of cereal demanded with a change in the price of cereal. In other words, what must happen to the price of cereal to cause the quantity of cereal demanded to *rise* by 9%? It is clear that the price of cereal must fall, because the law of demand suggests that there is an inverse relationship between price and quantity demanded. However, because we know the price elasticity of demand, we can actually determine how far the price of cereal needs to fall.

The price elasticity of demand for cereal is $\frac{\%\Delta Q}{\%\Delta P} = -0.75$. To offset the decline in cereal consumption caused by the rise in the price of milk, we need the percentage change in quantity demanded to be +9%. Therefore, we can plug 9% into the numerator of the ratio and solve for the denominator:

$$\frac{\%\Delta Q}{\%\Delta P} = -0.75$$

$$\frac{9}{\%\Delta P} = -0.75$$

$$\%\Delta P = \frac{9}{-0.75} = -12$$

The price of cereal would have to fall by 12% to exactly offset the effect of a rise in the price of milk on the quantity of cereal consumed.

2.10 Conclusion

This chapter introduced the concepts of supply and demand, two of the most important ideas in economics. Using the simplified supply and demand framework, we examined a variety of topics, including equilibrium price and quantity, the effects of shocks to supply and demand, and elasticities.

But, the various cases we looked at in this chapter are, for the most part, simplified and very abstract. In reality, measuring a market's demand and supply curves and determining the equilibrium price and quantity can be more challenging and complex. For example, firms hoping to make production decisions based on the types of analysis we've done here need to observe a wide range of data—prices, elasticities, demand curves, and so on—that are often not known exactly in the real world. As a result, producers might rely on more trial-and-error practices than allowed for in our simplified model. Indeed, our own experience with firms is that the people making the production decisions don't always approach and analyze them as economists would. If they did, firms might see more financial success. Beginning with Chapter 6 and continuing through Part 3, we talk more about situations that producers face in the real world, and the production decisions they have to make, such as how much of a product to produce, how to produce it, and whether they should enter a particular market at all. And we see how these decisions are reflected in a firm's supply curve. In the meantime, the simplified supply and demand framework we've developed here provides a valuable structure for delving into a deeper analysis of markets and equilibrium price and quantity in upcoming chapters.

Summary

1. Economists use models to analyze markets. Models employ simplifying assumptions to reduce the incredible complexity of the real world so that general insights can be learned. The supply and demand model is one of the most used analytical frameworks in economics. This model makes several assumptions about the market that is being analyzed, including that all goods bought and sold in the market are identical, they are all sold for the same price, and there are many producers and consumers in the market.

2. Demand describes the willingness of consumers to purchase a product. There are many factors that affect demand, including price, income, quality, tastes, and availability of substitutes. Economists commonly use the concept of a demand curve, which essentially divides these factors into two groups: price and everything else. A demand curve relates consumers' quantity demanded to the price of the good while holding every other factor affecting demand constant. A change in a good's price results in a movement along a given demand curve. If nonprice factors change, the quantity demanded at every price changes and the whole demand curve shifts.

3. Supply describes the willingness of producers to make and sell a product. Factors that affect supply include price, available production technologies, input prices, and producers' outside options. Supply curves isolate the relationship between quantity supplied and price, holding all other supply factors constant. A change in a good's price results in a movement along a given supply curve. If nonprice factors change, the quantity supplied at every price changes and the whole supply curve shifts.

4. Combining demand and supply curves lets us determine the market equilibrium price, which is where quantity demanded equals quantity supplied. This equilibrium can be determined because demand and supply curves isolate the relationships between quantities and the one factor that affects both demand and supply: price. At the equilibrium, every consumer who wants to buy at the going price can, and every producer who wants to sell at the current market price can as well.

5. Changes in the factors (other than price) that affect demand or supply will change the market equilibrium price and quantity. Changes that increase demand and shift out the demand curve will raise equilibrium price and quantity in the absence of supply shifts; when the changes decrease demand and shift the demand curve in, price and quantity will fall. Changes that increase supply and shift out the supply curve, assuming no change in the demand curve, will increase equilibrium quantity and reduce price. Changes that decrease supply and shift in the supply curve decrease quantity and raise price.

6. If both supply and demand shift, either the effect on equilibrium price or the effect on equilibrium quantity will be ambiguous. If demand and supply move in the same direction, equilibrium quantity will follow, but the impact on price is unknown. On the other hand, if demand and supply move in opposite directions, equilibrium price will move in the same direction as demand (increase when demand rises, fall when demand decreases) but we cannot say with certainty what the effect on equilibrium quantity will be.

7. Economists typically express the sensitivity of demand and supply to various factors, but especially price, in terms of elasticities. An elasticity is the ratio of the percentage changes in two variables. The price elasticity of demand is the percentage change in quantity demanded for a 1% change in price, and the price elasticity of supply is the percentage change in quantity supplied for a 1% price change.

8. Total expenditure and total revenue are both equal to price times quantity demanded. When demand is elastic ($|E^D| > 1$), an increase in price will lead to a fall in expenditures (revenue), while a decrease in price will lead expenditures (revenue) to increase. When demand is inelastic ($|E^D| < 1$), expenditure (revenue) rises when price rises and falls when price falls. When demand is unit elastic ($|E^D| = 1$), a change in price has no effect on total expenditure (revenue).

9. Other common demand elasticities measure the responsiveness of quantity demanded to changes in income and the prices of other goods. The income elasticity of demand is positive for normal goods and negative for inferior goods. The cross-price elasticity of demand is positive for substitutes and negative for complements.

Review Questions

1. There are four key assumptions underlying the supply and demand model. Name these assumptions.
2. Complements and substitutes of a given good affect the demand for that good. Define complements and substitutes.
3. What simplifying assumption do we make to build a demand curve? Why is the demand curve downward-sloping?
4. What is the difference between a change in quantity demanded and a change in demand?
5. Why is the supply curve upward-sloping?
6. What is an inverse supply curve? Why do economists often represent supply using the inverse supply curve?
7. What is the difference between a change in quantity supplied and a change in supply?
8. Define market equilibrium. What is true of the quantity supplied and demanded at the market equilibrium?
9. What happens when price is below the equilibrium price? Why?
10. In what direction will price and quantity move as a result of a demand shift?
11. In what direction will price and quantity move as a result of a supply shift?
12. Why is the direction of change of *either* price *or* quantity unknown when both supply and demand shift?
13. What happens to equilibrium price when demand and supply shift in the same direction? What happens to equilibrium quantity in the same situation?
14. What is the difference between an elasticity and slope?
15. We learned that economists have special terms for elasticities of particular magnitudes. Name the magnitudes for the following: inelastic, elastic, unit elastic, perfectly elastic, and perfectly inelastic.
16. What is total expenditure? Total revenue?
17. Why must you know the price elasticity of demand to be able to predict the effect of a change in price on total expenditure?
18. Using the concept of income elasticity of demand, describe normal, luxury, and inferior goods.
19. Using the concept of cross-price elasticity of demand, describe substitutes and complements.

Problems

1. Is there a difference between movements along a demand curve and shifts in a demand curve? How would you explain this difference to a friend who is taking this course and is confused about the issue?
2. The demand for organic carrots is given by the following equation:

$$Q_O^D = 75 - 5P_O + P_C + 2I$$

where P_O is the price of organic carrots, P_C is the price of conventional carrots, and I is the average consumer income. Notice how this isn't a standard demand curve that just relates the quantity of organic carrots demanded to the price of organic carrots. This demand function also describes how other factors affect demand—namely, the price of another good (conventional carrots) and income.
   a. Draw the demand curve for organic carrots when $P_C = 5$ and $I = 10$.
   b. Using the demand curve drawn in (a), what is the quantity demanded of organic carrots when $P_O = 10$?
   c. Using the demand curve drawn in (a), what is the quantity demanded of organic carrots when $P_O = 5$?
   d. Now, suppose $P_O = 10$ and $P_C = 15$ (I remains at 10). What is the quantity demanded of organic carrots? Compared with your answer in (b), has there been a change in demand or quantity demanded? Demonstrate using a graph.
   e. What happens to the demand for organic carrots when the price of conventional carrots increases? Are organic and conventional carrots complements or substitutes?
   f. What happens to the demand for organic carrots when the average consumer income increases? Are carrots a normal or an inferior good?
3. Out of the following events, which are likely to cause the demand for coffee to increase? Explain your answers.
   a. An increase in the price of tea
   b. An increase in the price of doughnuts
   c. A decrease in the price of coffee

d. The Surgeon General's announcement that drinking coffee lowers the risk of heart disease

e. Heavy rains causing a record-low coffee harvest in Colombia

4. How is each of the following events likely to shift the supply curve or the demand curve for fast-food hamburgers in the United States? Make sure you indicate which curve (curves) is affected and if it shifts out or in.

a. The price of beef triples.

b. The price of chicken falls by half.

c. The number of teenagers in the economy falls due to population aging.

d. Mad cow disease, a rare but fatal medical condition caused by eating tainted beef, becomes common in the United States.

e. The Food and Drug Administration publishes a report stating that a certain weight-loss diet, which encourages the intake of large amounts of meat, is dangerous to one's health.

f. An inexpensive new grill for home use that makes delicious hamburgers is heavily advertised on television.

g. The dollar rises relative to foreign currencies, so that it becomes expensive for foreign tourists to travel to the United States on vacation.

h. The minimum wage rises.

5. Your roommate remarks that it is strange that a flight from New York to Chicago costs more than a flight from New York to Orlando, since New York and Chicago are closer than New York and Orlando. What is your roommate assuming about the relationship between distance and price? How do you explain these prices?

6. Suppose that a hard freeze destroys a large portion of the Florida orange crop. At the same time, the *Journal of the American Medical Association* releases the results of a new study showing that drinking large quantities of orange juice substantially reduces one's risks of both heart disease and cancer. What is the likely effect of these two events on the price of orange juice? On the quantity of orange juice sold?

7. Suppose that you have been collecting vintage lightning rods for the past 30 years. When you began, finding lightning rods for sale meant drifting from town to town and antique store to antique store hoping that you would find a lightning rod for sale. The availability made possible by the Internet now means that you can easily find hundreds of lightning rods for sale at any given time.

a. Draw a diagram showing how the invention and popularization of the Internet have caused the demand curve for lightning rods to shift.

b. Suppose that the only change in the market for lightning rods is the change you described in (a). How would that change affect the equilibrium price of lightning rods and the equilibrium quantity of lightning rods sold?

8. In March 2002 the retail price of gasoline was $1.19 per gallon—exactly the same as it was in August 1990. Yet, total gasoline production and consumption rose from 6.6 million barrels per week in 1990 to 8.7 million barrels per week in 2002. Using the graph below, draw the appropriate shifts in the demand and supply curves to explain these two phenomena.

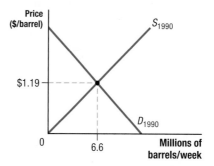

9. When the demand for toilet paper increases, the equilibrium quantity sold increases. Consumers are buying more, and producers are producing more.

a. How do producers receive the signal that they need to increase production to meet the new demand?

b. Does the increased production reflect an increase in supply, or an increase in the quantity supplied? Explain your answer, referring to (a).

10. Suppose the demand for towels is given by $Q^D = 100 - 5P$, and the supply of towels is given by $Q^S = 10P$.

a. Derive and graph the inverse supply and inverse demand curves.

b. Solve for the equilibrium price and quantity.

c. Suppose that supply changes so that at each price, 20 fewer towels are offered for sale. Derive and graph the new inverse supply curve.

d. Solve for the new equilibrium price and quantity.

11. Your university has an honors program that accepts exactly 40 freshmen each year. Every year before soliciting applications, students are informed of the standards for program participation. The admissions staff observed that whenever the difficulty of the program requirements increased (decreased), they received

fewer (more) applicants than in the previous year and have since begun to adjust requirements for each incoming group of students in an attempt to equate the number of applicants with the number of spots in the program. Though the system is not perfect, the administrators are able to estimate their applicant pool relatively accurately.

a. In this situation, what is the "price" that determines how many students will apply to the honors program? Also, assume that the people who run the honors program do not plan to expand or contract it. Depict the demand and supply curves that represent this situation.

b. How does the way "price" is determined in this situation differ from the way we normally think about the determination of equilibrium price?

c. Assume that applicants to the honors program are usually the most qualified students at the university. If the university began offering merit scholarships to incoming students, how would we expect the difficulty of the program to change over the next few years? Demonstrate your answer with a graph.

d. The president of the university became so impressed with the rigor of the first honors program that she decides to double its size. Assuming that the larger program accepts applicants in the same way, what will likely happen to the standards of the expanded honors program? Demonstrate your answer with a graph.

e. Instead of expanding the first honors program, the faculty recommends introducing a whole new one. Suppose the first was an honors program in science. How would standards change for the science honors program if the new honors program were in math? How about art history? Explain your answers.

12. Consider the market for van Gogh paintings and assume no forgeries are possible.

a. Is the supply of van Gogh paintings somewhat elastic, somewhat inelastic, perfectly elastic, or perfectly inelastic? Why?

b. Draw the supply curve for van Gogh paintings.

c. Suppose there are only 10 van Gogh paintings in the world, and the demand curve is $Q = 50 - 0.5P$. What is the equilibrium price?

d. A tragic fire destroys five of the paintings. What is the new equilibrium price?

13. Suppose the demand for down pillows is given by $Q^D = 100 - P$, and that the supply of down pillows is given by $Q^S = -20 + 2P$.

a. Solve for the equilibrium price.

b. Plug the equilibrium price back into the demand equation and solve for the equilibrium quantity.

c. Double-check your work by plugging the equilibrium price back into the supply equation and solving for the equilibrium quantity. Does your answer agree with what you got in (b)?

d. Solve for the elasticities of demand and supply at the equilibrium point. Which is more elastic, demand or supply?

e. Invert the demand and supply functions (in other words, solve each for P) and graph them. Do the equilibrium point and relative elasticities shown in the graph appear to coincide with your answers?

14. Suppose that budding economist Buck measures the inverse demand curve for toffee as $P = \$100 - Q^D$, and the inverse supply curve as $P = Q^S$. Buck's economist friend Penny likes to measure everything in cents. She measures the inverse demand for toffee as $P = 10{,}000 - 100Q^D$, and the inverse supply curve as $P = 100Q^S$.

a. Find the slope of the inverse demand curve, and compute the price elasticity of demand at the market equilibrium using Buck's measurements.

b. Find the slope of the inverse demand curve, and compute the price elasticity of demand at the market equilibrium using Penny's measurements. Is the slope the same as Buck calculated? How about the price elasticity of demand?

15. Suppose that innovations in agriculture lower the cost of producing lettuce by 10%. This cost reduction effectively shifts the inverse supply curve downward by 10% at every quantity.

a. Assume that the price of lettuce is determined by the forces of demand and supply. Graph the market for lettuce initially, and then illustrate the effects of the technological innovation.

b. Will lettuce growers be able to capture the cost savings provided by the new technology, or will they end up passing the savings along to consumers? Explain, using your graph.

c. How does your answer depend on the price elasticity of demand for lettuce? Explain, using two graphs to illustrate your point.

16. Some policy makers have claimed that the U.S. government should purchase illegal drugs, such as cocaine, to increase the price that drug users will face. Does this idea have any merit? Illustrate this logic in a simple supply and demand framework. How does the elasticity of demand for illegal drugs relate to the efficacy of this policy? Are

you more or less willing to favor this policy if you are told demand is inelastic?

17. Consider the following problems on elasticity:

a. When bottlers increased the price of canned soda from vending machines by 10%, sales dropped by 2.5%. Calculate the elasticity of demand for canned soda.

b. Refer to part (a). The total revenue received by bottlers from their sales of canned soda is equal to the price of canned soda times the number of cans sold ($TR = P_{\text{soda}} \times Q_{\text{soda}}$). In approximate percentage terms, what was the impact of the bottlers' price change on total revenue?

c. Sal the Sail Salesman's boss has just told him that if he fails to increase the volume of his sail sales by 8%, he'll be fired. In order to meet his goal, Sal is considering putting his sails on sale. If the price elasticity of demand for sales is −2.66, how much should Sal lower his price in order to meet his goal?

d. Yogi eats a sizable quantity of pizza by the slice, and generally pays $5 per slice at a vending cart outside his office. When a new vendor on the block begins offering pizza at $3 per slice, Yogi finds that his monthly total expenditures on pizza rise. What can we say about Yogi's elasticity of demand for pizza?

18. Suppose that a typical consumer has an inverse demand for frog's legs given by the following: $P = \dfrac{3}{Q^D}$. A graph of that inverse demand curve is given below:

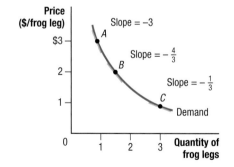

a. Show that the demand curve is unit-elastic.

b. If this customer came into your restaurant and asked for frog's legs, would you be better off charging a high price or a low price?

19. One type of elasticity that economists often use is the cross-price elasticity, which is measured as the percentage change in the quantity of a good when the price of a different good changes by 1%.

a. What sign might you expect the cross-price elasticity to have if the two goods are shampoo and hair conditioner? Why?

b. What sign might you expect the cross-price elasticity to have if the two goods are gasoline and ethanol? Why?

c. What sign might you expect the cross-price elasticity to have if the two goods are coffee and shoes? Why?

20. One type of elasticity that economists often use is the income elasticity, which is measured as the percentage change in the quantity of a good when the income of consumers changes by 1%.

a. What sign might you expect the income elasticity to have if the good in question is Swedish massages?

b. What sign might you expect the income elasticity to have if the good in question is Ramen noodles?

c. What sign might you expect the income elasticity to have if the good in question is table salt?

Using Supply and Demand to Analyze Markets

In Chapter 2, we introduced the tools of supply and demand analysis. We learned about the economic decisions that supply and demand curves embody, and defined what it means for a market to be in equilibrium. In this chapter, we put those tools to work to take a deeper look at how markets operate. We study how to measure the total benefits that consumers and producers gain in any given market, and how these benefits change when demand or supply shifts. We also see how various government interventions into markets affect the well-being of consumers and producers.

Governments often enact policies that affect how markets work. The purpose of these policies can be to serve a particular constituency, to raise necessary tax revenue, or (as we'll see in Chapter 16) to correct a market failure. For example, every time gas prices rise above the public's tolerance, some politicians predictably call for a top limit on gas prices (called a *price ceiling*). Judging from the opinion polls that are usually taken at such times, this policy strikes many people as being a good idea. Are they right? Whether changes in market conditions are the result of government market interventions or changes in any of the many factors that affect supply, demand, or both, we can use supply and demand analysis to figure out not only what happens to price and quantity, but also who benefits, who loses, and by how much.

consumer surplus
The difference between the amount consumers would be willing to pay for a good or service and the amount they actually have to pay.

3.1 Consumer and Producer Surplus: Who Benefits in a Market?

To begin to understand the market impact of any policy, we need a way to measure the benefit consumers and producers obtain from buying and selling goods and services in a market. Economists measure these benefits using the concepts of consumer and producer surplus.

Consumer Surplus

Consumer surplus is the difference between the price consumers would be willing to pay for a good (as measured by the height of their demand curves) and the price they actually have to pay. Consumer surplus is usually measured as an amount of money.

To see why we define consumer surplus this way, let's think like an economist. Say a person is lost in the desert with no water, is getting extremely thirsty, and has $1,000 in his pocket. He stumbles upon a convenience store in this desert where he sees a bottle of Dr Pepper for sale. What is he willing to pay for the drink? Quite likely, his entire $1,000. Applying the concept of elasticity from Chapter 2, we can say this guy's demand for something to drink is almost perfectly inelastic: He will demand the one bottle of Dr Pepper almost regardless of its price. Let's say the store is asking $1 for the bottle of Dr Pepper. Mr. Thirsty was willing to pay $1,000 for the Dr Pepper but only had to pay the $1 market price. After the transaction, he has his drink *and* $999 left in his pocket. That $999—the difference between what he was willing to pay and what he actually paid—is his consumer surplus.

We can take this one-person example and extend the consumer surplus to the demand curve for an entire market. For example, let's return to Pike Place Market but now consider the market for apples. The market demand curve in Figure 3.1 tells us how many pounds of apples consumers are willing to buy at any given price. Let's assume that the market price of apples is $3.50 per pound.

If every point along the market demand curve represents a different person's willingness to pay for a pound of apples, we can measure each person's consumer surplus just as we did for Mr. Thirsty. The person at point *A* on the demand curve is willing to pay up to $5 for a pound of apples. If the price is $3.50 per pound, she will buy the apples and also keep $1.50 of consumer surplus. Person *B* is willing to pay $4.50 per pound and receives $1 of consumer surplus, while Person *C* receives $0.50 of consumer surplus. The person at point *D* is willing to pay $3.50 for a pound of apples and must pay the market price of $3.50 a pound. Thus, there is no consumer surplus for this individual.[1] Person *E* will not buy any apples; he is only willing to pay $3 per pound, which is below the market price. If you want to know the total consumer surplus for the entire market, add up all of the gains for each individual who buys apples—person *A*, person *B*, and so on.

After adding up all the gains, you will find that the total consumer surplus in the entire Pike Place apple market is the area under the demand curve and above the price, the area of the shaded triangle *CS* in Figure 3.1. The base of the consumer surplus triangle is the quantity sold. The height of the triangle is the difference

---

[1] Some years ago, there was an economist who was hired away by another university. As part of the deal to lure him, the new school gave him a big raise. When he arrived at the new university in the fall, his new dean said that the school was happy he had decided to come. The economist responded that if they really were happy, then he hadn't asked for enough money. He wanted to leave them with no consumer surplus.

between the market price ($3.50) and the **demand choke price** ($5.50 per pound), the price at which quantity demanded is reduced to zero.[2]

In this example, the demand curve represented a collection of consumers, each with a different willingness to pay for a unit of the good. Those with a high willingness to pay are located at the upper left portion of the curve; those with a lower willingness to pay are down and to the right along the curve. The same logic also applies to an individual's demand curve, which reflects his declining willingness to pay for each additional unit of the good. For instance, an apple buyer might be willing to pay $5 for the first pound of apples he buys, but only $4 for the second pound and $3.50 for the third pound (maybe he has limited ability to store them, or just plain gets a bit tired of eating apples after a while). If the market price is $3.50 per pound, he will buy 3 pounds of apples. His consumer surplus will be $1.50 for the first pound, $0.50 for the second, and zero for the third, a total of $2. Doing this calculation for all apple buyers and adding up their consumer surpluses will give a total consumer surplus of the same type shown in the triangular area in Figure 3.1.

> **demand choke price**
> The price at which quantity demanded is reduced to zero.

Producer Surplus

Just as consumers gain surplus from engaging in market transactions, so do producers. **Producer surplus** is the difference between the price producers are willing to sell their goods for (measured by the height of the supply curve) and the price

> **producer surplus**
> The difference between the price at which producers are willing to sell their good or service and the price they actually receive.

Figure 3.1   Defining Consumer Surplus

Consumer surplus is the difference between the amount consumers are willing to pay and the amount they actually have to pay. The market demand curve shows how many pounds of apples consumers are willing to buy at a given price. The consumer at point A is willing to pay $5 for 1 pound of apples; at a market price of $3.50, this person has a consumer surplus of $1.50. Similarly, at the market price of $3.50, consumers at points B, C, and D have consumer surpluses of $1, $0.50, and $0, respectively. The consumer at point E does not purchase any apples. The total consumer surplus is the area under the demand curve and above the price, represented by the area of the shaded triangle CS, with the base of the triangle the total quantity sold and the height the difference between the market price and the demand choke price.

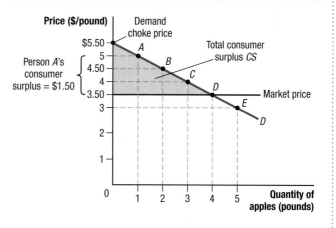

---

[2] There are two technicalities about this kind of calculation you should be aware of if you want to be completely precise. First, this area is a triangle only if the demand curve is a straight line. We use straight-line demand curves here because they are easy, but demand curves in real life are often curved. Second, calculating the total consumer surplus in dollars is only accurate if the marginal utility of income is constant. We discuss the idea of utility in Chapter 4. If a dollar of income is worth a lot more when income is low than when income is high, then we can't say for sure that all dollars of consumer surplus have the same impact on people's happiness.

they actually receive for the good. The supply curve in the Pike Place apple market (Figure 3.2) tells us how many pounds of apples producers are willing to sell at any given price. If we think of every point on the supply curve as representing a different apple seller, we see that Firm *V* would be willing to supply apples at a price of $2 per pound. Because it can sell apples at the market price of $3.50, however, it receives a producer surplus of $1.50.[3] Firm *W* is willing to sell apples for $2.50 per pound, and so receives $1 of producer surplus, while Firm *X* receives $0.50 of producer surplus. Firm *Y*, which is only willing to sell a pound of apples for $3.50, receives no surplus. Firm *Z* is shut out of the market; the market price of $3.50 per pound is less than its willingness to sell ($4). The total producer surplus for the entire market is the sum of producer surplus for every seller along the supply curve. This sum equals the triangle above the supply curve and below the price, the area of the shaded triangle *PS* in Figure 3.2. The base of the triangle is the quantity sold. The height of the triangle is the difference between the market price ($3.50) and the **supply choke price** ($1.50 per pound), the price at which quantity supplied equals zero. Here, that's $1.50 per pound; no seller is willing to sell apples below that price.

supply choke price
The price at which quantity supplied equals zero.

This particular supply curve represents a collection of producers that differ in their willingness to sell. The same logic applies to an individual producer's supply curve in cases where the firm's cost of producing additional output rises with its total output. In these cases, the firm must be paid more to sell additional units.[4] The firm's producer surplus is the sum of the differences between the market price and the minimum price the firm would need to receive to be willing to sell each unit.

Figure 3.2   Defining Producer Surplus

Producer surplus is the difference between the price at which producers are willing to sell their goods and the price they actually receive. The market supply curve shows how many pounds of apples sellers are willing to supply at a given price. The seller at point *V* is willing to sell his apples at a price of $2 per pound; at a market price of $3.50, this person receives a $1.50 producer surplus. Similarly, at the market price of $3.50, sellers at points *W*, *X*, and *Y* receive producer surpluses of $1, $0.50, and $0, respectively. The seller at point *Z* does not sell any apples. The total producer surplus is the area above the supply curve and below the price, represented by the area of the shaded triangle *PS*, with the base of the triangle the total quantity sold and the height the difference between the market price and the supply choke price.

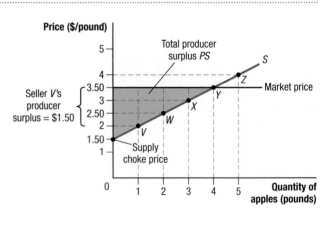

---

[3] Resist the temptation to call producer surplus "profit." While it seems natural to do this here, we will see in later chapters that the term "profit" has a precise meaning in economics, and it's not exactly this.

[4] We're also assuming here that the firm takes the market price as given. We'll discuss firms' supply behavior in this and the alternative case where a firm has price-setting power in Chapters 8 and 9.

3.1 figure it out

The demand and supply curves for newspapers in a Midwestern city are given by

$$Q^D = 152 - 20P$$
$$Q^S = 188P - 4$$

where Q is measured in thousands of newspapers per day and P in dollars per newspaper.

a. Find the equilibrium price and quantity.

b. Calculate the consumer and producer surplus at the equilibrium price.

Solution:

a. Equilibrium occurs where $Q^D = Q^S$. Therefore, we can solve for equilibrium by equating the demand and supply curves:

$$Q^D = Q^S$$
$$152 - 20P = 188P - 4$$
$$156 = 208P$$
$$P = \$0.75$$

Therefore, the equilibrium price of a paper is $0.75. To find the equilibrium quantity, we need to plug the equilibrium price into either the demand or supply curve:

$$Q^D = 152 - 20P \qquad\qquad Q^S = 188P - 4$$
$$= 152 - 20(0.75) \qquad\qquad = 188(0.75) - 4$$
$$= 152 - 15 \qquad\qquad = 141 - 4$$
$$= 137 \qquad\qquad = 137$$

Remember that Q is measured in terms of thousands of papers each day, so the equilibrium quantity is 137,000 papers each day.

b. To calculate consumer and producer surplus, it is easiest to use a graph. First, we need to plot the demand and supply curves. For each curve, we can identify two points. The first point is the equilibrium, given by the combination of equilibrium price ($0.75) and equilibrium quantity (137). The second point we can identify is the choke price for demand and supply. These can be determined by setting Q^D and Q^S equal to zero and solving for P:

$$Q^D = 152 - 20P \qquad\qquad Q^S = 188P - 4$$
$$0 = 152 - 20P \qquad\qquad 0 = 188P - 4$$
$$20P = 152 \qquad\qquad 4 = 188P$$
$$P = 7.6 \qquad\qquad P = 0.02$$

So the demand choke price is $7.60 and the supply choke price is $0.02.

The demand and supply curves are graphed in the figure below. Consumer surplus is the area below demand and above the price (area A). Its area can be calculated as

$$CS = \text{area } A = \frac{1}{2} \times \text{base} \times \text{height} = (0.5) \times (137{,}000 - 0) \times (\$7.60 - \$0.75)$$
$$= (0.5) \times 137{,}000 \times \$6.85 = \$469{,}225$$

Producer surplus is the area below price and above supply (area B):

$$PS = \text{area } B = \frac{1}{2} \times \text{base} \times \text{height} = (0.5) \times (137{,}000 - 0) \times (\$0.75 - \$0.02)$$
$$= 0.5 \times 137{,}000 \times \$0.73 = \$50{,}005$$

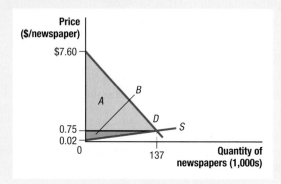

application

The value of innovation

Equipped with the concepts of consumer and producer surplus, we can do a quick analysis of one of the most important issues in economics—the introduction of new products. Economists emphasize the importance of innovation and new goods in raising a society's standard of living. In any discussion of the value of innovation, we need a way to compute how much benefit a new product gives to consumers.

A simple suggestion for valuing a new product would be to just add up what people paid for it. However, that approach would not be correct because, in reality, many consumers value the product at much more than the price they paid to get it. Consumer surplus, however, *does* measure the full benefit of the new product because it tells us how much consumers value the product *over and above* the price they pay.

A key factor in determining the amount of potential consumer surplus in a market for a new good is the steepness of the demand curve: All else equal, the steeper it is, the bigger the consumer surplus. That's because steep demand curves mean that at least some consumers (those accounting for the upper-left-hand side of the demand curve) have very high willingness to pay for the good. (You can see this on a price-quantity demand curve diagram. First, draw a horizontal line representing an equilibrium market price. Next, draw various demand curves with different slopes that intersect this price at the same point—i.e., so that the equilibrium quantity demanded is the same. You will see that the consumer surplus triangles will be larger for steeper demand curves.)

Let's look at eyeglasses as an example. Economist Joel Mokyr explained in his book *The Lever of Riches* that the invention of eyeglasses around the year 1280 allowed craftsmen to do detailed work for decades longer than they could before. If we think of glasses as a "new technology" circa 1280, we can visualize what the demand curve for glasses might have looked like. Because many people in 1280 would be quite blind without glasses, the demand curve was probably very steep—there was a set of individuals with a very high willingness to pay for glasses. This would also imply that demand wasn't particularly sensitive to prices. This steepness of the demand curve probably remained stable for the next 700 years, until the first commercially available contact lenses came on the market in the latter half of the twentieth century.

In Chapter 2, we learned that readily available substitute goods are likely to make demand more elastic. This is true of glasses, too: When contact lenses became available, the demand for glasses became more price elastic. How would this change in elasticity affect the consumer surplus people get from the existence of eyeglasses? Figure 3.3 illustrates the answer. Consumer surplus in 1950 is large because the demand for glasses D_1 is inelastic—if you want to see better, glasses are the only game in town. The consumer surplus is the area above the price and below D_1, or area $A + B$. Many people would be willing to buy glasses even if the price were much higher than P. (That's what having an inelastic demand means.)

When contact lenses become available, the demand for glasses becomes much more elastic, as shown by curve D_2. Even if just as many people buy glasses at the equilibrium price as before, a sharp rise in the price of glasses would cause many people to stop buying them because now they have an alternative. The figure shows that the consumer surplus from glasses declines after contacts come on the market. The area below the new, flatter demand curve and above the price is only area B.

After contacts are available, glasses are not worth as much to consumers because there are now other ways in which they can improve their eyesight. If glasses are the only way to fix your eyesight, you might be willing to pay thousands of dollars for them. Once you can buy contacts for $300, however, there is a limit to how much you would pay for glasses. You might still buy the glasses for $200, but you would certainly not be willing to pay $1,000 for them, and the change in consumer surplus reflects that change. Glasses are a miracle invention if they are the only way to correct one's vision (so they yield a higher consumer surplus). Remember that consumer surplus depends on the *most* that people would be willing to pay for the product. That maximum price goes down if alternatives are available. When alternative methods of vision correction are available, however, glasses are just another option rather than a virtual necessity, and the consumer surplus associated with them falls.

If you're concerned these examples imply innovation destroys surplus, remember that the substitute goods create surpluses of their own. They have their own demand curves, and the areas under those curves and above the substitute goods' prices are

---

Figure 3.3 :   **Consumer Surplus and the Elasticity of Demand**

D_1 represents the demand for glasses in 1950 before a popular substitute good, contact lenses, were available. D_1 is relatively inelastic, and the total consumer surplus, $A + B$, is large. D_2 represents the demand for glasses after contact lenses were put on the market. D_2 is now relatively elastic, and the total consumer surplus B is relatively small.

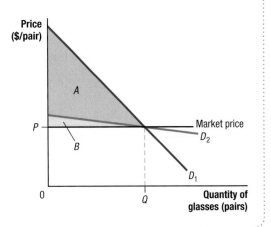

also consumer surplus. For example, while the invention of contact lenses does reduce the consumer surplus provided by glasses, it creates a lot of surplus in the new contact lens market. ∎

 **application**

What is LASIK eye surgery worth to patients?

Laser-assisted in situ keratomileusis, commonly known as LASIK surgery, gives some people with vision problems an alternative to glasses and contact lenses. In the procedure, doctors use a laser to change the shape of the cornea to improve vision, usually to a point where patients can get rid of their corrective lenses.

Suppose we wanted to know how valuable LASIK surgery is to the patients who receive it. According to a market study commissioned by AllAboutVision.com, in 2010, the procedure cost about $2,150 per eye when performed by a reputable doctor. There were an estimated 800,000 LASIK procedures in 2010. A simple estimate for the value of this new procedure would be the number of surgeries times the cost (800,000 times $2,150, or about $1.7 billion). By now, however, you should realize that this measure of value is not a correct measure of the procedure's benefit to consumers because many people value the procedure at more than the price they paid. To determine the full benefit, we need to compute the consumer surplus—the benefit people receive from LASIK above and beyond what they have to pay for it.

To begin this computation, we need a demand curve for LASIK surgery. Because glasses and contacts are substitutes for LASIK, the demand curve will be flatter than if there were no substitutes. If LASIK were the only way to correct vision problems, then the nearly 70 million people now using corrective lenses in the United States would be willing to pay a lot for it. Because alternatives exist, however, if the price of LASIK goes up too much, many people will not opt for it, implying that LASIK's demand curve isn't very steep.

A hypothetical but realistic demand curve for LASIK procedures in 2010 is

$$Q_{\text{LASIK}} = 2,400,000 - 750P_{\text{LASIK}}$$

where Q_{LASIK} is the quantity of LASIK procedures demanded and P_{LASIK} is the price per eye of the procedure. Plugging in a price of $2,150 per eye gives a quantity demanded of 787,500 procedures, right around the 2010 estimate. This demand curve is graphed in Figure 3.4. We can use this demand curve to determine the consumer surplus from LASIK.

We know the consumer surplus is the area of the triangle that is under the demand curve but above the price:

$$CS = \frac{1}{2} \times \text{base} \times \text{height}$$

$$= \frac{1}{2} \times (\text{quantity sold}) \times (\text{demand choke price} - \text{actual price})$$

Note that, for this demand curve, the demand choke price ($P_{D\,\text{Choke}}$) occurs where Q_{LASIK} is equal to zero, or

$$Q_{\text{LASIK}} = 0 = 2,400,000 - 750P_{D\,\text{Choke}}$$

$$750P_{D\,\text{Choke}} = 2,400,000$$

$$P_{D\,\text{Choke}} = 2,400,000/750 = 3,200$$

Figure 3.4 : Valuing LASIK Eye Surgery

The demand curve for LASIK is shown by the equation $Q = 2,400,000 - 750P$. The shaded triangle represents the consumer surplus in the LASIK market. We can use the actual price ($2,150), the choke price ($3,200), and the equilibrium quantity sold (787,500) to calculate the triangle's height (demand choke price − actual price) and base (quantity sold). The equation for the total consumer surplus thus becomes $CS = \frac{1}{2} \times$ (quantity sold) × (demand choke price − actual price), yielding a consumer surplus of approximately $413 million.

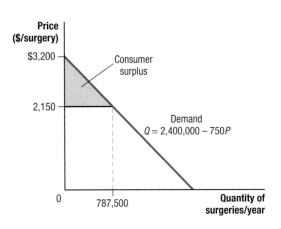

So the consumer surplus from LASIK is

$$CS = \frac{1}{2}(\text{quantity sold})\,(P_{D\,\text{Choke}} - \text{actual price})$$

$$= \frac{1}{2}(787,500)\,(\$3,200 - \$2,150)$$

$$= \frac{1}{2}(787,500)\,(\$1,050)$$

$$= \$413 \text{ million}$$

This calculation suggests that the people who got LASIK surgery in 2010 valued the surgery by about $413 million above and beyond what they paid for it. They paid about $1.7 billion for the surgery, but would have been willing to pay as much as 25% more. Because LASIK didn't exist as a product a couple of decades ago, that value was only created once the procedure was invented and a market established for it. This example suggests how important new goods can be for making consumers better off and raising the standard of living.

We can do the same sorts of calculations to compute the amount of producer surplus in a market. You'll see such an example in the next section. ∎

3.2 The Distribution of Gains and Losses from Changes in Market Conditions

One nice thing about our definitions of producer and consumer surpluses is that we can analyze the impact of any changes on either side of a market in a way that builds on the analysis we started in Chapter 2. There, we learned how shocks to supply and demand affect prices, quantity demanded, and quantity supplied. Now we can show how these shocks affect the benefits producers and consumers receive from participating in a market.

Figure 3.5 shows the initial supply and demand in the market for donuts. We see that at the market price P_1, the donut buyers' benefit from buying donuts is greater than the price they pay for the donuts (reflected in the consumer surplus area $A + B + C + D$). Similarly, the donut makers' benefit from making the donuts is greater than the price at which they sell the donuts (reflected in the producer surplus area $E + F + G$).

Figure 3.5 | **Changes in Surplus from a Supply Shift**

S_1 and D are the initial supply and demand for donuts. At market price P_1, consumer surplus is the area $A + B + C + D$, and producer surplus is the area $E + F + G$.

An increase in the manufacturing costs of donuts causes the supply curve to shift leftward from S_1 to S_2. At the new equilibrium price (P_2) and quantity (Q_2), consumer surplus has been reduced to the area A. The new producer surplus is shown by $B + E$. The effect of a supply shift on producer surplus is ambiguous. This ambiguity results because the lower equilibrium quantity acts to reduce producer surplus (by area $F + G$), while the higher equilibrium price increases producer surplus (by area B).

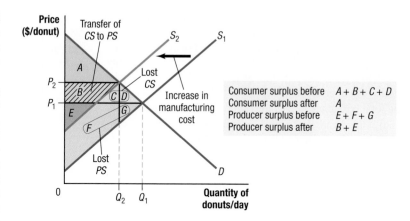

Consumer surplus before	$A + B + C + D$
Consumer surplus after	A
Producer surplus before	$E + F + G$
Producer surplus after	$B + E$

Now let's suppose that a shock hits the donut market. Because of a poor berry harvest, the price of jelly filling goes up. (We're assuming that the filling the bakers use actually has some real fruit in it!) When this shock hits, the cost of making donuts rises, and suppliers are no longer willing to supply as many donuts at any given price. The supply of donuts falls, as reflected in the inward shift of the donut supply curve from S_1 to S_2. In response to the jelly shock, the equilibrium price of donuts rises to P_2, and the quantity of donuts bought and sold in the donut market falls to Q_2.

These changes affect both consumer and producer surplus. The higher equilibrium price and lower equilibrium quantity both act to reduce consumer surplus. Compared to triangle $A + B + C + D$ in Figure 3.5, triangle A is much smaller. While these price and quantity effects imply that inward supply shifts must reduce consumer surplus, there is no general rule for their impact on producer surplus. The lower equilibrium quantity that results from the supply shift reduces producer surplus, but the higher price increases it. These opposing effects can be seen in Figure 3.5. Some of the producer surplus before the shift—specifically, the space $G + F$ between the old and new supply curve and below the demand curve—is lost. But the price increase shifts some of what was consumer surplus before to producer surplus. This shifted surplus is area B. These effects on consumer and producer surplus are reversed for outward supply shifts.

We can also do a similar analysis for the effects of demand shifts. An inward shift in demand leads to a lower equilibrium price and quantity, both of which reduce *producer* surplus. The impact on consumer surplus, however, is ambiguous. Having a smaller equilibrium quantity reduces consumer surplus, but this reduction is counteracted by the drop in price. Similar to the supply shift case above (but in the opposite direction), the inward demand shift transfers to consumers part of what was producer surplus before. We see these effects in the application that follows.

application

How much did 9/11 hurt the airline industry?

After terrorists attacked the United States on September 11, 2001, the demand for air travel fell substantially, bringing the airline industry to its knees. Many congressional leaders wanted to compensate the airlines for the losses they suffered as a result, but there was a great debate over how much money was at stake. Using supply and demand industry analysis and our consumer and producer surplus tools, we can estimate the reduction in producer surplus that the airlines suffered after 9/11.

Statistics from the U.S. Department of Transportation (DOT) show that in the fourth quarter (October through December) of 2000, there were about 148.9 million enplanements (an enplanement is defined as one passenger getting on a plane).[5] In the fourth quarter of 2001, the first full quarter after the attack, there were only 123.6 million enplanements, a drop of 17% from the previous year. According to the DOT data, the average ticket price that airlines received per enplanement in the fourth quarter of 2000 was $122.22. In the fourth quarter of 2001, this average revenue had fallen to $104.82. This change in average revenue measures the price change over the period.

To figure out the damage to the industry, we need to compute the change to producer surplus.[6] Let's think of September 11th as creating a negative shift of the demand curve and assume no changes to the supply curve to make it easy: At every price, consumers demanded a lower quantity of plane travel. This shift is illustrated in Figure 3.6. Prices and quantities decreased in response to this event—just as the model suggests.

Figure 3.6   Airlines and September 11

After September 11, the demand curve for air travel shifted inward, from D_{2000} to D_{2001}. In 2000 the equilibrium price and quantity were $122.22 and 148.9 million enplanements, respectively, and the producer surplus was the total shaded area, $A + B + C$. After September 11, the equilibrium price and quantity fell to $104.82 and 123.6 million enplanements, respectively, and the producer surplus was reduced to the area C. The area $A + B$ represents the loss in producer surplus to the airlines and was over $2.3 billion.

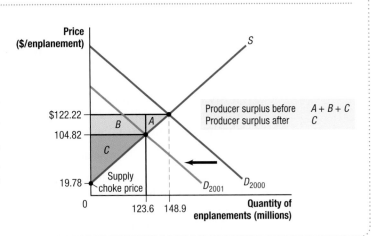

---

[5] Enplanements is one of many standard airline measures of quantity. If you fly a non-stop round-trip flight from Los Angeles to Chicago, for example, that would count as two enplanements because you got onto the airplane two times in your trip. We could have used a different measure of quantity such as revenue passenger miles (the number of miles that paying customers flew), and the answer would be very similar.

[6] We simplify our analysis by ignoring the modest supply effects of increases in costs from increased security requirements that the government did not pay for directly.

Figure 3.6 shows that the producer surplus fell when the demand curve shifted. Before the attack, producer surplus was the area above the supply curve and below the price, or $A + B + C$. After the attack, price and quantity fell and producer surplus fell to just area C. The loss to the airlines, then, was the area $A + B$.

To calculate the producer surplus in this market, we need to know the equation for the supply curve. If we assume the supply curve is linear, we can use the data from our two equilibrium points to derive the equation for our inverse supply curve. The slope of the supply curve is the ratio of the change in equilibrium prices over the change in equilibrium quantities:

$$\text{slope} = \frac{P_2 - P_1}{Q_2 - Q_1} = \frac{\$122.22 - \$104.82}{148.9 - 123.6} = 0.688$$

Now that we have the slope, we can use either (or even better both!) equilibrium points to determine the supply choke price (the vertical intercept of the supply curve):

$$122.22 = P_{S\text{Choke}} + 0.688(148.9) \qquad \text{or} \qquad 104.82 = P_{S\text{Choke}} + 0.688(123.6)$$

$$P_{S\text{Choke}} = 122.22 - 102.44 \qquad\qquad\qquad P_{S\text{Choke}} = 104.82 - 85.04$$

$$= \$19.78 \qquad\qquad\qquad\qquad\qquad = \$19.78$$

So now we know that the industry's inverse supply curve is $P = 19.78 + 0.688Q$. Using the inverse supply equation allows us to match up the equation with the diagram in Figure 3.6.

With this inverse supply curve equation in hand, we can now calculate producer surplus before and after 9/11. Before 9/11, producer surplus is the area below the equilibrium price of \$122.22 per enplanement and above the supply curve, for the entire quantity of 148.9 million enplanements. This would be areas $A + B + C$ in the graph. Since these three areas combine to form a triangle, we can calculate producer surplus before 9/11 as

$$\text{producer surplus} = \frac{1}{2} \times \text{base} \times \text{height} = \frac{1}{2}(148.9)(\$122.22 - \$19.78) = \$7,626.66$$

(The units of this producer surplus value are millions of dollars, because the quantity number is in millions of enplanements and the price is in dollars per enplanement.)

After 9/11, the equilibrium price fell to \$104.82 per enplanement and the equilibrium quantity fell to 123.6 million enplanements. This means that producer surplus became only area C after 9/11, which was equal to

$$\frac{1}{2} \times \text{base} \times \text{height} = \frac{1}{2}(123.6)(\$104.82 - \$19.78) = \$5,255.47$$

These calculations indicate that the producer surplus in the airline industry fell by \$2,371.19 million, or over \$2.3 billion, as a result of the terrorist attack on 9/11.

One interesting thing to note about this calculation is that even after the 9/11 attack, the producer surplus is a big number. Comparing the \$5.255 billion of producer surplus in 2001 Q4 to that quarter's reported (in the Air Carrier Financial Statistics) operating profit of –\$3.4 billion (i.e., a \$3.4 billion *loss*) for the industry leaves a puzzle. How can there be such a large producer surplus if the airlines had such a large loss? In reality, the puzzle is not so puzzling because producer surplus and profit are distinct concepts. The key distinction is the fixed costs firms pay—the expenses each must incur even if it doesn't produce a thing. Those costs aren't reflected in the supply curve, so they don't count against producer surplus. But they do come out of the firm's profits (and airlines have a lot of fixed costs). We learn more about fixed costs, the nature of the supply curve, and the connection between producer surplus and profit in Chapters 7 and 8.

By the way, if all we cared about was the drop in producer surplus after 9/11, there was another way to do the calculation we just did. We could have computed the size of areas A and B directly without actually solving for the supply curve. Rather than computing $A + B + C$ and subtracting C, we could have computed the size of rectangle B and triangle A using just the quantity and price data. This calculation would have given us the same answer for the *change* in producer surplus, but it would not have let us compute the *overall size* of the producer surplus before and after 9/11. ■

3.2 figure it out

A local tire market is represented by the following equations and in the diagram on the next page:

$$Q^D = 3{,}200 - 25P$$

$$Q^S = 15P - 800$$

where Q is the number of tires sold weekly and P is the price per tire. The equilibrium price is $100 per tire, and 700 tires are sold each week.

Suppose an improvement in the technology of tire production makes them cheaper to produce so that sellers are willing to sell more tires at every price. Specifically, suppose that quantity supplied rises by 200 at each price.

   a. What is the new supply curve?

   b. What are the new equilibrium price and quantity?

   c. What happens to consumer and producer surplus as a result of this change?

Solution:

   a. Quantity supplied rises by 200 units at every price, so we simply add 200 to the equation for Q^S:

$$Q_2^S = 15P - 800 + 200 = 15P - 600$$

   b. The new equilibrium occurs where $Q^D = Q_2^S$:

$$3{,}200 - 25P = 15P - 600$$

$$3{,}800 = 40P$$

$$P = \$95$$

We can find the equilibrium quantity by substituting the equilibrium price into either the supply or demand equation (or both):

$$Q^D = 3{,}200 - 25(95) \qquad\qquad Q_2^S = 15(95) - 600$$

$$= 3{,}200 - 2{,}375 \qquad\qquad = 1{,}425 - 600$$

$$= 825 \qquad\qquad\qquad\qquad = 825$$

The new equilibrium quantity is 825 tires per week. Notice that because supply increased, the equilibrium price fell and the equilibrium quantity rose just as we would predict.

c. The easiest way to determine the changes in consumer and producer surplus is to use a graph such as the one below. To calculate all of the areas involved, we need to make sure we calculate the demand choke price and the supply choke prices before and after the increase in supply.

The demand choke price is the price at which quantity demanded is zero:

$$Q^D = 0 = 3{,}200 - 25P$$
$$25P = 3{,}200$$
$$P = \$128$$

The demand choke price is $128.

The supply choke price is the price at which quantity supplied is zero. Because supply is shifting, we need to calculate the supply choke price for each supply curve:

$$Q_1^S = 0 = 15P - 800$$
$$15P = 800$$
$$P = \$53.33$$
$$Q_2^S = 0 = 15P - 600$$
$$15P = 600$$
$$P = \$40$$

The initial supply choke price is $53.33 but falls to $40 when supply increases.

With the choke prices and the two equilibrium price and quantity combinations, we can draw the supply and demand diagram.

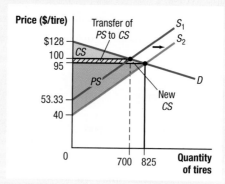

Consumer surplus: The initial consumer surplus is the area of the triangle below the demand curve but above the initial equilibrium price ($100):

$$CS_{\text{initial}} = \frac{1}{2} \times \text{base} \times \text{height}$$
$$= \frac{1}{2} \times (700 - 0) \times (\$128 - \$100) = (0.5)(700)(\$28) = \$9{,}800$$

The new consumer surplus is the area of the triangle below the demand curve and above the new equilibrium price ($95):

$$CS_{\text{new}} = \frac{1}{2} \times \text{base} \times \text{height}$$
$$= \frac{1}{2} \times (825 - 0) \times (\$128 - \$95) = (0.5)(825)(\$33) = \$13{,}612.50$$

So, after the outward shift in supply, consumer surplus rises by $3,812.50.

Producer surplus: The initial producer surplus is the area of the triangle below the initial equilibrium price and above the initial supply curve (S_1):

$$PS_{initial} = \frac{1}{2} \times base \times height$$

$$= \frac{1}{2} \times (700 - 0) \times (\$100 - \$53.33) = (0.5)(700)(\$46.67) = \$16,334.50$$

The new producer surplus is the area of the triangle below the new equilibrium price and above the new supply curve (S_2):

$$PS_{new} = \frac{1}{2} \times base \times height$$

$$= \frac{1}{2} \times (825 - 0) \times (\$95 - \$40) = (0.5)(825)(\$55) = \$22,687.50$$

The increase in supply also led to a rise in producer surplus by $6,353.

3.3 Price Regulations

Politicians call regularly for price ceilings on products whose prices have risen a lot. In this section, we explore the effects of direct government interventions in market pricing. We look both at regulations that set maximum prices (like a gas price ceiling) and minimum prices (price floors like a minimum wage).

Price Ceilings

A **price ceiling** establishes the highest price that can be paid legally for a good or service. Price ceilings get passed all the time. At various times, there have been price ceilings for cable television, auto insurance, flood insurance, electricity, telephone rates, gasoline, prescription drugs, apartments, food products, and many other goods.

price ceiling
A price regulation that sets the highest price that can be paid legally for a good or service.

   To look at the impact of a price ceiling, let's suppose the city council of a college town passes a pizza price control regulation. With the intent of helping out the college's financially strapped students, the city council says no pizzeria can charge more than $8 for a pizza. Let's say the demand curve for pizzas in a month during the school year is described by the equation $Q^D = 20,000 - 1,000P$. The cheaper pizzas get, the more students will eat them, so the demand curve slopes downward as usual. If the price were zero, 20,000 pizzas will be sold per month (it's not that big of a college, and there are only so many meals one can eat). The demand choke price is $20 per pizza—if the price were $20 per pizza, no pizzas would be sold.

   Let's say the supply of pizzas is given by $Q^S = 2,000P - 10,000$. Supply slopes upward because when prices are higher, the pizzerias will make more pizzas. If the price is below $5, they make no pizzas. For each $1 increase in the price of a pizza after that, an additional 2,000 pizzas per month would be supplied.

   Figure 3.7 graphs the supply and demand curves described by these two equations. It shows that the free-market equilibrium is at point w; that is, before price controls the equilibrium price for a pizza is $10, and at that price, 10,000 pizzas are supplied and demanded. Given these baseline market conditions, we can study the impact of the price ceiling using the graph or the equations. Let's start with the graph.

Figure 3.7   The Effects of a Price Ceiling

A price ceiling affects both producer and consumer surpluses. Before price controls in the pizza market, consumers pay $10 per pizza, and producers supply 10,000 pizzas per week at the equilibrium point w. Consumer surplus is the triangle $A + B + C$, and producer surplus is $D + E + F$. When a price ceiling of $8 is put in place, pizzerias supply only 6,000 pizzas (point x), but consumers demand 12,000 pizzas (point y), creating a shortage of 6,000 pizzas. Because pizzerias are now selling fewer pizzas at a lower price, producer surplus is reduced to area F. The new consumer surplus is the area $A + B + D$, and the net gain to consumers is $D − C$. The shaded area $C + E$ is the deadweight loss created by the price ceiling.

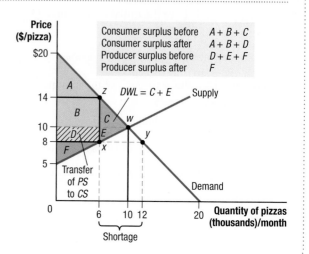

Graphical Analysis   Before any price controls, the consumer surplus for pizza-eating students is given by the area below the demand curve and above the $10 free-market price, $A + B + C$. The producer surplus is the area above the supply curve but below the price, $D + E + F$.

When the city council implements the price control regulation, the highest price the pizzerias can charge is $8 per pizza, which is less than the market-clearing price of $10. At $8, students demand a total of 12,000 pizzas (point y). This quantity demanded is larger than the 10,000 pizzas demanded at the free-market equilibrium because the price ceiling price is lower than the free-market price. At an $8 price, however, pizzerias are only willing to supply 6,000 pizzas. Because the quantity demanded exceeds the quantity supplied at that price, there is a shortage of 6,000 pizzas (sometimes this condition is also referred to as excess demand). Because the actual quantity of pizzas is limited to the number that suppliers are willing to sell, we end up with 6,000 pizzas sold at $8, and a large number of students frustrated that they cannot buy the additional 6,000 pizzas they would like to even though they are willing to pay the $8 per pie price.

Now let's consider the consumer and producer surplus to figure out how much better or worse off the two groups are as a result of the price controls. It's clear that the pizzerias are worse off. In the free market, they would have sold more pizzas (10,000 versus 6,000) at a higher price ($10 versus $8). The producer surplus after the price control law is everything below the capped price and above the supply curve; producer surplus shrinks from area $D + E + F$ to area F.

The law was passed to benefit students by lowering pizza prices. But we can't actually say for sure whether they are better off as a result. The new consumer surplus is the area below the demand curve and above the price, area $A + B + D$. The consumer surplus now includes area D because the price is lower. We call area D a **transfer** from producers to consumers, because imposing price controls shifted that area from being part of producer surplus to being part of consumer surplus. However, fewer pizzas are bought after the price cap law, resulting in consumers losing area C. Therefore, the net impact of the price cap on consumers depends on the

transfer
Surplus that moves from producer to consumer, or vice versa, as a result of a price regulation.

relative sizes of the surplus transferred from the producers (area *D*) and loss reflected in area *C*. For those students who are able to buy the 6,000 pizzas in a month at a price that is $2 lower than they did before the law was enacted, life is good. They are the ones to whom area *D* is transferred. But for the students who would have enjoyed 4,000 more pizzas in the free market that they can no longer buy, life is a hungry proposition.

The producer surplus and consumer surplus represented by areas *C* + *E* have disappeared because of the price ceiling. No one receives these surpluses anymore. Their combined areas are known as a **deadweight loss (DWL).** Deadweight loss is the difference between the maximum total surplus that consumers and producers could gain from a market and the combined gains they actually reap after a price regulation, and it reflects the inefficiency of the price ceiling. It's called a deadweight loss because it represents a set of surplus-generating transactions (pizza purchases, in this case) that would have occurred in an unregulated market with a customer who was willing to buy and a producer who was willing to sell at the market price. Area *C* is the deadweight loss suffered by consumers; area *E* is lost by producers.

Why is there a loss in consumer surplus if the students get to keep the money that they're not spending on pizza? Remember, the students missing out on the 4,000 pizzas after the price control law don't want to save the $10—they want the pizza! The reason there is a loss of consumer surplus is that the pizzas those students would have gotten in a market without a price control would be worth *more* than $10 to them. People who buy are on the part of the demand curve that is above the market price (except that individual right *at* the market price); their willingness to pay is greater than the price they have to pay. The price control results in their losing that difference.

Some producer surplus also becomes deadweight loss as a result of the price ceiling. There are pizzerias that would be willing to sell pizzas for more than $8 but less than the $10 equilibrium price. Once the $8 price ceiling is in place, pizzerias will pull 4,000 pizzas off the market because $8 is not enough to cover their costs of making those extra pizzas. So both students and pizzerias were benefiting from transactions that took place before the price control; once the price ceiling is imposed, however, those transactions no longer take place and these benefits are lost.

Analysis Using Equations   Now let's compare the free and regulated markets for pizzas using the supply and demand equations we described earlier. To determine the free-market equilibrium using the equations, we set quantity supplied equal to quantity demanded and solve for the market clearing price *P*:

$$Q^S = Q^D$$

$$2{,}000P - 10{,}000 = 20{,}000 - 1{,}000P$$

$$3{,}000P = 30{,}000$$

$$P = \$10$$

Plugging that price back into either the supply or demand equation gives an equilibrium quantity of 10,000 pizzas:

$$
\begin{aligned}
Q^S &= 2{,}000P - 10{,}000 & &\text{or} & Q^D &= 20{,}000 - 1{,}000P \\
&= 2{,}000(10) - 10{,}000 & & & &= 20{,}000 - 1{,}000(10) \\
&= 20{,}000 - 10{,}000 & & & &= 20{,}000 - 10{,}000 \\
&= 10{,}000 & & & &= 10{,}000
\end{aligned}
$$

deadweight loss (DWL)
The reduction in total surplus that occurs as a result of a market inefficiency.

The consumer surplus in the free market is the triangle $A + B + C$. The area of that triangle is

$$CS = \frac{1}{2} \times (\text{base}) \times (\text{height})$$

$$= \frac{1}{2} \times (\text{quantity sold}) \times (\text{demand choke price} - \text{market price})$$

The demand choke price is the price at which $Q^D = 0$. In this case,

$$0 = 20{,}000 - 1{,}000(P_{D\text{Choke}})$$

$$1{,}000(P_{D\text{Choke}}) = 20{,}000$$

$$(P_{D\text{Choke}}) = \$20$$

The consumer surplus triangle is

$$CS = \frac{1}{2} \times (\text{quantity sold}) \times (P_{D\text{Choke}} - \text{market price})$$

$$= \frac{1}{2}(10{,}000)(\$20 - \$10)$$

$$= (5{,}000)(\$10) = \$50{,}000 \text{ per month}$$

(Remember that quantities are measured in pizzas per month, so the consumer surplus is measured in dollars per month.)

The producer surplus is the triangle $D + E + F$ in the graph. The area of that triangle is $PS = \frac{1}{2} \times (\text{quantity sold}) \times (\text{market price} - \text{supply choke price})$.

The supply choke price is the price at which quantity supplied is zero:

$$Q^S = 2{,}000P - 10{,}000$$

$$0 = 2{,}000(P_{S\text{Choke}}) - 10{,}000$$

$$P_{S\text{Choke}} = 10{,}000/2{,}000 = \$5$$

Plugging this price into the equation for producer surplus, we find

$$PS = \frac{1}{2}(\text{quantity sold}) \times (\text{market price} - P_{S\text{Choke}})$$

$$= \frac{1}{2}(10{,}000)(\$10 - \$5)$$

$$= (5{,}000)(\$5)$$

$$= \$25{,}000 \text{ per month}$$

Now let's consider the impact of the price ceiling. The price of a pizza cannot rise to $10 as it did in the free market. The highest it can go is $8. We saw in the graphical analysis that this policy led to a shortage. The shortage is the difference between the quantity demanded and the quantity supplied at the price ceiling (P_c):

$$Q^D_{pc} = 20{,}000 - 1{,}000P_c$$

$$= 20{,}000 - 1{,}000(8)$$

$$= 12{,}000$$

$$Q^S_{pc} = 2{,}000P_c - 10{,}000$$

$$= 2{,}000(8) - 10{,}000$$

$$= 6{,}000$$

The shortage is $12,000 - 6,000$ or 6,000 pizzas per month. This means that there are students ringing pizzerias' phones off the hook trying to order 6,000 more pizzas, but whose orders the pizzerias won't be willing to fill at the new market price.

Next, we compute the consumer and producer surpluses after the price control is imposed. Producer surplus is area F.

$$PS_c = \frac{1}{2}(Q_{pc}^S) \times (P_c - P_{SChoke})$$

$$= \frac{1}{2}(6,000)(\$8 - \$5)$$

$$= (3,000)(\$3) = \$9,000 \text{ per month}$$

which is just over one-third of the $25,000 of producer surplus pizzerias were making before the price ceiling. It is no wonder that producers fight against laws like this one.

The consumer surplus is now areas $A + B + D$. An easy way to figure the value for this surplus is to add the area of triangle A to the area of the rectangles B and D. Triangle A has an area of

$$\text{Area of } A = \frac{1}{2}(Q_{pc}^S) \times (P_{DChoke} - \text{price at point } z)$$

where the price at point z is the price at which quantity demanded equals the new quantity supplied of 6,000 pizzas. To figure out this price, set $Q^D = Q_{pc}^S$ and solve for the price:

$$Q^D = 20,000 - 1,000P_z = Q_{pc}^S$$

$$20,000 - 1,000P_z = 6,000$$

$$20,000 - 6,000 = 1,000P_z$$

$$P_z = 14,000/1,000 = \$14$$

This means that, if the price of a pizza were actually $14, exactly 6,000 pizzas would be demanded. With this value for the price at point z, we can now calculate:

$$\text{Area of } A = \frac{1}{2}(Q_{pc}^S) \times (P_{DChoke} - P_z)$$

$$= \frac{1}{2}(6,000)(\$20 - \$14)$$

$$= (3,000)(\$6)$$

$$= \$18,000 \text{ per month}$$

The area of rectangle B is

$$B = Q_{pc}^S \times (P_z - \text{free-market price})$$

$$= (6,000)(\$14 - \$10)$$

$$= \$24,000 \text{ per month}$$

and the rectangle D is

$$D = Q_{pc}^S \times (\text{free-market price} - P_c)$$

$$= (6,000)(\$10 - \$8)$$

$$= \$12,000 \text{ per month}$$

Adding these three areas, we find that total consumer surplus after the pizza price ceiling is $A + B + D = \$54,000$ per month.

Therefore, consumers *as a group* are better off than they were under the free market: They have $4,000 more of consumer surplus per month. However, this outcome hides a big discrepancy. Those students lucky enough to get in on the 6,000 pizzas for $8 rather than $10 are better off, but there are 4,000 pizzas that would have been available in the free market that are no longer being supplied. Students who would have consumed those missing pizzas are worse off than they were before.

What is the deadweight loss from the inefficiency of the price-controlled market outcome? The full DWL is the area of triangle $C + E$ in the figure, so

$$\text{DWL} = \frac{1}{2} \times (\text{free-market quantity} - Q_{pc}^S) \times (P_z - P_c)$$

$$= \frac{1}{2}(10{,}000 - 6{,}000)(\$14 - \$8)$$

$$= \frac{1}{2}(4{,}000)(\$6)$$

$$= \$12{,}000 \text{ per month}$$

The Problem of Deadweight Loss   As we have seen, a price ceiling creates a deadweight loss. This deadweight loss is just that: lost. It's surplus that was formerly earned by consumers (C) or producers (E) that neither gets when there is a price ceiling. This analysis has shown that price ceilings and other mandates and regulations can come with a cost, even if they don't involve any direct payments from consumers or producers (as taxes do).

A natural way to think about the size of the deadweight loss is as a share of the transfer D. Because the price control was designed to transfer surplus from pizzerias to students, the deadweight loss tells us how much money gets burned up in the process of transferring surplus through this regulation. In this case, the deadweight loss ($12,000) is just as large as the transfer. In other words, in the process of transferring income from pizzerias to students through the price ceiling, one dollar of surplus is destroyed for every dollar transferred.

This example illustrates the dilemma of using regulations to transfer income. If somehow the city council could get the producers to directly pay the consumers the amount $D - C$ without changing the price, the consumers would be just as happy as with the price control, because that's all they net in the deal after losing the deadweight loss. The producers would be better off as well. Rather than being left with just F, they would have their free-market producer surplus of $D + E + F$ minus their payment of $D - C$. The areas D in these two values cancel, leaving the pizzerias $E + F + C$, which is larger than the F in producer surplus they get under the price ceiling law. Deadweight loss occurs because the price-control regulation transfers income by changing prices, and price changes affect incentives and lead to inefficiency. Practically speaking, though, it's difficult to figure out how to organize the payment of $D - C$ without changing the price. A per pizza subsidy paid by pizzerias to students, for example, would have the same result as reducing the price and would thus have its own deadweight loss as we describe in Section 3.6.

Importance of Price Elasticities   The elasticities of supply and demand are the keys to the relative sizes of the deadweight loss and the transfer. Consider two different pizza markets in Figure 3.8. In panel a, the curves are relatively inelastic and show little price sensitivity. In panel b, the relatively elastic supply and demand curves reflect a greater amount of price sensitivity. It's clear from the figure that if the same price control rule is applied to both markets, the deadweight loss

Figure 3.8   :   **Deadweight Loss and Elasticities**

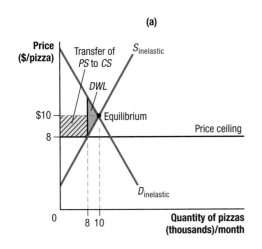

(a)

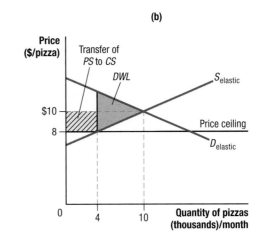

(b)

(a) $S_{inelastic}$ and $D_{inelastic}$ show little price sensitivity. With price controls, relatively few buyers and sellers who would have traded in the free market are kept out of the market, and the transfer is much larger than the deadweight loss created.

(b) In a market with a more elastic supply and demand curve, $S_{elastic}$ and $D_{elastic}$, a relatively large group of buyers and sellers who would have traded in the free market are kept out of the market, and the deadweight loss created by the price control is much larger than the transfer.

will be larger as a share of the transfer in the market with more elastic supply and demand.

The intuition behind this result is that the price ceiling's deadweight loss comes about because it keeps a set of sellers and buyers who would be willing to trade in the market at the free-market price from doing so. If the number of people in this set is small (in other words, the quantity after the regulation is close to the quantity before), then the deadweight distortion is small. How large that number of people is depends on how sensitive demand and supply are to prices. If demand and supply are relatively inelastic, the number of people and firms changing their quantity demanded or supplied will be small, and the DWL will be small. If demand and supply are relatively elastic, the number of people and firms who change their quantity demanded or supplied will be large.

Nonbinding Price Ceilings   In the pizza example, the price ceiling was below the free-market equilibrium price. What if a ceiling were set above the equilibrium price? Suppose the city council passed a law that limited the price of pizzas to $12 instead of $8, for example.

In such cases, the price ceiling has no effect. Because it is set at a level above where the market would clear anyway ($10 in the pizza case), it won't distort market outcomes. There will be no impact on price, no excess demand, and no deadweight loss. Price ceilings at levels above the equilibrium price are said to be **nonbinding,** because they do not bind or keep the market from arriving at its free-market outcome.

nonbinding price ceiling
A price ceiling set at a level above equilibrium price.

If conditions in the market change, however, a price ceiling that was once non-binding could become binding. Suppose, for example, that enrollment increases at the college, and as a result, the demand for pizzas shifts out to a point at which the equilibrium price would be $13. If this shift were to occur, a $12 price ceiling would start to bind, leading to excess demand and deadweight loss in the market. (A large inward shift in the supply curve from the original equilibrium could also make a formerly nonbinding ceiling start to bind.)

Price Floors

price floor (or price support)
A price regulation that sets the lowest price that can be paid legally for a good or service.

The other major type of price regulation is a **price floor** (sometimes called a **price support**), a limit on how low a product's price can go. Lawmakers around the world use price floors to prop up the prices of all sorts of goods and services. Agricultural products are a favorite, especially in wealthier countries. As early as the 1930s, the United States federal government began setting price supports for agricultural goods such as milk, corn, wheat, tobacco, and peanuts. The goal was to guarantee farmers a minimum price for their crops to protect them from fluctuating prices. Many of these price supports remain today. We will use the tools of consumer and producer surplus to analyze price floors just as we used them for price ceilings.

Let's look at the market for peanuts. The unregulated market for peanuts is shown in Figure 3.9. The equilibrium quantity of peanuts is 20 million tons, and the equilibrium price of peanuts is $500 per ton. The government decides that farmers should be getting more than $500 per ton for their peanuts, so it passes a regulation that peanuts must sell for no less than $1,000 per ton.

Immediately, we know there is going to be a problem. At the higher price, peanut farmers want to sell a whole lot of peanuts—30 million tons. But at that price, quantity demanded is much lower—only 10 million tons. (Peanut butter sandwiches are just too expensive when peanuts cost $1,000 per ton.) This imbalance leads to excess supply in the market: Sellers want to sell more of the product at that price than buyers want to buy. This is indicated in the figure by the 20-million-ton difference between the quantity of peanuts supplied and the quantity demanded at the price floor.

Figure 3.9   **The Effects of a Price Floor**

A price floor affects both producer and consumer surpluses. Before price controls in the peanut market, consumers pay $500 per ton, and producers supply 20 million tons of peanuts. Consumer surplus is the triangle $A + B + C$, and producer surplus is $D + E + F$. When a price floor of $1,000 per ton is put in place, peanut farmers supply 30 million tons of peanuts (point y), but consumers demand only 10 million tons of peanuts (point x), creating an excess supply of 20 million tons of peanuts. Consumer surplus is reduced to A. Producer surplus is now $B + D + F$, and the net gain to producers is $B - E$. The deadweight loss is $C + E$.

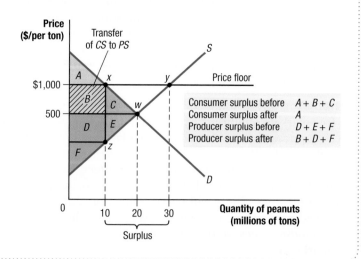

Consumer surplus before	$A + B + C$
Consumer surplus after	A
Producer surplus before	$D + E + F$
Producer surplus after	$B + D + F$

The goal of the price floor policy is to help farmers, so we need to look at the producer surplus to know how well the policy accomplishes its goal. Before the regulation, producer surplus was the area $D + E + F$. After the regulation, prices go up for all the peanut farmers who are still able to find buyers, so producers gain area B as a transfer from consumers. The farmers sell 10 million tons of peanuts and receive $500 per ton more than they were receiving in the free market. But peanut growers lose some of their market. The reduction in quantity demanded from 20 million to 10 million tons knocks out producers who used to sell peanuts at market prices and made a small amount of producer surplus from it. This area E then becomes the producers' part of the deadweight loss (DWL) from the regulation.

Overall, the producers gain surplus of $B - E$. If supply and demand are sufficiently elastic (i.e., if both curves are flat enough), producers could actually be made *worse off* from the price floor that was put in place to help them. This is because area E—the producers' share of the DWL—may be larger than the transfer from consumers, area B. This outcome is another application of our discussion above about how the deadweight loss grows as the supply and demand curves become more elastic.

How do consumers fare when the price floor is enacted? You can probably guess: Consumer surplus falls from $A + B + C$ to A. Area B is the surplus transferred from consumers to producers and area C is the consumer part of the DWL.

The price floor policy therefore transfers income from consumers to peanut farmers, but only by burning $C + E$ (the DWL) to do it. Again, if there were some way for the consumers to directly pay the peanut farmers a set amount equal to area B, the farmers would obtain more surplus than they get with the regulation (producer surplus of B versus $B - E$), and the consumers would be better off too (consumer surplus of $A + C$ instead of A). By changing the actual price of peanuts instead of making a transfer unrelated to quantity, the price support distorts people's incentives and leads to inefficiency as reflected by the DWL of $C + E$.

This analysis also illustrates the everlasting dilemma of price supports. The quantity supplied at the price floor is greater than the quantity demanded. So what happens to the extra peanuts? They accumulate in containers rather than being sold on the market. To avoid this outcome, a government will often pay the producers who can't sell their output in the regulated market to *stop* producing the extra output (20 million extra tons of peanuts in our example). The United States Department of Agriculture, for example, oversees various programs to reduce the surplus of price-supported crops on the market. One such program, the Conservation Reserve Program (CRP), paid farmers $1.85 billion in 2010 (an average of about $55 per acre) for holding land out of production. The program does have environmental benefits that mitigate some of the losses, but it also serves to reduce the quantity of subsidized crops that is grown, effectively by replacing those subsidies with CRP payments. There are also a number of programs that distribute millions of dollars annually ($871 million in 2010) of commodity foods—like peanut butter!—to school lunch programs and needy individuals on the condition that the foods will not be resold. Again, these programs serve to take surplus crops off the market.

Another example of a price support is a minimum wage. Here, the "product" is labor and the "price" is the wage, but the analysis is the same. If the government tries to help college students save tuition money by mandating that all summer internships pay at least $40 an hour, the quantity of labor supplied for internships will be much greater than the quantity demanded. As a result, there will be a lot of unemployed intern-hopefuls who would have been working at the equilibrium wage.

Just as with our earlier examples, how many people a minimum wage adds to the number of unemployed (the excess quantity supplied in the price floor figure), the amount of income transferred to workers (the change in producer surplus), and the size of the deadweight loss all depend on the elasticity of labor supply and labor demand. The price floor's deadweight loss arises because a set of sellers and buyers who would be willing to trade in the market at the free-market price will not do so at the regulated price. When suppliers and demanders are relatively insensitive to price, the number of transactions that the price floor prevents from happening is relatively small, and therefore so is the deadweight loss. Large price elasticities imply a large number of destroyed transactions and a large deadweight loss.

Nonbinding Price Floors   If a price floor is set below the free-market equilibrium price, it will have no effect on the market. **Nonbinding price floors** have no effect on price and do not create excess supply or deadweight loss. Just as with nonbinding price ceilings, however, conditions in a market may change to make a price floor that was once unbinding start to bind. Suppose the peanut price floor had been set at $400, below the equilibrium price of $500. If there is a sufficiently large outward shift in supply or inward shift in demand, the free-market equilibrium price may fall below $400, causing the price floor to start to affect the market.

nonbinding price floor
A price floor set at a level below equilibrium price.

3.4 Quantity Regulations

Sometimes, rather than regulating prices, governments impose quantity regulations. We discuss some of these regulations and analyze their effects on market outcomes in this section.

Quotas

quota
A regulation that sets the quantity of a good or service provided.

A **quota** is a regulation mandating that a certain quantity of a good or service be provided. Quotas are occasionally used to force firms to produce a certain amount of a good (say, a vaccine in preparation for a flu epidemic or armaments during a war), but most often they are used to limit the amount of a good that is produced.

For example, countries wanting to limit imports but not wanting to publicly announce tariffs (taxes on imports) can limit imports by establishing a quota. The U.S. government imposes quotas on the amount of sugar that can be imported from various countries, for example.[7] In other circumstances, a government may limit the amount of fish people can catch or the production of milk or oil.[8] The nation of Bhutan has a quota on the number of foreign tourists that can visit in a given year. France limits the amount of U.S. television shows that can be broadcast on TV. Singapore limits the number of cars that people can buy. London's Heathrow Airport limits the number of direct flights from U.S. airports. Taxis need medallions to operate, and doctors need licenses to practice.

[7] Legally, the current sugar quotas aren't completely binding. If a country goes over its quota allocation, it can still export sugar to the United States, but it must pay an additional tariff to do so. In practice, however, this tariff is so high that it all but eliminates shipments beyond the quota allocation.

[8] As we will see in Chapter 16 when we discuss externalities, there may be reasons for governments to limit the production of certain goods. For now, we just want to know what effects quotas have in a standard market situation.

Zoning laws impose another type of quota. Most towns and cities have zoning laws that limit the amount or type of construction that can go on in a certain area. A common zoning restriction limits the number of certain businesses considered by some to be unsavory, such as pawn shops or tattoo parlors. Such restrictions can be thought of as quotas on the amount of services these stores can provide in a local market. Let's consider as an example the impact of a quota on the amount of tattoo services that can be provided in the fictional town of River City.

Suppose the city's demand curve for tattoos is $Q_d = 2{,}500 - 20P$, and the supply curve is $Q_s = 100P - 3{,}500$, where the quantities demanded and supplied are both measured in the number of tattoos per year. We can analyze the effects of a quota on price and quantity by using graphs and equations.

Graphical Analysis   In the free market, the equilibrium quantity of tattoos supplied and demanded for tattoos in River City is 1,500 tattoos per year and a price of $50 per tattoo (Figure 3.10). The consumer surplus in this market is $A + B + C$ and the producer surplus is $D + E + F$.

Suppose that River City's mayor becomes convinced that tattoo shops are a blight on society and rules that no more than 500 tattoos can be purchased per year in the city. He enforces this quota by requiring everyone who wants a tattoo to buy a tattoo permit before getting inked.

The quota creates a regulatory bend in the supply curve so that it becomes vertical at the quantity of 500. In other words, no matter what the price of tattoos is, parlors cannot supply more than 500. When this happens, the supply curve becomes perfectly inelastic at 500, making the new supply curve S_2 look like the red line in Figure 3.10. Now the demand curve intersects supply at point z rather than at point x, and the price rises from $50 to $100. Consumer surplus falls from area $A + B + C$ to area A, which is the only area that is below the demand curve and above the post-quota price P_{quota}. The post-quota producer surplus is above the supply curve and below the new price. This area $B + D + F$ includes a surplus transfer B from consumers to producers. The area $C + E$ is the deadweight loss.

Figure 3.10   The Effects of a Quota

In the free market for tattoos in River City, producers supply 1,500 tattoos per year at a price of $50 per tattoo at the equilibrium (point x). Consumer surplus is $A + B + C$, and producer surplus is $D + E + F$. After the mayor of River City enacts a law requiring a permit to get a tattoo, the supply for tattoos becomes vertical at the quantity of 500 tattoos. At the new equilibrium (point z), producers supply 500 tattoos at the increased price of $100 per tattoo. Consumer surplus is reduced to A. Producer surplus is $B + D + F$, and the net gain to producers is $B - E$. The deadweight loss is $C + E$.

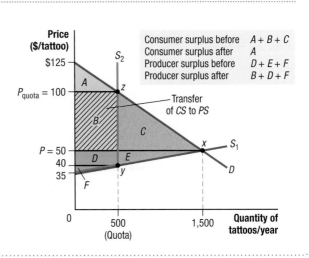

Consumer surplus before	$A + B + C$
Consumer surplus after	A
Producer surplus before	$D + E + F$
Producer surplus after	$B + D + F$

Analysis Using Equations   The equilibrium price is the price that exists when quantity supplied equals quantity demanded:

$$Q^D = Q^S$$

$$2{,}500 - 20P = 100P - 3{,}500$$

Solving for P and Q, we find

$$P = 50 \text{ and}$$

$$Q^D = 2{,}500 - 20(50) = 1{,}500 \qquad \text{or} \qquad Q^S = 100(50) - 3{,}500 = 1{,}500$$

At the free-market equilibrium price and quantity, the consumer surplus is

$$CS = \frac{1}{2} \times (\text{base}) \times (\text{height})$$

$$= \frac{1}{2} \times Q \times (P_{D\text{Choke}} - P)$$

The demand choke price $P_{D\text{Choke}}$ is the price at which $Q^D = 0$, which in this case is

$$Q^D = 2{,}500 - 20(P_{D\text{Choke}}) = 0$$

$$20P_{D\text{Choke}} = 2{,}500$$

$$P_{D\text{Choke}} = \$125$$

Consumer surplus is therefore

$$CS = \frac{1}{2} \times Q \times (P_{D\text{Choke}} - P)$$

$$= \left(\frac{1}{2}\right)(1{,}500)(\$125 - \$50)$$

$$= (750)(\$75) = \$56{,}250$$

The producer surplus is the triangle $D + E + F$ in the graph. That triangle's area is

$$PS = \frac{1}{2} \times Q \times (P - P_{S\text{Choke}})$$

The supply choke price $P_{S\text{Choke}}$ is the price at which quantity supplied is zero:

$$Q^S = 100 \times P_{S\text{Choke}} - 3{,}500 = 0$$

$$P_{S\text{Choke}} = 3{,}500/100 = \$35$$

Producer surplus in the unregulated tattoo market is then

$$PS = \frac{1}{2} \times Q \times (P - P_{S\text{Choke}})$$

$$= \frac{1}{2} \times 1{,}500 \times (\$50 - \$35)$$

$$= (750)(\$15) = \$11{,}250$$

After the 500-tattoo quota is implemented, the supply curve is the same up to $Q_S = 500$, at which point it becomes perfectly inelastic (point y). The equilibrium price will be

$$Q^S = Q^D$$

$$500 = 2{,}500 - 20P_{\text{quota}}$$

$$P_{\text{quota}} = \$100$$

At this price, the consumer surplus is the area A:

$$CS = \frac{1}{2} \times Q_{\text{quota}} \times (P_{D\,\text{Choke}} - P_{\text{quota}})$$

$$= (\frac{1}{2})(500)(\$125 - \$100)$$

$$= (250)(\$25) = \$6{,}250$$

This is dramatically reduced from the free-market surplus of $56,250. Sorry, River City tattoo fans.

The producer surplus is measured by the areas $B + D + F$. We can break out each of these areas separately:

$$\text{Area } F = \frac{1}{2} \times Q_{\text{quota}} \times (\text{price at point } y - P_{S\,\text{Choke}})$$

The price at point y is the price at which the quantity supplied is equal to the quota. It can be determined by setting $Q^S = 500$ and solving for P:

$$Q^S = 100(\text{price at point } y) - 3{,}500 = 500$$

$$100(\text{price at point } y) = 4{,}000$$

$$\text{price at point } y = 4{,}000/100 = \$40$$

So, this means

$$\text{Area } F = \frac{1}{2} \times 500 \times (\$40 - \$35) = \$1{,}250$$

The rectangle B is

$$\text{Area } B = Q_{\text{quota}} \times (P_{\text{quota}} - P)$$

$$= 500(\$100 - \$50) = \$25{,}000$$

and the rectangle D is

$$\text{Area } D = Q_{\text{quota}} \times (P - \text{price at } y)$$

$$= 500(\$50 - \$40) = \$5{,}000$$

Thus, the total producer surplus equals $F + B + D = \$31{,}250$.

Let's compare the quota outcomes to those of the free, unregulated River City tattoo market. Consumers are much worse off after the quota because their surplus has fallen from $56,250 to only $6,250. This decrease reflects, in part, the losses of the additional 1,000 people who would be willing to get a tattoo in River City in a free market but cannot with the quota in place. But the loss in consumer surplus also reflects the fact that the quota increases the price of tattoos even for those people who get one. This price increase shrinks the gap between what they are willing to pay for the tattoo and the price they actually have to pay.

On the supply side, the tattoo parlors do just fine. They lose the producer surplus in area E when the quota is imposed, but the quantity restriction leads to much higher prices for their output—they get a huge transfer from consumers (area B), which makes their total producer surplus $31,250 under the quota instead of $11,250 without it. This gain could explain why the tattoo parlors may not complain about an ordinance that would reduce the total number of tattoos they could sell, although a noneconomist might expect they would.

The quantity-restricting quota drives up the price of tattoos. In doing this, the quota transfers a bunch of surplus from tattoo buyers to tattoo parlors and creates a significant amount of deadweight loss (area $C + E$, which based on our calculations above totals $25,000 + $5,000 = $30,000).

Government Provision of Goods and Services

The quota example we just discussed set a maximum quantity for the tattoo market. What if a government wanted to mandate a *minimum* amount of a good or service instead? For legal reasons, it can be difficult for a government to actually force companies to provide a certain quantity of a product that they do not want to produce. However, governments can and sometimes do produce goods themselves. In the market for higher education, for example, states run public colleges and universities that directly compete with private colleges and universities. In the insurance market, the government provides flood insurance. Research and development (R&D) conducted by private firms competes with R&D funded by the federal government through institutions like the National Institutes of Health or the National Science Foundation. Weather forecasting from the National Weather Service competes against Accuweather, The Weather Channel, and others. The U.S. Postal Service competes with UPS and Federal Express in package delivery.

To understand the effects of direct government provision of goods and services, let's use the supply and demand model to analyze the college education market. The price in this market is tuition per credit hour, and the quantity is the total number of credit hours taken.[9] In Figure 3.11, we start with the equilibrium that would exist in the market if higher education were provided only by private schools. The demand curve for education is D and the supply curve is S_{priv}. The equilibrium price and quantity are P_1 and Q_1.

If the government decides that getting more people to attend college is important, it can do so in many ways. It could help pay part of students' costs of attending a private school. (We analyze the impact of such payments, called subsidies, in Section 3.6.) Alternatively, the government could impose a price ceiling on college tuition so that more students could afford it. This price ceiling would have the disadvantage we learned about earlier in this chapter: There would be a shortage of education

---

Figure 3.11 : **The Effects of Government Provision of Education**

In a market with only private colleges, supply would be S_{priv}, demand would be D, and the equilibrium price and quantity would be P_1, Q_1. When the government opens a new university, there is an outward shift in the supply curve equal to the number of credit hours provided by the government, the quantity Q_{gov}. At the equilibrium, the price decreases to P_{tot}, and the quantity increases to $Q_{tot} = Q_{gov} + Q_{priv}$. Because the increase in the equilibrium quantity is less than Q_{gov}, the quantity supplied by private universities must have been crowded out.

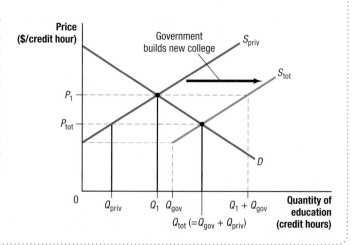

---

[9] In using the supply and demand model here, we are assuming that all colleges, private and public, offer identical educations.

because more students would want a college education and fewer colleges would be willing to offer this education. Finally, the government could start a public university to directly enable more students to attend college. That's the case we'll look at here.

Let's say the government provides Q_{gov} credit hours at the new state-run university. This increase in credit hours shifts the supply curve from S_{priv} to S_{tot}. Notice that because the government's additional quantity supplied doesn't depend on price, this leads to a parallel outward shift in the supply curve by an amount Q_{gov}.

With this shift in supply, the market tuition falls from P_1 to P_{tot} per credit hour. However—and this is key—the number of credit hours taken will rise less than Q_{gov}, the amount provided by the government. We can see this in Figure 3.11. As we just noted, the horizontal distance between S_{priv} and S_{tot} is Q_{gov}. For the equilibrium quantity of credit hours to rise by an amount equal to Q_{gov}, the equilibrium price would have to remain at P_1, making the quantity of credit hours equal to $Q_1 + Q_{gov}$. The price doesn't stay at P_1, though, because the demand for credit hours is downward-sloping. The equilibrium price instead falls to P_{tot}, and the quantity rises by an amount less than Q_{gov}, to Q_{tot}. Because the total quantity of credit hours increases by less than the amount the government provides, private schools must now supply a number of credit hours (call this Q_{priv}) that is less than Q_1, the quantity they supplied before the government stepped in.

This decline in the quantity supplied by the private schools is known as **crowding out,** a reduction in private economic activity created by greater government presence in a market. Here, crowding out is the equivalent of the deadweight loss seen in our earlier examples. The government pays to provide Q_{gov} credit hours, but it increases the total number of credit hours in the market by less than this amount. Some credit hours formerly offered by private schools and willingly purchased by students are no longer produced. The larger the number of these lost credit hours—that is, the smaller the increase in the equilibrium quantity of credit hours relative to the government-provided quantity—the greater is the inefficiency from crowding out.

The intuition behind why crowding out occurs lies in the fact, seen in the example above, that the equilibrium quantity rises less than the quantity the government produces because demand is downward-sloping. By stepping in and increasing output, the government drives down the market price. This reduces the quantity supplied by private producers. At the original equilibrium price, private producers were willing to supply a certain quantity. At the lower, post-government market price, however, the private producers find it is no longer worth supplying their initial amount.

The same intuition explains how large crowding out will be in a market. When demand is relatively elastic, the increase in supply due to the government won't reduce the equilibrium price much. As a result, private producers won't cut back production a lot, and crowding out will be small. In the extreme case, when demand is perfectly elastic (i.e., if the demand curve were flat), government production won't change the equilibrium price at all. As we just discussed, in this case, the equilibrium quantity will rise by exactly the amount the government produces. On the other hand, if demand is relatively inelastic, government supply will reduce the equilibrium price a great deal. This will lead to large cutbacks in private production and a lot of crowding out. In the extreme case of perfectly inelastic (vertical) demand, crowding out is complete: Price falls and private firms cut back on production one-for-one for each unit the government produces. This makes sense: If quantity demanded is fixed at some specific amount regardless of price, any government provision will only serve to replace private production.

crowding out
A reduction in private economic activity created by greater government presence in a market.

theory and data

Does Public Health Insurance Crowd Out Private Insurance?

The role of the government in providing health insurance is constantly debated in countries where coverage is provided by both private and public payers. The United States is a country with a heavy mix of the two. In 2010 about 150 million Americans were covered by private insurers, but another 50 or so million people were on Medicare, the government-provided health insurance for seniors, and just under 60 million were enrolled in Medicaid, government-provided insurance for low-income individuals and families. Another 50 million were uninsured.

In mixed-payer countries, government-provided coverage is often targeted at population segments like the elderly and poor that many believe would have a difficult time obtaining private coverage. Many policy makers and economists nevertheless believe that public coverage and private coverage might be close enough substitutes to cause expansion of public coverage to crowd out private coverage. In other words, if the government tries to expand coverage in order to reduce the number of uninsured, some of the increased enrollees will be individuals who would have still been covered by private insurance otherwise.

In a well-known study, health economists David Cutler and Jonathan Gruber measured the amount of crowding out that occurred during significant expansions of Medicaid.[*] Specifically, they used law changes that occurred in the late 1980s and early 1990s that greatly expanded the number of women and children eligible for Medicaid coverage. They measured crowding out by looking at the period of this large shift in the quantity of publicly provided insurance and determining if there were any corresponding drops in private insurance among the same population. In terms of Figure 3.12, they compared Q_{gov} (here, the amount of additional Medicaid coverage) to the difference between Q_e and Q_{priv} (respectively, the amount of private coverage before and after the Medicaid expansion).

Using this approach, Cutler and Gruber found evidence of substantial crowding out. For example, the expansion of coverage eligibility led to an additional 1.5 million children obtaining Medicaid coverage. Thus $Q_{gov} = 1.5$ million in Figure 3.12. However, they estimated about 600,000 of these new enrollees had been covered by private insurance beforehand; that is, $Q_e - Q_{priv} = 0.6$ million. Therefore the net change in children covered by medical insurance, $Q_1 - Q_{gov}$, was only about 900,000. This implies a crowd-out rate of

Figure 3.12

Government Provision of Health Insurance

In a market with only private health insurance, supply would be S_{priv}, demand would be D, and the equilibrium price and quantity would be P_e, Q_e. When the government offers health insurance (in the form of Medicaid), the supply curve shifts out to S_{tot}. At the equilibrium, the price decreases to P_1, and the quantity increases to $Q_1 = Q_{priv} + Q_{gov}$. The quantity supplied by private insurers is crowded out since the total rise in the quantity of insurance coverage falls short of Q_{gov}.

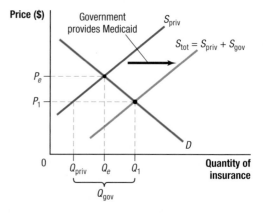

[*] David M. Cutler and Jonathan Gruber, "Does Public Insurance Crowd Out Private Insurance?" *Quarterly Journal of Economics* 111, no. 2 (1996): 391–430.

40 percent—for every 10 additional Medicare enrollees, 4 were simply exchanging their private insurance for public insurance. Another way to quantify this is in terms of the changes in uninsured children due to the policy. Before the expansion of coverage there were about 8.6 million uninsured children. Had all of the 1.5 million new enrollees come from this group, it would have cut the number of uninsured children by about 17 percent. But crowding out meant it reduced the number of uninsured by only 10 percent.

This result raises an interesting question about what the mechanism was through which the reduction in private insurance occurred. One possibility is that newly Medicaid-eligible individuals were less likely to pay for private coverage available to them through their employers or other channels. Another possible mechanism is that employers, knowing additional public coverage has been made available, reduced the quality or raised the price of the insurance plans they offered their employees. Cutler and Gruber found some evidence that employers did pare back their plans, but most of the crowding out appeared to have arisen because individuals who were newly eligible for Medicaid avoided using their employer-provided insurance options.

Just as with deadweight loss, the relative size of crowding out inefficiencies depends on elasticities. But there is a difference. While both supply and demand elasticities determine the amount of deadweight loss, only the demand elasticity matters for crowding out. This is because we've assumed the quantity supplied by the government doesn't depend on the price. As a result, for a given demand curve, the drop in equilibrium price after the government enters the market only depends on how much supply shifts (i.e., how much the government produces), not on the slope of the private supply curve.[10]

3.5 Taxes

Governments at all levels (local, state, federal) tax all kinds of things, and they do it in different ways. Sometimes, suppliers are legally required to remit the tax. Stores in the United States collect sales taxes and send them to state revenue agencies, for example, just as producers in Canada and Europe collect and remit value-added tax (VAT). Sometimes the legal burden falls on consumers, like "use taxes" that states levy on purchases their residents make in other states. In still other cases, the legal burden is shared. For instance, half of the U.S. federal payroll tax (which funds the Social Security and Medicare programs) is paid by employers before workers get their wages, and the other half is paid by workers through a deduction from their wages.

In this section, we use the supply and demand model to show one of the most striking findings in economics: In a competitive market, it doesn't matter whether the buyer or the seller is required by law to actually sign the check and remit the tax to the government; the impact on consumers and producers is always the same. That is, we could change the law so that consumers paid sales tax instead of sellers, or employers have to pay the entire payroll tax, and market outcomes would not change. The total impact of a tax on consumers and sellers depends only on the steepness of the supply and demand curves, not on the identity of the payer. Before we can understand why this is true, however, we first need to look at how taxes affect a market.

---

[10] If, for some reason, the government's quantity supplied *is* sensitive to price, then the elasticity of the supply curve (both the private and government components) will affect the amount of crowding out, just as the demand elasticity does.

Tax Effects on Markets

We start with a no-tax market that is in equilibrium, the market for movie tickets in Boston, Massachusetts (Figure 3.13). The equilibrium is at point x, with a price of P_1, and the quantity of movie tickets sold is Q_1. In 2003 the mayor of Boston, Tom Menino, proposed adding a 50 cent tax to movie tickets to help balance a budget deficit. Many thought Menino proposed the tax because a large number of movie-goers in Boston are college students who live in the Greater Boston area but are not Boston voters. Regardless of his motivation, the tax was defeated by the state legislature.

If it had been enacted, the tax would have required theater owners to pay 50 cents per ticket to the government. Let's look at how such a change would affect the market for movie tickets. The tax is much like a 50 cent per ticket increase in the theaters' costs. We know from Chapter 2 that increases in production costs cause suppliers to supply a smaller quantity at any given price. Therefore, in response to the tax, the supply curve shifts up by the amount of the tax (50 cents) to S_2, and the equilibrium quantity of movie tickets sold falls to Q_2.[11]

But taxes do something different from a typical supply shift: They drive a wedge between the price buyers pay (the market price) and the price that producers ac-tually receive (the market price minus the tax). With a normal supply curve, the price at any point on the supply curve is the price a producer receives for selling

---

Figure 3.13   Effect of a Tax on Boston Movie Tickets

The figure shows the effect of a $0.50 movie tax on the market for Boston movie tickets. In the pre-tax market, supply S_1 and demand D intersect at the equilibrium price of $8 and the equilibrium quantity of 400,000 movie tickets. The consumer surplus is $A + B + C$, and the producer surplus is $D + E + F$. The addition of the $0.50 tax per movie ticket results in an inward shift of the supply curve from S_1 to S_2 by the amount of the tax and decreases the equilibrium quantity to 340,000 tickets. The resulting tax wedge creates two prices: $8.30, the price the buyer faces, and $7.80, the price the seller actually receives. The new consumer surplus is A, and the producer surplus is F. Area $B + D$ is government tax revenue, while area $C + E$ is the deadweight loss.

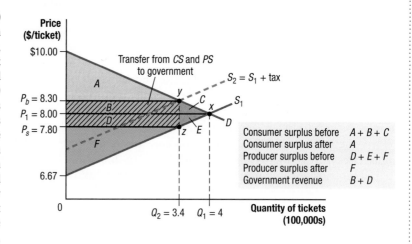

Consumer surplus before	$A + B + C$
Consumer surplus after	A
Producer surplus before	$D + E + F$
Producer surplus after	F
Government revenue	$B + D$

---

[11] A tax expressed in percentage terms, such as a sales tax of 6%, is called an *ad valorem* tax (as opposed to a *specific tax* that is a set dollar amount, like the 50 cents per ticket here). An ad valorem tax version of this tax would shift the supply curve, but not by a fixed amount at every point. Instead, it would rotate the curve by a fixed percent around the point at which quantity supplied is zero.

its product. With a tax, the product sells for the price P_b (we denote the price the buyers pay with a "b"), but the sellers only receive P_s (we denote the price the seller receives with an "s"). This is the buyers' price minus the tax: $P_s = P_b -$ tax. In other words, the buyers have to pay 50 cents more for any quantity, but the movie theaters don't get to keep the extra money—they only receive the higher price minus the tax.

Because of this wedge, the new equilibrium in the Boston movie market involves *two* prices. The first, point *y*, is the price ($8.30) that the buyers pay at the theater that includes the 50 cent tax. Thus, $8.30 is the market price. The second, point *z*, is the price ($7.80) that the suppliers receive after taking the 50 cents out of the higher market price and sending it to the government.

There are two key characteristics to note about the post-tax market equilibrium. First, the price of movie tickets increases, but not by the full 50 cents of the tax. This can be seen in Figure 3.13. The size of the tax is reflected in the vertical distance between P_b ($8.30) and P_s ($7.80). The rise in the price of movie tickets, however, is the distance between $8.30 and the equilibrium price with no tax, $8.00. The reason for this discrepancy is that the tax wedge drives some of the highest-cost theaters out of the market: Once the tax is added to the price, these theaters would have to sell their tickets at a price that is too high for buyers. The second characteristic to note is that the government generates revenue from the tax. The total revenue equals the 50 cent tax times Q_2, the new quantity of tickets sold.

We can apply all the familiar concepts from consumer and producer surplus analysis to this new equilibrium. We just need to remember that the tax creates a second supply curve that we have to keep track of, rather than moving a single supply curve as before. The supply curve that the theater owner cares about is S_1, the initial supply curve. The number of tickets that theaters are willing to supply at any particular price is still given by this curve, even after the tax is imposed, because the level of S_1 reflects the after-tax dollars theater owners take home from selling tickets. But the supply curve actually facing the buyers is S_2. It has been shifted up by the amount of the tax, because that is the price that moviegoers have to pay for a particular quantity supplied.

To make things clearer, let's work through this example in more detail. In Figure 3.13, the demand curve for movie tickets in Boston is $Q^D = 20 - 2P$ and the supply of movie tickets is $Q^S = 3P - 20$, where both quantities demanded and supplied in these curves are measured in hundreds of thousands of tickets. If the legislature passes the tax, all theater owners will be required to remit to the city 50 cents per ticket sold. We can analyze the tax's effect on the market using graphs or equations.

Graphical Analysis   With no taxes, solving the model our usual way gives a free-market equilibrium price P_1 and quantity Q_1 and the resulting consumer and producer surpluses (Figure 3.13).

The tax means buyers now face a new supply curve S_2, equal to S_1 shifted up by $0.50, the amount of the tax. This reduces the number of movie tickets bought in the market from 400,000 to 340,000. At that quantity, the price the buyers are paying rises from $8.00 to $8.30. Because the law requires suppliers (the theater owners) to pay the government a 50 cent tax for every ticket they sell, the suppliers don't get to keep $8.30; they only get to keep $7.80 = $8.30 - 0.50.

What happens to consumer and producer surplus in the post-tax market? The new consumer surplus is smaller than before. In the no-tax market, consumer surplus was $A + B + C$. Now it is only A, the area below the demand curve but above the price that the buyers have to pay, $8.30.

The new producer surplus is also smaller than before. Before the tax, it was $D + E + F$. After the tax, it is only F, the area above the supply curve and below the price that the suppliers receive after they pay the tax, $7.80.

Imposing the tax reduces total producer and consumer surplus from area $(A + B + C) + (D + E + F)$ to just area $A + F$. Where has the surplus in areas B, C, D, and E gone? The area $B + D$ is no longer consumer *or* producer surplus; it is government tax revenue, the tax times the quantity sold after the tax is implemented. With a tax, there is no surplus transfer between producers and consumers, as we saw in earlier examples. Instead, both producers and consumers transfer some of their surpluses to the government. This tax revenue is then "returned" to consumers and producers in the form of government services, so it is not lost.

Areas C and E are the deadweight loss from the tax. They are surplus that moviegoers and theater owners formerly got from buying and selling tickets at the competitive price. This surplus is gone now because consumers buy fewer tickets at the higher post-tax price and sellers supply fewer tickets at their lower post-tax price.

Just as in the price regulation cases, a natural way to look at the size of the deadweight loss is as a fraction of the surplus transfer. Before, that transfer was from producers to consumers (for a price ceiling) or from consumers to producers (for a price floor). Now, it's from both to the government. The ratio in this case is the area $C + E$ to the area $B + D$, which is the DWL as a share of revenue.

Analysis Using Equations The no-tax market equilibrium equates quantity demanded and quantity supplied:

$$Q^D = Q^S$$

$$20 - 2P = 3P - 20$$

$$5P = 40$$

$$P_1 = 40/5 = \$8 \text{ per ticket}$$

$$Q^D = 20 - 2(\$8) = 4 \quad \text{or} \quad Q^S = 3(\$8) - 20 = 4$$

Therefore, before the tax, the equilibrium price is $8 and 400,000 tickets are sold.

The pre-tax consumer surplus is the triangle above the price and below the demand curve, as shown in Figure 3.13:

$$CS = \frac{1}{2} \times Q \times (P_{D\,\text{Choke}} - P_1)$$

Again, the choke price is found by determining the price that pushes the quantity demanded to zero:

$$Q^D = 20 - 2P_{D\,\text{Choke}} = 0$$

$$P_{D\,\text{Choke}} = \$10$$

In other words, this demand curve says that if tickets cost $10, no one will go to theaters in the city of Boston (perhaps because theaters in the suburbs are an attractive alternative).

Plugging the demand choke price into the CS formula gives a consumer surplus of

$$CS = \frac{1}{2}(400,000)(\$10 - \$8)$$

$$= \$400,000$$

The producer surplus is the triangle above the supply curve and below the price:

$$PS = \frac{1}{2} \times Q \times (P_1 - P_{S\,\text{Choke}})$$

The supply choke price is the price that moves quantity supplied to zero:

$$Q^S = 3P_{S\,Choke} - 20 = 0$$

$$P_{S\,Choke} = \$6.67$$

That is, at any price below $6.67 a ticket, no theaters would operate in Boston. Plugging this supply choke price into the PS formula gives a producer surplus of

$$PS = \frac{1}{2}(400{,}000)(\$8 - \$6.67)$$

$$= \$266{,}667$$

What happens to consumer and producer surplus when Mayor Menino applies his 50 cent tax? Theaters must pay the state for each ticket they sell. This creates a dual-supply-curve situation. The supply curve for the theater owners is the same as the initial supply curve. The theater is still willing to supply whatever number of tickets the supply curve says at the market price. But now, the supply curve facing buyers is shifted up by the amount of the tax: At each price, the tickets supplied to consumers now cost $0.50 more. The difference between the supply curve that the buyers face and the supply curve that the sellers face is the amount of the tax. In words, the theaters' supply curve says they would be willing to sell 400,000 tickets if they receive $8 per ticket (after the tax gets paid), but for theaters to get $8 per ticket, buyers would actually have to pay $8.50 per ticket because $0.50 of tax needs to be paid out of the price received by the theaters. The prices that result for both the buyer and the seller are summed up in the equation $P_b = P_s + \$0.50$.

To solve for the post-tax quantity and prices, we substitute this expression, which links the two supply prices into our supply and demand equations:

$$Q^D = Q^S$$

$$20 - 2P_b = 3P_s - 20$$

$$20 - 2(P_s + 0.50) = 3P_s - 20$$

$$20 - 2P_s - 1 = 3P_s - 20$$

$$5P_s = 39$$

$$P_s = 39/5 = \$7.80$$

Therefore, the buyers face the following price:

$$P_b = P_s + 0.50 = \$7.80 + 0.50 = \$8.30$$

Now if we plug the buyer price into the demand curve equation and the supplier price into the supply curve equation, they will both give the same after-tax market quantity:

$$Q_2 = 20 - 2(8.30) = 3.4 \quad \text{or} \quad Q_2 = 3(7.80) - 20 = 3.4$$

Only 340,000 tickets will be sold once the tax is put into place.

The consumer surplus after a tax is the area below the demand curve but above the price that the buyer pays:

$$CS = \frac{1}{2}(340{,}000)(\$10.00 - \$8.30)$$

$$= \$289{,}000$$

The producer surplus is the area above the supply curve and below the price that the suppliers receive:

$$PS = \frac{1}{2}(340{,}000)(\$7.80 - \$6.67)$$

$$= \$192{,}667$$

So the tax makes consumer surplus fall by \$111,000 and producer surplus fall by \$74,000 from their values in the no-tax market equilibrium. Some of that \$185,000 in lost surplus flows to the government in the form of revenue from the tax, however. That revenue is equal to \$0.50 per ticket times the number of tickets sold after the tax, or

$$\text{Revenue} = 0.50Q_2$$

$$= \$0.50(340{,}000) = \$170{,}000$$

Notice that the total amount of the lost surplus, \$185,000, is more than the amount of revenue that the government generated, \$170,000. The difference of \$15,000 is the deadweight loss of the tax.

A different way to calculate DWL is to compute the area of the triangle whose base is the change in quantity and whose height is the amount of the tax:

$$\text{DWL} = \frac{1}{2} \times (Q_1 - Q_2) \times (P_b - P_s) = \frac{1}{2} \times (Q_1 - Q_2) \times \text{tax}$$

$$= \frac{1}{2}(400{,}000 - 340{,}000)(\$0.50) = \$15{,}000$$

That's about 9% of the revenue generated by the tax. In other words, this tax burns up about \$1 of surplus in DWL for every \$11 of revenue it generates.

Why Taxes Create a Deadweight Loss

Just as we showed in the case of price and quantity regulations, the main determinant of the DWL from a tax as a share of revenue is how much the quantity changes when the tax is added. The size of that change depends, in turn, on how sensitive supply and demand are to prices. The deadweight loss from pizza price controls, for example, came about because there were consumers and suppliers who would like to trade at market prices and would have earned surplus from doing so but were prevented from engaging in these transactions by the price ceiling. With taxes, there are no forbidden transactions. The source of the loss is the same, however. There are people who would have bought tickets at the market price without a tax and would have gained some surplus from doing so. Once the government adds a tax, the after-tax price rises enough so that these consumers no longer want to buy tickets. They get to keep their money, but they were previously able to buy something with it that gave them surplus. Likewise, movie houses lose surplus because some would have shown movies at the pre-tax market price but find the after-tax price too low to justify operating. These lost surpluses are the DWL of the tax.

Why a Big Tax Is Much Worse Than a Small Tax

An interesting result of our analysis is that it implies the inefficiency represented by the size of the deadweight loss gets much bigger as the size of a tax becomes larger. In the movie ticket tax example (Figure 3.13), we saw that the DWL from the tax was area $C + E$ and that the revenue generated was $B + D$. What would happen if Mayor Menino decided to *increase* the ticket tax? How much more revenue and how much more DWL would this large tax increase create?

Figure 3.14 : The Effect of a Larger Tax on Boston Movie Tickets

After an increase in the tax on movie tickets in Boston from t_1 to t_2, the tax wedge between the price consumers pay and the price movie theaters receive increases, while the quantity of movie tickets at the equilibrium (Q_3) decreases. The tax revenue is now $B + D + G$. Area E, a part of the government's tax revenues under the lower tax, is a part of the deadweight loss, $C + E + F + H$. Since the incremental DWL is $C + E + H$ and the revenue gain is only $B + G - E$, the incremental revenue created by the second larger tax is more inefficient than that of the first smaller tax.

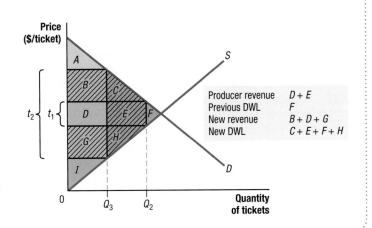

Producer revenue	$D + E$
Previous DWL	F
New revenue	$B + D + G$
New DWL	$C + E + F + H$

Figure 3.14 illustrates the outcome for a general case. The larger tax reduces the quantity even further, from Q_2 to Q_3. The DWL under the larger tax is area $C + E + F + H$ (remember that it was only area F with the smaller tax). Government revenue, which was area $D + E$ with a smaller tax, is now area $B + D + G$. That is, the government gains areas B and G because the people who still buy tickets are paying more in taxes. However, the government loses area E, because some people stop buying movie tickets after the tax is raised. If we look at the DWL as a share of the revenue generated, it is clear that the *incremental* revenue generated by increasing this tax causes more inefficiency than the smaller tax did. Initially, the DWL was F, with a revenue gain of $D + E$. But the incremental DWL here is $C + E + H$, while the revenue gain is only $B + G - E$. In fact, if taxes are high enough, the increase in revenue per ticket from the tax will be more than offset by the reduction in the quantity of tickets sold, and there will be no revenue gain at all!

A general rule of thumb is that the DWL of a tax rises with the square of the tax rate.[12] That is, doubling the tax rate quadruples the DWL. That's why economists tend to favor tax policies that exhibit what is called "low rates and broad bases." That is just a way of saying that, all else equal, taxing ten things at a low rate is better than taxing five things at zero and five things at a high rate. Because DWL rises with the square of the tax rate, the overall DWL will be larger with the five high rates than with the ten low rates.

The Incidence of Taxation: The Payer Doesn't Matter

An important thing to note about the movie ticket example is that although we supposed that it would be the theater owners who were legally obligated to remit the

---

[12] To see where this intuition comes from, notice that with linear supply and demand curves, the DWL from a tax is a triangle with a height equal to the quantity reduction caused by the tax and a base equal to the tax. Because the supply and demand curves are linear, the quantity reduction is proportional to the tax. Specifically, it will be $\Delta Q = A * t$, where A is some number that depends on the slope of the demand and supply curves. Therefore, the area of the DWL triangle is $\frac{1}{2} * A * t * t = \frac{1}{2} * A * t^2$. This area is proportional to the square of the tax. For nonlinear demand and supply curves, this formula is only an approximation, but if they aren't too nonlinear, the intuition remains the same.

50 cents per ticket tax to the City of Boston, they don't bear the complete burden of the tax. Before the tax came in, the theater owners received $8 dollars per ticket and moviegoers paid $8 a ticket. After the $0.50 tax, moviegoers pay $8.30 a ticket. After they send in the tax, however, the theaters only end up with $7.80 per ticket. Therefore, of the 50 cents going to the government, 30 cents (60%) of it is coming out of consumers' pockets because their price went up by 30 cents. Movie theaters send the tax check to the government, but they are able to pass on much of the tax to consumers through higher prices. This means that the price realized by the suppliers goes down by only 20 cents. Who *really* bears the burden of a tax is called **tax incidence.** The incidence of this tax is 60% on the buyers and 40% on the suppliers.

tax incidence
Who actually pays a tax.

Now let's say Boston changed the rule for who pays the tax to the government. Instead of the theater sending the tax payment to the government, moviegoers would pay the tax by, after buying their ticket at whatever price the theater charges, dropping two quarters in a "Menino Box" as they enter the theater (silly, yes, but this is just to make a point).

Does this change alter the tax incidence? It does not. The equations below show that the tax formula doesn't matter whether you subtract the tax from what the supplier receives or add the tax to what the buyer pays.

$$P_s = P_b - \text{tax}$$

is the same as

$$P_s + \text{tax} = P_b$$

This can also be seen graphically. The original case where the theater remits the tax is shown in Figure 3.15a. When the tax is instead paid by buyers, their quantity demanded depends on the price including the tax. But the price suppliers receive at this quantity demanded is only the price without the tax. To account for this differ-

Figure 3.15   Tax Incidence

(a)

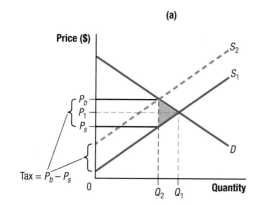

(b)

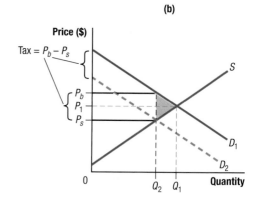

(a) The tax incidence is unaffected by whether the seller or buyer pays the tax. When the seller pays the tax, the supply curve shifts inward by the amount of the tax, $P_b - P_s$, from S_1 to S_2. The equilibrium quantity decreases from Q_1 to Q_2. The seller now faces price P_s at the equilibrium, while the buyer pays price P_b.

(b) When the buyer pays the tax, the demand curve shifts inward by the amount of the tax, $P_b - P_s$, from D_1 to D_2. The equilibrium quantity decreases from Q_1 to Q_2. As in panel a, the seller now faces price P_s at the equilibrium, while the buyer pays price P_b.

ence, we shift down the demand curve by the amount of the tax, from D_1 to D_2 in Figure 3.15b. But the result hasn't changed: Quantity demanded is still Q_2 and the difference between the buyer's price and the seller's price still equals the amount of the tax. Thus, the incidence of a tax does not depend on who is legally bound to pay it.

That's why a helpful way to picture taxes on a graph is to just forget about whether the tax is moving the supply curve up or the demand curve down. Instead, start from the initial no-tax equilibrium point and move left until the vertical space between the supply and demand curves is the amount of the tax. This gives you the right answer regardless of whether the tax is being legally applied to suppliers or buyers.

This point about tax incidence is fundamental. If you have ever had a job, you probably know that the government takes many taxes out of your pay. Some of these are payroll taxes that appear on your pay stub as FICA (Federal Insurance Contributions Act). They are collected to pay for Social Security and Medicare. In the United States, payroll taxes are legally split evenly between workers and employers. In other words, if you earn wages of $1,000, you have to pay 7.65% of that in payroll taxes and the employer has to pay another 7.65% on its own.[13] Would U.S. workers be better or worse off if the law changed so that the company paid 15.3% and workers paid nothing, or if it instead made the employee pay 15.3% and his or her employers paid nothing? The analyses we've just completed suggest that such changes wouldn't make any difference. In a competitive market, the wage would adjust to the same level regardless of which side of the market actually pays the tax.

It turns out that the only thing that matters about the economic effects of this tax is how elastic the supply and the demand for labor are. To see why, let's consider the two extremes.

Elastic Demand with Inelastic Supply   In a market characterized by an elastic demand and an inelastic supply, buyers are very sensitive to price and the suppliers are not. Most labor economists tend to think of the labor market in this way, so that

make the grade

Did I measure deadweight loss correctly?

A few simple tricks will help you nail problems involving deadweight loss. First, whenever the quantity consumed falls as a result of a government policy, a deadweight loss occurs. (This isn't *exactly* correct; if externalities are present, government policies can actually improve market outcomes. We learn more about externalities in Chapter 16.) If the quantity doesn't get distorted, no deadweight loss occurs. Second, the deadweight loss almost always takes the shape of a triangle, and moreover, that triangle points at the efficient market equilibrium with no market distortion. Why? Because deadweight loss measures the consumer and producer surplus destroyed. As we have seen, this loss in surplus grows as we move further and further away from the efficient equilibrium. The growing distance between the sides of the triangle reflects this fact.

---

[13] FICA taxes apply only to "earned" income like wages and salaries. In 2011 the Social Security tax applied to the first $106,800 of wages per person. After that, only the Medicare part of the tax applied (that rate is 2.9%). The limit is subject to increases from year-to-year, typically at a rate tied to inflation. Also in 2011, Congress temporarily reduced the Social Security rate workers were responsible for, making workers' legal share of the tax less than half.

the 15.3% FICA tax (the combined tax rate on the two sides) applies to a market in which labor supply is fairly inelastic (people work a similar amount even if their wage goes up or down) and firms' demand for labor is fairly elastic. This market is illustrated in Figure 3.16a.

Applying the methods we've used throughout this section, we see that the tax is borne almost entirely by the suppliers—here, workers supplying labor. With a tax, employers have to pay wages W_b that are a bit higher than wages without the tax, W_1. But after taxes, the workers receive a wage W_s that is much less than W_1. Therefore, workers are a lot worse off after the tax than employers. And we know from the discussion that we just had on tax incidence that even if the government switched the payroll tax rules so that employers paid the entire amount, workers would not do any better. Their wages would fall almost as much as the employers' tax went up.

Inelastic Demand with Elastic Supply   Figure 3.16b shows a market characterized by inelastic demand (buyers are not sensitive to price) and elastic supply (suppliers are very sensitive to price). In the market for cigarettes, for instance, many buyers are addicted and tend to buy a similar amount no matter how much the price goes up. Cigarette supply is more elastic. You can see in the figure that in this case, consumers bear the brunt of the tax. A tax on cigarettes causes the buyers' price to rise from P_1 to P_b, almost the entire amount of the tax. Suppliers are only a bit worse off than they were before, because they can pass on the higher costs to the inelastic consumers.

Figure 3.16   **Tax Incidence and Elasticities**

(a)

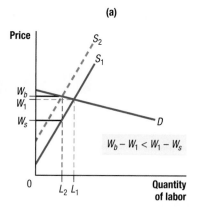

(b)

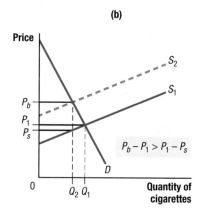

(a) In a labor market where demand is elastic and supply inelastic, we begin with supply curve S_1, demand D, and equilibrium price and quantity (W_1, L_1). The implementation of the tax $W_b - W_s$ shifts the supply curve inward from S_1 to S_2 and decreases the equilibrium quantity of labor from L_1 to L_2. Because laborers in this market are not very sensitive to price and employers are, the effect of the tax on the wages laborers receive is much larger than its effect on the wage employers pay, $W_b - W_1 < W_1 - W_s$.

(b) In the market for cigarettes where demand is inelastic and supply elastic, we begin with supply curve S_1, demand D, and equilibrium price and quantity (P_1, Q_1). The implementation of the tax $P_b - P_s$ shifts the supply curve inward from S_1 to S_2 and decreases the equilibrium quantity of cigarettes from Q_1 to Q_2. Because smokers in this market are not very sensitive to price and cigarette companies are, the effect of the tax on the price consumers pay is much larger than its effect on the price companies receive, $P_b - P_1 > P_1 - P_s$.

We could do this entire analysis using equations, as we did in the movie ticket example. It turns out that there is a general formula that will approximate the share of the tax that is borne by the consumer and the share borne by the producer. Not surprisingly given what we've just discussed, these shares depend on elasticities:

$$\text{Share borne by consumer} = \frac{E^S}{E^S + |E^D|}$$

$$\text{Share borne by producer} = \frac{|E^D|}{E^S + |E^D|}$$

If the price elasticity of supply (E^S) is infinite, the consumers' share is equal to 1; that is, consumers bear the whole burden when supply is perfectly elastic. If the absolute value of the price elasticity of demand ($|E^D|$) is infinite, the consumers' share of the tax burden is zero, and suppliers bear the whole burden of the tax.

3.3 figure it out

Consider the demand and supply for cola in a market represented by the following equations:

$$Q^D = 15 - 10P$$
$$Q^S = 40P - 50$$

where Q is millions of bottles per year and P measures dollars per bottle. The equilibrium price of cola is $1.30 per bottle, and 2 million bottles are sold each year.

a. Calculate the price elasticity of demand and the price elasticity of supply at the equilibrium price and quantity.

b. Calculate the share of a tax that would be borne by consumers and the share borne by producers.

c. If a tax of $0.15 per bottle is created, what would be the expected price buyers will have to pay? What price will sellers receive after the tax?

Solution:

a. The formula for price elasticity of demand is

$$E^D = \frac{\Delta Q^D}{\Delta P} \times \frac{P}{Q^D}$$

From the demand curve, we can calculate $\frac{\Delta Q^D}{\Delta P}$. Each time P changes by one unit, Q^D falls by 10. Therefore,

$$\frac{\Delta Q^D}{\Delta P} = -10$$

Substituting into the formula for elasticity, we get

$$E^D = \frac{\Delta Q}{\Delta P} \times \frac{P}{Q} = -10 \times \frac{1.3}{2} = \frac{-13}{2} = -6.25$$

The formula for price elasticity of supply is

$$E^S = \frac{\Delta Q^S}{\Delta P} \times \frac{P}{Q^S}$$

From the supply curve, we can see that $\frac{\Delta Q^S}{\Delta P} = 40$. Note that each time P increases by one unit, Q^S rises by 40.

Thus, the price elasticity of supply is

$$E^S = \frac{\Delta Q^S}{\Delta P} \times \frac{P}{Q^S} = 40 \times \frac{1.3}{2} = \frac{52}{2} = 26$$

b. The proportion of the tax borne by buyers will be

$$\frac{E^S}{E^S + |E^D|} = \frac{26}{26 + |-6.5|} = \frac{26}{32.5} = 0.8$$

The proportion of the tax borne by sellers will be

$$\frac{|E^D|}{E^S + |E^D|} = \frac{|-6.5|}{26 + |-6.5|} = \frac{6.5}{32.5} = 0.2$$

So, buyers will bear 80% of the tax and sellers will bear only 20% of the tax.

c. If there is a tax of $0.15 per bottle, buyers will bear 80% of the tax:

$$\text{Increase in } P_b = (0.80)(\$0.15) = \$0.12$$

The price buyers pay will rise from $1.30 per bottle (the original equilibrium price) to $1.42.

Sellers will bear the other 20% of the tax:

$$\text{Decrease in } P_s = (0.2)(\$0.15) = \$0.03$$

The price sellers receive will fall from $1.30 per bottle to $1.27.

3.6 Subsidies

subsidy
A payment by the government to a buyer or seller of a good or service.

A **subsidy** is a payment by the government to a buyer or seller of a good or service. It is, in essence, the exact opposite of a tax. In fact, when we analyze the effects of subsidies on markets, we can treat the subsidy as a negative tax. Thus, the price the buyer pays is *lower* than the price the supplier receives after the subsidy. If the government subsidizes gasoline by $1 per gallon, for example, then buyers might pay $3.50 per gallon at the pump, but gas stations receive $4.50 per gallon because they get to add the government dollar to the $3.50. This relationship is

$$P_b + \text{subsidy} = P_s$$

where P_b is the price the buyer pays (the market price) and P_s is the price the seller receives after the subsidy is paid.

Governments tax a lot, but they also subsidize the production of many different goods and services. Let's look at the effects of the U.S. government subsidy for the domestic production of ethanol, a corn-based fuel additive that can be mixed with gasoline. (A common rationale given for the subsidy is to reduce the dependence of the United States on imported oil, though not coincidentally politicians from large corn-producing states have been vocal backers of the policy.) Let's say the government gives fuel producers $1 for every gallon of gas-ethanol mix they sell. This means that if the original supply curve S_1 is what suppliers receive, the supply curve that buyers face will be *shifted down* by the amount of the subsidy, to S_2 (Figure 3.17).

The supply curve that buyers face is lower because the amount people pay to fill their tank is less than the amount the gas station receives, since the government is footing part of the bill (the effects of a tax are just the opposite).

Before the subsidy was in place, consumer surplus was everything below the demand curve and above the price that consumers pay (P_1), area $A + B + C$ in Figure 3.17. After the subsidy, consumer surplus will change. But it will not get smaller, as in the case of a tax. It will get larger. The new consumer surplus is the area below the demand curve and above the price that the consumers have to pay (the new lower price, P_b). This is the old consumer surplus $A + B + C$ *plus* the new part $F + G + H$. This additional surplus comes from the lower price and the additional sales at that price.

Before the subsidy, the producer surplus was everything above the supply curve but below the price the suppliers received (P_1), area $F + G + J$. After the subsidy, producer surplus gets bigger, too. The area above the producers' own supply curve S_1 and below the price that the suppliers receive (P_s) is now $F + G + J$ plus $B + C + D$. (We calculate producer surplus using the *producers'* supply curve (S_1) to compute producer surplus because this is the supply curve that embodies the suppliers' costs of production.)

Note that parts of the consumer and producer surplus areas overlap in this case (areas $B + C + F + G$) because both sides are getting more surplus than before. The only way this is possible, however, is if someone else foots the bill. In this case, it's the government. The subsidy costs money. The cost of the subsidy is the subsidy amount times the quantity produced, $Q_1 \times (P_s - P_b)$, which amounts to the rectangle $B + C + D + E + F + G + H + I$.

Figure 3.17   The Impact of a Producer Subsidy

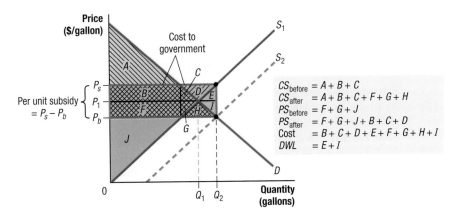

In the pre-subsidy market for gasoline, the supply curve S_1 intersects with the demand curve D at the equilibrium price P_1 and equilibrium quantity Q_1. The consumer surplus is $A + B + C$, and the producer surplus is $F + G + J$. After a government subsidy is put in place, the supply curve shifts down by the amount of the subsidy, $P_s - P_b$, to S_2. At the equilibrium, the quantity increases to Q_2, the price facing suppliers is P_s, and the price facing buyers is P_b. Consumer surplus is now $A + B + C + F + G + H$, and producer surplus is $F + G + J + B + C + D$. The cost of the subsidy is $B + C + D + E + F + G + H + I$, and the deadweight loss is $E + I$. Therefore, the costs associated with the subsidy are larger than the sum of the benefits to producers and consumers.

This isn't the only cost of the subsidy, however. Like any other price regulation, a subsidy also creates deadweight loss. It might seem odd at first that there would be DWL when both consumers *and* producers are better off after the subsidy. The key is to compare how much their surplus goes up to how much the subsidy costs the government. While consumer surplus went up by $F + G + H$ and producer surplus by $B + C + D$, total government outlays for the subsidy were $(F + G + H) + (B + C + D) + (E + I)$. Therefore, the subsidy's DWL is $E + I$. Society as a whole pays more for the subsidy than the added benefit it gave to consumers and producers. If somehow the government could just turn over the subsidy revenue to consumers without changing the price, society would be better off. By changing the price, it gets some extra people to buy gasoline (with ethanol added) who really were not interested in buying before.

When we looked at the market interventions earlier in this chapter, the DWL derived from the surplus lost by people who would have bought if there were no tax or regulation, but do not buy when the tax is in place and the price is too high. Here, it is the other way around. The DWL comes from people who would *not* have made a purchase in a competitive market. They only make a purchase because the subsidy lowers the price. The amount they value the extra quantity is less than it costs the government to move them to buy it.

A different way to see how this deadweight loss occurs is to think about people giving presents to each other. Economist Joel Waldfogel asked microeconomics students who received Christmas presents how much they thought the gifts they received cost the people who bought them.[14] Then he asked the students how much the gifts were worth to them, apart from the sentimental value. The students valued the presents they got by about 15% less than the cost of the presents. This 15% DWL from Christmas presents is just like the DWL from a subsidy. When the government subsidizes a product, it gives consumers a gift: The consumers value the gift (as measured by the consumer surplus) less than it costs the government to buy it (as measured by the revenue cost).

 **application**

The cost of the black-liquor loophole

A recent example of an (accidental) subsidy gone awry is the so-called black-liquor loophole in the law that gave companies tax credits for using alternative fuels. The tax credit is given to businesses that combine alternative fuels with traditional fossil fuels used in their operations, with the idea of encouraging companies to reduce their fossil fuel use in doing so.

It turns out that there is a chemical by-product of paper making called "black liquor" that paper companies have traditionally recycled to use as fuel in their plants. The government determined that this chemical qualified as an alternative fuel under the definition in the law. However, the paper companies couldn't qualify for the tax credit unless they *combined* the alternative fuel with a fossil fuel. So they started adding a bit of diesel fuel—a fossil fuel they weren't using at all before—to the black liquor before burning it. This led to two results. First, paper companies used more diesel than they did before, even though the point of the tax credit was

---

[14] Joel Waldfogel, "The Deadweight Loss of Christmas," *American Economic Review* 83, no. 5 (1993): 1328–1336. Leave it to an economist to point out the deadweight loss of Christmas!

to encourage movement away from use of fossil fuels. Second, paper companies got paid (in the form of tax credits) to burn the black liquor they were already using without payment. They got paid a lot too: This tax credit, originally projected to cost the government $61 million, ended up costing an estimated $6 to $8 *billion* in tax credits in 2009, almost all of it going to paper companies.

How does our analysis in this section explain what happened? The tax credit became, in practice, a diesel subsidy for the paper industry. By tying the credit to the use of blended fuels, it lowered the effective price of diesel that the paper companies faced. Before, when they had to pay the market price, their quantity demanded for diesel to fuel their plants was zero—they had a plentiful and cheap alternative in the black liquor. But now every gallon of diesel they bought came with a big tax credit attached—meaning they faced a downward-shifted supply curve for diesel. The quantity of diesel they demanded at these lower supply prices became positive.

As a result of this policy, the paper companies and the diesel sellers are better off because of the subsidy. (The former very much so in this case.) But the costs are large. First, there is deadweight loss: An industry that wasn't using diesel before because it had a superior alternative now demands it, even though the industry values it at less than the cost of supplying it. Second, the government has to pay the subsidy. And as noted above, that's a really big number. So big, in fact, that Congress closed the loophole in 2010 because they decided that we couldn't afford it. ∎

3.4 figure it out

Suppose the demand and supply of ethanol in a small town are as follows:

$$Q^D = 9,000 - 1,000P$$
$$Q^S = 2,000P - 3,000$$

where Q measures gallons per day and P represents price per gallon. The current equilibrium price is $4, and the current equilibrium quantity is 5,000 gallons per day.

Now, suppose that the government wants to create a subsidy of $0.375 per gallon to encourage the use of ethanol.

a. What will happen to the price buyers pay per gallon, the price sellers receive per gallon, and the number of gallons consumed each day?

b. How much will this subsidy cost the government (and ultimately taxpayers)?

Solution:

a. Determining the prices that buyers and sellers face under a subsidy is done in a way similar to how we determined the prices for buyers and sellers in the presence of a tax. However, there is one big difference. Now, the price sellers receive is actually larger than the price paid by buyers (due to the subsidy):

$$P_s = P_b + \text{subsidy}$$

So, now we know that in our problem

$$P_s = P_b + 0.375$$

Remember that we need to start with the supply and demand equations in the following form:

$$Q^D = 9,000 - 1,000P_b$$
$$Q^S = 2,000P_s - 3,000$$

Once we have these, we can substitute for P_s in the supply equation so that it becomes

$$Q^S = 2,000P_s - 3,000$$
$$Q^S = 2,000(P_b + 0.375) - 3,000 = 2,000P_b + 750 - 3,000 = 2,000P_b - 2,250$$

Now, we can equate Q^D and Q^S to solve for P_b

$$9,000 - 1,000P_b = 2,000P_b - 2,250$$
$$3,000P_b = 11,250$$
$$P_b = 3.75$$
$$P_s = P_b + 0.375$$
$$P_s = 4.125$$

To solve for the quantity of ethanol sold after the subsidy is put in place, we can substitute P_b into the demand equation or substitute P_s into the supply equation. (It is a good idea to do both to check your work.)

$$Q^D = 9,000 - 1,000P_b = 9,000 - 1,000(3.75) = 9,000 - 3,750 = 5,250$$
$$Q^S = 2,000P_s - 3,000 = 2,000(4.125) - 3,000 = 8,250 - 3,000 = 5,250$$

So, buyers will pay $3.75 per gallon, sellers will receive $4.125 per gallon, and 5,250 gallons will be sold each day. This can be seen in the figure below.

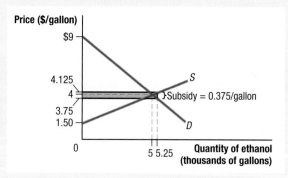

b. The cost of the subsidy will be the subsidy per gallon multiplied by the number of gallons sold:

$$\text{Cost of subsidy} = (\$0.375)(5,250) = \$1,968.75 \text{ per day}$$

freakonomics

Can Economic Incentives Get You Pregnant?

In many countries around the world, the number of babies being born has declined dramatically. In places like China, which instituted a one child per family policy in 1978, the government wanted fewer babies to control the size of the population. In many other parts of the world, especially Europe and Japan, declining fertility poses a problem for governments. Fewer babies mean an aging population. In the next 20 years, the number of retired people worldwide who depend on government pensions will skyrocket, but there will be fewer people of working age to pay the taxes that fund these pensions.

What can governments do about this? One approach would be for governments to run budget surpluses now to cover potential shortfalls in the future. But that sort of austerity is not very popular among elected officials: They would pay the political price of high taxes today but wouldn't be in office 20 years from now to reap the benefits. Another approach would be to encourage additional immigration of working-age individuals. This is another tough sell politically in many countries. Instead, some countries such as France and Sweden are now considering adopting a different economic solution: paying cash to people who have babies.

Can government subsidies encourage the production of babies? You may think this is preposterous—that a couple's decision to become parents is completely unconnected to economics. If so, it just means you don't yet think like an economist. (It is only Chapter 3, though, so there is plenty of time to fix that.) The data suggest that the demand curve for babies slopes downward; that is, when the "price" of having a baby falls, people have more babies. In Israel, which has paid parents to have kids since 1959, economists Alma Cohen, Rajeev Dehejia, and Dmitri Romanov found sizable impacts of government subsidies on fertility.* In fact, they estimate that a 2003 reduction in the subsidy offered to new parents decreased the number of children born in 2004 by 12%. Given Israel's population, that amounts to approximately 5,400 babies who would have been born had the old, higher subsidy remained in effect. This pricing effect was seen across all ethnicities and religious groups too, with payouts affecting the family planning of Orthodox Jews as well as Arab Muslims in the country.

Countries of the former Soviet bloc didn't explicitly pay for children, but they encouraged baby-making in other ways. During the Communist reign, many of these countries such as Czechoslovakia and East Germany offered free child care, giving mothers the opportunity to quickly return to work. The allocation of housing was often tied to children; in Prague, for example, a couple had to be married with a child to be eligible for a government apartment.

The despotic ruler of Romania, Nicolae Ceausescu, used a different approach: In 1966, without warning, he banned abortion, which was the primary form of birth control in Romania at the time. The number of children born skyrocketed in the short run, with the fertility rate nearly doubling from 1.9 children per woman in 1966 to 3.7 children per woman, on average, in 1967. The large number of births accomplished Ceausescu's goal of having more boys who could eventually serve in his army. The problem with suddenly banning abortion, however, was that the babies who were born were not wanted or planned for by their parents. This outcome made the parents angry and led to unwanted children who faced much more difficult lives than the typical Romanian child born prior to 1966. Compared to Romanian children born just a year earlier, the cohorts of children born after the abortion ban would do worse in every measurable way: They would test lower in school, they would have less success in the labor market, and they would also prove much more likely to become criminals. Eventually, young protesters born after the abortion ban would overthrow Ceausescu in 1989, and he would be executed.

If Ceausescu had been a better economist, he would have realized that changing prices (in this case, by offering subsidies for babies) can be a more efficient way of incentivizing behavior than outright prohibition. In other words, economics might even have saved Ceausescu's life.

*Alma Cohen, Rajeev Dehejia, and Dmitri Romanov, "Do Financial Incentives Affect Fertility?" NBER working paper (2007).

3.7 Conclusion

In this chapter, we took the supply and demand hammer and pounded every nail in sight. We saw how you can compute the consumer and producer surplus generated by transactions in a market, learned how to value new goods, and learned what deadweight loss is. We learned to use supply, demand, and total surplus to analyze industries and the ways in which they change in response to changes in the market, particularly to price and quantity regulations, taxes, and subsidies. Being able to do so much with such a simple model makes supply and demand the workhorse of microeconomics.

Summary

1. Consumer surplus is the value that consumers receive from participating in market transactions. It is the difference between the most they would pay for something and the price they actually have to pay for it. On a supply and demand graph, consumer surplus is measured by the area under the demand curve and above the price. Producer surplus is the benefit that producers receive from participating in market transactions. It is the difference between what they sell their product for and the least they would be willing to receive to sell their product. On a supply and demand graph, producer surplus is measured by the area above the supply curve and below the price.

2. Using consumer and producer surplus, we can compute how shifts in supply and demand affect the well-being of customers and of companies. An inward shift in supply will cause consumer surplus to fall because both the increase in the equilibrium price and the decrease in the equilibrium quantity this shift causes act to reduce consumer surplus. An outward shift in supply, on the other hand, raises consumer surplus. An inward shift in demand leads to a drop in producer surplus because it decreases both the equilibrium price and quantity. Outward demand shifts have the opposite effect.

3. If the government imposes a price regulation—either a maximum price or price ceiling like rent control or a minimum price or price floor like the minimum wage—the quantities supplied and demanded will differ at the market price, resulting in either excess demand or excess supply of the good. Such regulations also create a deadweight loss that arises because some of the surplus-creating transactions that took place before the regulation was enacted do not take place in the regulated environment. A direct transfer of income from one side to the other without changing the price would be a more efficient way to help consumers and suppliers. Deadweight losses are largest when supply and demand are most elastic.

4. If the government imposes a cap on output (a quota) or provides output itself, this action will change the market and create a deadweight loss, just as a price regulation does. These actions do not create excess demand or supply, though, because prices are able to adjust and clear the market.

5. Taxes reduce output and raise price. In doing so, they reduce consumer and producer surplus but generate tax revenue. The revenue they generate is less than the damage they do to surplus, and the difference is the deadweight loss of the tax. The concept of tax incidence tells us who really bears the burden of a tax: It does not matter who actually pays a tax by law. All that matters is the elasticities of demand and supply. The more elastic side of the market will bear less of the burden because it can more easily shift away from the taxed good.

6. Subsidies increase both consumer and producer surplus relative to the free-market equilibrium. They still create a deadweight loss, though, because the outlay cost of the subsidy exceeds the amount by which it increases the surplus of the two groups.

Review Questions

1. Define consumer and producer surplus.
2. What is the demand choke price? How does this price relate to consumer surplus?
3. What is the supply choke price? How does this price relate to producer surplus?
4. How does a supply shift affect consumer and producer surplus in a given market? Consider both inward and outward shifts of the supply curve.
5. How does a demand shift affect consumer and producer surplus in a given market? Consider both inward and outward shifts of the demand curve.
6. What is a price ceiling? Why does a price ceiling create excess demand for (shortage of) a good?
7. What is a price floor? Why does a price floor create an excess supply of (surplus of) a good?
8. What is a deadweight loss? If the price elasticity of a good is large, would you expect the deadweight loss to be large or small?
9. When is a price ceiling nonbinding? When is a price floor nonbinding?
10. What is a quota? How does it differ from a price ceiling or a price floor?
11. What is crowding out? Why does it occur?
12. Why is the relative size of crowding out inefficiencies dependent only on the elasticity of demand and not on the elasticity of supply?
13. What happens to the equilibrium price and quantity of a good when a tax is imposed on the good? Why does a tax create a wedge between the price the consumer pays and the price the producer receives?
14. How does a tax affect consumer and producer surplus? Why does a tax create a deadweight loss?
15. What is the tax incidence? What factors determine the tax incidence?
16. What is a subsidy?
17. How does a subsidy affect consumer and producer surplus?
18. Why does a subsidy create a deadweight loss?

Problems

1. If the supply curve for snowboards in the United States is described by the equation $Q^S = 400P - 8,000$ (where Q is the number of snowboards and P is in dollars per snowboard), compute the producer surplus at a price of $120. What happens to producer surplus if the price falls to $100?
2. The demand for air travel is summarized in the equation $Q^D = 800 - 2P$, where quantity is in millions of enplanements per quarter and price is in dollars per enplanement. How much would consumer surplus change if the rising cost of fuel led airlines to raise the price from $150 to $200?
3. Consider the demand for broadband Internet service, given as follows: $Q^D = 224 - 4P$, where Q is the number of subscribers in a given area (in hundreds) and P is the price in dollars per month. This demand relationship is illustrated in the diagram on the right. Assume that the price of broadband service is $25 per month. Determine the following, paying particular attention to the units in which quantity is denominated:
   a. The total number of subscribers at that price
   b. The total amount paid by subscribers for broadband service, area B
   c. The consumer surplus received by subscribers, area A
   d. The total value to consumers of the broadband service they received, areas A and B

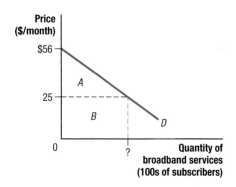

4. Consider the diagram on the next page, which depicts the supply of broadband Internet service. The supply of broadband service is given by $Q^S = 12.5P - 150$, where Q is the quantity of services (in hundreds) and P is the price per month. Assume that the price of broadband service is $25 per month. Determine the following, paying particular attention to the units in which quantity is denominated:
   a. The total number of services providers will supply at that price
   b. The total amount received by producers for that service, areas D and E
   c. The producer surplus received by suppliers, area D

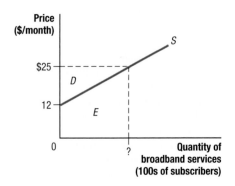

5. Combine the graphs and equations from questions 3 and 4 and determine the following:
   a. The equilibrium price of broadband Internet service
   b. The equilibrium quantity of broadband Internet service
   c. Consumer surplus
   d. Producer surplus
   e. The total surplus received by producers and consumers together
6. Holding price and quantity constant, why does the consumer surplus from a product decline if the demand curve becomes more elastic?
7. Neco Marine in the Republic of Palau estimates that the demand for its scuba diving services is given by $Q^D = 6{,}000 - 20P$, where Q is the number of divers served each year and P is the price of a two-tank dive. The supply of Neco's diving services is given by $Q^S = 30P - 2{,}000$.
   a. Solve for the equilibrium price and quantity.
   b. Find the value of the consumer surplus received by Neco divers. (*Hint:* It may help to draw a graph.)
   c. Find the value of Neco Marine's producer surplus. (*Hint:* It may help to draw a graph.)
   d. Suppose that the demand for scuba diving services increases, and that the new demand is given by $Q^D = 7{,}000 - 20P$. Calculate the impact of this change in demand on the values you calculated in parts (a) through (c).
   e. Are consumers better off or worse off as a result of the demand increase?
8. Is it possible that a regulation like the minimum wage, which is specifically designed to help low-income people, could actually reduce their income? If so, under what supply and demand conditions might this happen?
9. Low-skilled workers operate in a competitive market. The labor supply is $Q^S = 10W$ (where W is the price of labor measured by the hourly wage) and the demand for labor is $Q^D = 240 - 20W$.

Q measures the quantity of labor hired (in thousands of hours).
   a. What is the equilibrium wage and quantity of low-skilled labor working in equilibrium?
   b. If the government passes a minimum wage of $10 per hour, what will be the new quantity of labor hired? Will there be a shortage or surplus of labor? How large?
   c. What is the deadweight loss of this price floor?
   d. How much better off are low-skilled workers in this case (in other words, how much does producer surplus change) and how much worse off are employers?
10. The diagram below illustrates the market for beef. Suppose that the government has instituted a price support program for beef by placing a price floor at $4.00 per pound. Under the program, any unsold beef will be purchased by the government and placed in long-term storage.

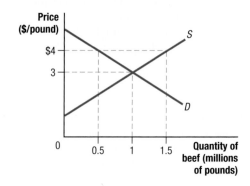

   a. What is the cost to consumers in lost surplus?
   b. What is the cost to taxpayers to purchase the unsold beef?
   c. How much producer surplus do sellers of beef gain?
   d. What is the loss to society of the beef program?
   e. The president of the National Cattleman's Association makes the following semi-extortionary offer to consumers: "Pay us $2.2 million per month forever and we'll lobby our congressmen to abandon the price support program." Should consumers pay the Cattleman's Association? Why or why not?
11. Draw a graph illustrating the impact of imposing a quota on production in a market, where the quota is less than the current equilibrium quantity. What happens to the price of the good, producer surplus, and consumer surplus? Show the deadweight loss from the quota.
12. For decades, the mob ran a "numbers game" in which participants who matched three numbers chosen at random would win a prize. In the

1970s, state governments began authorizing state lottery commissions; those commissions typically offered games similar in structure to the numbers game. Using supply and demand analysis:

a. Predict the effect of the creation of state lotteries on the number of people playing numbers-type games.

b. Predict the effect of the creation of state lotteries on the number of people playing mob-run numbers games.

c. Predict the effect of the creation of state lotteries on the price of playing a numbers-type game.

d. Numbers games are unusual in that tickets don't typically vary in their nominal price—most tickets sell for exactly $1. Given that the nominal price is fixed, how might the price change you indicated in (c) be achieved?

13. Why do taxes create a deadweight loss the same way that regulations do? If a tax and a quota raise prices by the same amount, which causes more deadweight loss? Explain.

14. Consider the market for Cheese Puff Snacks (Q is in bags of Cheese Puffs). The demand for Cheese Puff Snacks is $Q^D = 30 - P$ and the supply is $Q^S = 3P - 10$. To pay for classes about healthy snacking, the government imposes a $4 per bag tax on Cheese Puffs.

a. What are the price paid by buyers, price received by sellers, and the number of bags of Cheese Puffs sold both before and after the tax?

b. What are the deadweight loss and revenue generated from this tax?

c. If the government decides to expand the healthy snacking program and raises the tax by $8 per bag (to the $12 total), what is the *additional* DWL and revenue from increasing taxes by this amount (that is in addition to the DWL and revenue that resulted from the $4 tax)?

15. The demand for ice cream is given by $Q^D = 20 - 2P$, measured in gallons of ice cream. The supply of ice cream is given by $Q^S = 4P - 10$.

a. Graph the supply and demand curves, and find the equilibrium price and quantity of ice cream.

b. Suppose that the government legislates a $1 tax on a gallon of ice cream, to be collected from the buyer. Plot the new demand curve on your graph. Does demand increase or decrease as a result of the tax?

c. As a result of the tax, what happens to the price paid by buyers? What happens to the price received by sellers? How many gallons of ice cream are sold?

d. Who bears the greater burden of the tax? Can you explain why this is so?

e. Calculate consumer surplus both before and after the tax.

f. Calculate producer surplus both before and after the tax.

g. How much tax revenue did the government raise?

h. How much deadweight loss does the tax create?

16. Social Security taxes are taxes on the sale of labor services. Half of Social Security taxes are generally collected from the employer and half from the employee. Does this seem like a good way to structure the tax collection? Can the government dictate who bears what share of the burden of a tax? Explain.

17. Draw a graph for a competitive market with a relatively elastic demand curve and inelastic supply curve. Illustrate on the graph the impact of imposing a per unit tax on the suppliers of the good in terms of consumer and producer surplus, prices and quantities, as well as how much deadweight loss the tax creates and the revenue it generates for the government. Who bears the larger burden of this tax?

18. The U.S. Senate is considering a bill that would tax the sale of laptop computers in order to fund a computer education program for presidential hopefuls. The Congressional Budget Office (CBO) estimates that if it implements a low tax of $12 per laptop, revenue should be sufficient to exactly fund the program. The CBO also estimates that a high tax of $230 per laptop will exactly fund the program.

a. How can a low tax and a high tax raise exactly enough money to fund the program? Illustrate your answer using a graph.

b. Suppose that you are an economic advisor to the Senate Finance Committee, tasked with analyzing the economic impact of the tax proposals. Which proposal do you recommend, and why?

19. Consider the following fiscal scheme designed to directly transfer welfare from coffee drinkers to coffee vendors: The government will impose a $1.00 tax, collected from buyers, for each cup of coffee sold. The government will then subsidize coffee vendors $1.00 for each cup of coffee sold.

a. What will happen to the equilibrium price of coffee?

b. What will happen to the equilibrium quantity of coffee?

c. How will the outcome of this scheme differ from one in which the government collects a $1.00 tax for each cup of coffee sold, and divides the total tax collections equally among all coffee vendors? (It is safe to assume that all coffee vendors are identical.)

Consumer Behavior 4

This chapter is about one key question: Given the seemingly unlimited array of products and services that consumers can buy, how do they decide which ones (and how much of each) to consume? In addition to serving as the building block for the demand curve in the basic supply and demand model, understanding the answer to this simple question is incredibly powerful and its potential applications are enormous.

■ Suppose you're Jeff Bezos at Amazon in 2006, trying to develop the Kindle for introduction to the market the following year. What features do you want to include in this device to maximize profitability? Much of the answer to that question depends on consumers' preferences: what they like to read, where they read, their willingness to pay for screen size, and their distaste for carrying heavy objects, just to name a few examples. Your profitability will also depend on consumers' ability to pay—their income. If you can figure out how all those forces interact, Mr. Bezos, you can build an attractive, desirable digital text display device that could make you bazillions. (You must have figured well: Kindle books now outsell print books on

Amazon, and while Amazon doesn't release figures on the number of devices it sells, some estimate that 8 million units sold in 2010, and Amazon's Kindle-generated revenue including both the devices and the books approached $5 billion a year.)

■ Suppose you manage a grocery store. Pepsi offers to cut your wholesale price if you run a promotion over the coming week. If you drop Pepsi prices by 20%, how much more shelf space should you give to Pepsi instead of Coke? How many customers will switch from buying Coke to Pepsi? How many customers who wouldn't have bought any soft drinks before the promotion will buy them now? Deciding how to handle this situation is another case in which understanding how consumers behave can help someone make the right decision and earn some profit by doing so.

■ Suppose you're an economic analyst working for a development nongovernmental organization (NGO) that needs projections of how a country's consumption patterns will change as its citizens become wealthier. Such projections will help the organization plan and create the infrastructure to move new goods to the country's growing markets. Again, a key part of the answer lies in understanding how consumers make their choices.

■ Suppose you are trying to decide whether to buy a ticket to see your favorite performer live or pay a share to rent a beach house with 10 friends for spring break. How do you make *all* your choices about what to spend your money on? Is your method of making such decisions "right," or could you do better? In this chapter, we examine some simple rules about how you (and other consumers) make choices. You might find that your decision-making methods violate these rules. If so, changing your behavior to take them into account will probably help you make decisions that improve your day-to-day well-being and happiness.

In addition to preparing you to analyze specific applications like these examples, this chapter also illustrates a broader point about the study of economics. Like so many problems in economics (and life), the consumer's decision is a *constrained optimization* problem. Consumers try to do the best they can (they try to *optimize*) given that they are limited or *constrained* by the amount of money they have to spend. They have to make tradeoffs but do it in the smartest way they can. The set of techniques and ways of thinking we use to analyze consumers' constrained optimization problems will reappear over and over, in slightly modified ways and different settings, throughout this book and in any economics courses you may take in the future. If you become adept at solving the kind of constrained optimization problem we solve in this chapter, you will have gone a long way toward being able to answer *any* constrained optimization problem.

We begin the chapter by discussing the nature of consumers' preferences (what they like and don't like) and how economists use the concepts of utility—a measure of a consumer's well-being—and utility functions to summarize consumers' preferences. Consumers maximize their utility by trading off the purchase of one good against the purchase of others in a way that makes them the happiest. We'll see how such tradeoffs depend on a consumer's preferences, the amount of income the consumer has to spend, and the prices of the goods. Once we have these concepts in hand, we can combine them to analyze how real-world consumers behave, for example, why people buy less of something when its price rises (i.e., why demand curves slope down), and why they might consume not just more but different things as they become wealthier.

4.1 The Consumer's Preferences and the Concept of Utility

Consumers' preferences underlie every decision they make. Economists think of consumers as making rational choices about what they like best, given the constraints that they face when they make their choices.

Assumptions about Consumer Preferences

Consumers make many choices every day about what to buy and what not to buy. These choices involve many different goods: Buy a giant bag of Twizzlers and walk home, or buy a bus ticket and leave a sweet tooth unsatisfied? Buy a new video game or buy a new water pump for the car? Buy a ticket to the ball game or go to a bar for drinks with friends and watch the game on TV? To make it possible to understand how consumers form their preferences for thousands of goods and services, we need to make some simplifying assumptions. Specifically, we assume that all consumers' decisions about what to buy share four properties and that these properties help consumers determine their preferences over all the combinations of goods and services they might consume.

1. **Completeness and rankability.** This assumption implies consumers can make comparisons across all sets of goods that they consider. Economists use the term **consumption bundle** (or just *bundle*) to describe any collection of these goods. The assumption means that, given any two bundles, a consumer can determine whether she prefers the first bundle to the second bundle, the second to the first, or is indifferent between the two (i.e., views them equally). This assumption is important because it means that we can apply economic theory to any bundle of goods we want to discuss. Whether the bundle includes sapphires and SUVs; movies, motorcycles, modern art, and marshmallows; or iPods, Ikea furniture, and iceberg lettuce, the consumer can decide which bundle she likes better. This assumption does not, however, tell us what kinds of bundles the consumer will like more than others. It just implies she is able to determine if one is better than the other.

   consumption bundle
   A set of goods or services a consumer considers purchasing.

2. **For most goods, more is better than less (or at least more is no worse than less).** In general, we think that more of a good thing is good. If we like a car that is safe in a crash, we would like that car even better if it were even safer.[1] We also assume that consumers can discard unwanted goods at no cost, a concept economists call "free disposal." If you can get rid of things for free, then having more of something will never hurt you, even if it does not make you better off. The free disposal assumption may not always be strictly true in the real world, but it is a useful simplification in our basic economic model of consumer behavior.

3. **Transitivity.** For any three bundles of goods (call them *A, B,* and *C*), if a consumer prefers *A* to *B* and also prefers *B* to *C,* then the consumer must also prefer *A* to *C.* For example, if Claire prefers an apple to an orange, and prefers an orange to a banana, then transitivity implies that Claire must also prefer an apple to a banana. Note that, as always, we are holding everything else constant when making

---

[1] There may come a point at which more of a good thing stops being better. Economists call this a *satiation point.* For instance, the first jelly bean may make us happy, but the 1,437th jelly bean might actually make us sick if we ate it, making us worse off than had we eaten only 1,436. However, because people can sometimes save extra jelly beans for later, trade them to someone else for something they want, or just give them away, satiation points tend not to be very important in practice.

these comparisons. Transitivity does *not* mean that Claire has to prefer apples to bananas in all situations, but rather that at a given moment, she prefers apples to bananas. Transitivity imposes a logical consistency on the consumer.

4. **The more a consumer has of a particular good, the less she is willing to give up of something else to get even more of that good.** The idea behind this assumption is that consumers like variety. If you like birthday cake and haven't had cake lately, you might be willing to give up a lot for some cake. You might pay a high price for a cake, take the afternoon to bake a cake, or trade away your last carton of milk for some cake. On the other hand, if you've just polished off two-thirds of a cake, you are unlikely to be willing to pay much money for more, and you may very well want to trade the rest of the cake to get back some of that carton of milk. Like free disposal, it is possible to think of special cases in which the assumption of consumers liking variety will be violated (e.g., most people would prefer having either two water skis or two snow skis to having one of each). Nonetheless, we will almost always adopt this assumption because it holds true in a large number of situations and greatly simplifies our analysis.

The Concept of Utility

Given these assumptions about utility, we could create a list of a consumer's preferences between any bundles she might consume. The problem is that such a list would be a very long and unwieldy one. If we try to analyze a consumer's choices based on millions of pairwise comparisons over these bundles, we would get hopelessly lost.

Economists use the concept of utility and a mathematical relationship called a utility function to describe preferences more concisely. **Utility** describes how satisfied a consumer is. For practical purposes, you can think of utility as being a fancy word for happiness or well-being. It is important to realize that utility is *not* a measure of how rich a consumer is. Income may affect utility, but it is just one of many factors that do so.

A **utility function** summarizes the relationship between what consumers consume and their level of well-being. A function is a mathematical relationship that links a set of inputs to an output. For instance, if you combine the inputs eggs, flour, sugar, vanilla, butter, frosting, and candles in just the right way, you end up with the output of a birthday cake. In consumer behavior, the inputs to a utility function are the different things that can give a person utility. Examples of inputs to the utility function include traditional goods and services like cars, candy bars, health club memberships, and airplane rides. But there are many other types of inputs to utility as well, including scenic views, a good night's sleep, spending time with friends, and the pleasure that comes from giving to charity. The output of the utility function is the consumer's utility level. By providing a mapping between the bundles a consumer considers and a measure of the consumer's level of well-being—this bundle provides so much utility, that bundle provides so much utility, and so on—a utility function gives us a concise way to rank bundles.

Utility functions can take a variety of mathematical forms. Let's look at the utility someone enjoys from consuming Junior Mints and Milk Duds. Generically, we can write this utility level as $U = U(J, M)$, where $U(J, M)$ is the utility function and J and M are, respectively, the number of Junior Mints and Milk Duds the consumer eats. An example of a specific utility function for this consumer is $U = J \times M$. In this case, utility equals the product of the number of Junior Mints and Milk Duds she eats. But it could instead be that the consumer's (or maybe another consumer's) utility equals the

utility
A measure of how satisfied a consumer is.

utility function
A mathematical function that describes the relationship between what consumers actually consume and their level of well-being.

total number of Junior Mints and Milk Duds eaten. In that case, the utility function is $U = J + M$. Yet another possibility is that the consumer's utility is given by $U = J^{0.7}M^{0.3}$. Because the exponent on Junior Mints (0.7) is larger than that on Milk Duds (0.3), this utility function implies that a given percentage increase in Junior Mints consumed will raise utility more than the same percentage increase in Milk Duds.

These are just a few examples from the large variety of possible utility functions we could imagine consumers having for these or any other combination of goods. At this point in our analysis of consumer behavior, we don't have to be too restrictive about the form any particular utility function takes. Because utility functions are used to represent preferences, however, they have to conform to our four assumptions about preferences (rankability and completeness, more is better, transitivity, and variety is important).

Marginal Utility

One of the most important concepts related to utility functions is **marginal utility,** the extra utility the consumer receives from a one-unit increase in consumption.[2] Each good in a utility function has its own marginal utility. Using the Junior Mints and Milk Duds utility function, for example, the marginal utility of Junior Mints, MU_J, would be

$$MU_J = \frac{\Delta U(J,M)}{\Delta J}$$

where ΔJ is the small (one-unit) change in the number of Junior Mints the consumer eats and $\Delta U(J,M)$ is the change in utility she gets from doing so. Likewise, the marginal utility of consuming Milk Duds is given by

$$MU_M = \frac{\Delta U(J,M)}{\Delta M}$$

Later in this chapter, we see that marginal utility is the key to understanding the consumption choices a person makes.

Utility and Comparisons

One important but subtle point about the four preference assumptions is that they allow us to rank all bundles of goods for a particular consumer, but they do not allow us to determine how much more a consumer likes one bundle than another. In mathematical terms, we have an *ordinal* ranking of bundles (we can line them up from best to worst), but not a *cardinal* ranking (which would allow us to say exactly how much one bundle was preferred to another). The reason for this is that the units in which we measure utility are essentially arbitrary.

An example will make this clearer. Let's say we define a unit of measurement for utility that we call a "util." And let's say we have three bundles: *A, B,* and *C,* and a consumer who likes bundle *A* the most and bundle *C* the least. We might then assign these three bundles values of 8, 7, and 6 utils, respectively. The difficulty is that we just as easily could have assigned the bundles values of 8, 7, and 2 utils (or 19, 17, and 16 utils; or 67, 64, and 62 utils, etc.) and this would still perfectly describe the situation. Because there is no real-world unit of measure like dollars, grams, or inches with which to measure utility, we can shift, stretch, or squeeze a utility

marginal utility
The additional utility a consumer receives from an additional unit of a good or service.

---

[2]Marginal utility can be calculated for any given utility function.

function without altering any of its observable implications, as long as we don't change the ordering of preferences over bundles.[3]

Does it matter that we only have an ordinal ranking of utility, rather than a cardinal ranking? For the most part, not really. We can still provide answers to the important questions about how individual consumers behave, and how this behavior results in a downward-sloping demand curve.

The one set of questions we will not be able to answer so easily is how to make *interpersonal comparisons,* that is, comparisons of one consumer's utility and another's. Based on utility functions alone, it's impossible to determine which consumer values, say, a set of concert tickets more, or whether society as a whole will be made better off if we take the tickets away from one consumer and give them to another. (We can determine, however, that if one person prefers, say, tickets to Concert A over tickets to Concert B, and the other person prefers Concert B to Concert A, then both consumers will be better off if we give the tickets to Concert A to the first person and the tickets to Concert B to the second.) These important questions are addressed in the area known as **welfare economics,** which we discuss in several places in the book. For now, however, we focus on one consumer at a time.

welfare economics
The area of economics concerned with the economic well-being of society as a whole.

Just as important as the assumptions we make regarding utility functions are the assumptions that we *do not* make. For one, we do not impose particular preferences on consumers. An individual is free to prefer dogs or ferrets as pets, just as long as the four preference assumptions are not violated. Moreover, we typically don't make value judgments about what consumers should or shouldn't prefer. It isn't "right" or "wrong" to like bluegrass music instead of R&B or classical; it is just a description of how a person feels. We also don't require that preferences remain constant over time. Someone may prefer sleeping to seeing a movie tonight, but tomorrow, the opposite may be true.

The concepts of utility and utility functions are general enough to let us account for a consumer's preferences over any number of goods and the various bundles into which they can be combined. As we proceed in building our model of consumer behavior, though, we focus on a simple model in which a consumer buys a bundle with only two goods. This approach is an easy way to see how things work, but the basic model works with more complicated situations, too. In the rare situations in which this is not the case, we will point out how and why things change once there are more than two goods.

4.2 Indifference Curves

As we discussed in the previous section, the right way to think about utility is in relative terms; that is, in terms of whether one bundle of goods provides more or less utility to a consumer than another bundle. An especially good way of understanding

---

[3] In mathematical parlance, these order-preserving shifts, squeezes, or stretches of a utility function are called *monotonic* transformations. Any monotonic transformation of a utility function will imply exactly the same preferences for the consumer as the original utility function. Consider our first example of a utility function from consuming Junior Mints and Milk Duds, $U = J \times M$. Suppose that it were $U = 8J \times M + 12$ instead. For any possible bundle of Junior Mints and Milk Duds, this new utility function will imply the same ordering of the consumer's utility levels as would the old function. (You can put in a few specific numbers to test this.) Because the consumer's relative preferences don't change, she will make the same decisions on how much of each good to consume with either utility function.

utility is to take the special case in which a consumer is **indifferent** between bundles of goods. In other words, each bundle provides her with the same level of utility.

Consider the simple case in which there are only two goods to choose between, say, square feet in an apartment and the number of friends living in the same building. Michaela wants a large apartment, but also wants to be able to easily see her friends. First, Michaela looks at a 750-square-foot apartment in a building where 5 of her friends live. Next, she looks at an apartment that has only 500 square feet. For Michaela to be as happy in the smaller apartment as she would be in the larger apartment, there will have to be more friends (say, 10) in the building. Because she gets the same utility from both size/friend combinations, Michaela is indifferent between the two apartments. On the other hand, if her apartment were a more generous 1,000 square feet, Michaela would be willing to make do with (say) only 3 friends living in her building and feel no worse off.

Figure 4.1a graphs these three bundles. The square footage of the apartment is on the horizontal axis and number of friends is on the vertical axis. These are not the only three bundles that give Michaela the same level utility; there are many different bundles that accomplish that goal—an infinite number of bundles, in fact, if we ignore that it might not make sense to have a fraction of a friend (or maybe it does!).

The combination of all the different bundles of goods that give a consumer the same utility is called an **indifference curve**. In Figure 4.1b, we draw Michaela's indifference curve, which includes the three points shown in Figure 4.1a. Notice that it

indifferent
The special case in which a consumer derives the same utility level from each of two or more consumption bundles.

indifference curve
A mathematical representation of the combination of all the different consumption bundles that provide a consumer with the same utility.

Figure 4.1 | **Building an Indifference Curve**

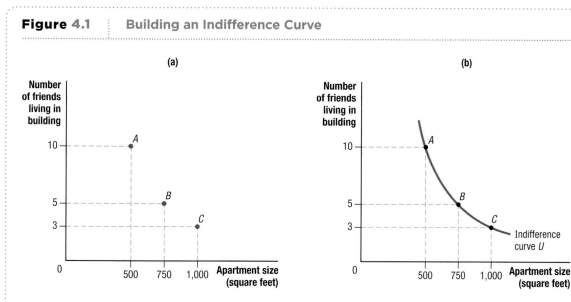

(a) Because Michaela receives utility from both the number of friends in her apartment building and the square footage of her apartment, she is equally happy with 10 friends in her building and a 500-square-foot apartment or 5 friends in her building and a 750-square-foot apartment. Likewise, she is willing to trade off 2 more friends in her building (leaving her with 3) to have a 1,000-square-foot apartment. These are three of many combinations of friends in her building and apartment size that make her equally happy.

(b) An indifference curve connects all bundles of goods that provide a consumer with the same level of utility. Bundles A, B, and C provide the same satisfaction for Michaela. Thus, the indifference curve represents Michaela's willingness to trade off between friends in her apartment building and the square footage of her apartment.

contains not just the three bundles we discussed, but many other combinations of square footage and friends in the building. Also notice that it always slopes down: Every time we take away a friend from Michaela, we need to give her more square footage to leave her indifferent. (Equivalently, we could say every time we take away apartment space, we need to give her more friends in the building to keep her equally as well off.)

For each level of utility, there is a different indifference curve. Figure 4.2 shows two of Michaela's indifference curves. Which corresponds to the higher level of utility? The easiest way to figure this out is to think as a consumer would. One of the points on the indifference curve U_1 represents the utility Michaela would get if she had 5 friends in her building and a 500-square-foot apartment. Curve U_2 includes a bundle with the same number of friends and a 1,000-square-foot apartment. By our "more is better" assumption, indifference curve U_2 must make Michaela better off. We could have instead held the apartment's square footage constant and asked which indifference curve had more friends in the building, and we would have found the same answer. Still another way of capturing the same idea is to draw a ray from the origin—zero units of both goods—through the two indifference curves. The first indifference curve the ray hits has bundles that give lower utility. Remember that by the definition of an indifference curve, utility is the same at every point on any given indifference curve, so we don't even need to check any other points on the two curves to know Michaela's utility is higher at every point on U_2 than at any point on U_1.

Characteristics of Indifference Curves

Generally speaking, the positions and shapes of indifference curves can tell us a lot about a consumer's behavior and decisions. However, our four assumptions about utility functions put some restrictions on the shapes that indifference curves can take.

1. **We can draw indifference curves.** The first assumption, completeness and rankability, means that we can always draw indifference curves: All bundles have a utility level, and we can rank them.

Figure 4.2   A Consumer's Indifference Curves

Each level of utility has a separate indifference curve. Because we assume that more is preferred to less, an indifference curve lying to the right and above another indifference curve reflects a higher level of utility. In this graph, the combinations along curve U_2 provide Michaela with a higher level of utility than the combinations along curve U_1. Michaela will be happier with a 1,000-square-foot apartment than a 500-square-foot apartment, holding the number of friends living in her building equal at 5.

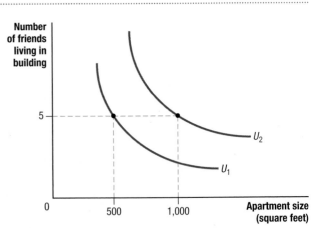

2. **We can figure out which indifference curves have higher utility levels and why they slope downward.** The "more is better" assumption implies that we can look at a set of indifference curves and figure out which ones represent higher utility levels. This can be done by holding the quantity of one good fixed and seeing which curves have larger quantities of the other good. This is exactly what we did when we looked at Figure 4.2. The assumption also implies that indifference curves never slope up. If they did slope up, this would mean that a consumer would be indifferent between a particular bundle and another bundle with more of *both* goods. There's no way this can be true if more is always better.

3. **Indifference curves never cross.** The transitivity property implies that indifference curves for a given consumer can never cross. To see why, suppose our apartment-hunter Michaela's hypothetical indifference curves intersect with one another, as shown in Figure 4.3. The "more is better" assumption implies she prefers bundle *E* to bundle *D*, because *E* offers both more square footage and more friends in her building than does *D*. Now, because *E* and *F* are on the same indifference curve U_2, Michaela's utility from consuming either bundle must be the same by definition. And because bundles *F* and *D* are on the same indifference curve U_1, she must also be indifferent between *those* two bundles. But here's the problem: Putting this all together means she's indifferent between *E* and *D*, because each makes her just as well off as *F*. We know that can't be true. After all, she must like *E* more than *D* because it has more of both goods. Something has gone wrong. What went wrong is that we violated the transitivity property by allowing the indifference curves to cross. Intersecting indifference curves imply that the same bundle (the one located at the intersection) offers two different utility levels, which can't be the case.

4. **Indifference curves are convex to the origin.** The fourth assumption of utility—the more you have of a particular good, the less you are willing to give up of something else to get even more of that good—implies something about the way indifference curves are curved. Specifically, it implies they will be convex to the origin; that is, they will bend in toward the origin as if it is tugging on the indifference curve, trying to pull it in.

Figure 4.3   Indifference Curves Cannot Cross

Indifference curves cannot intersect. Here, Michaela would be indifferent between bundles *D* and *F* and also indifferent between bundles *E* and *F.* The transitivity property would therefore imply that she must also be indifferent between bundles *D* and *E.* But this can't be true, because more is preferred to less, and bundle *E* contains more of both goods (more friends in her building and a larger apartment) than *D.*

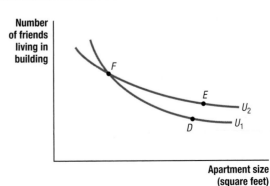

To see what this curvature means in terms of a consumer's behavior, let's think about what the slope of an indifference curve embodies. Again, we'll use Michaela as an example. If the indifference curve is steep, as it is at point *A* in Figure 4.4, Michaela is willing to give up a lot of friends to get just a few more square feet of apartment space. It isn't just coincidence that she's willing to make this tradeoff at a point where she already has a lot of friends in the building but a very small apartment. Because she already has a lot of one good (friends in the building), she is less willing to give up the other good (apartment size) to have yet another friend. On the other hand, where the indifference curve is relatively flat, as it is at point *C* of Figure 4.4, the tradeoff between friends and apartment size is reversed. At *C*, the apartment is already big, but Michaela has few friends around, so she now needs to receive a great deal of extra space in return for a small reduction in friends to be left as well off.

Because tradeoffs between goods generally depend on how much of each good a consumer would have in a bundle, indifference curves are convex to the origin. Virtually every indifference curve we draw will have this shape. As we discuss later, however, there are some special cases in which either curvature disappears and indifference curves become straight lines, or where they become so curved that they have right angles.

make the grade

Draw some indifference curves to really understand the concept

Indifference curves, like many abstract economic concepts, are often confusing to students when they are first introduced. But one nice thing about indifference curves is that preferences are the only thing necessary to draw your own indifference curves, and everybody has preferences! If you take just the few minutes of introspection necessary to draw your own indifference curves, the concept starts to make sense.

Start by selecting two goods that you like to consume—maybe your favorite candy bar, pizza, hours on Facebook, or trips to the movies. It doesn't matter much what goods you choose (this is one of the nice things about economic models—they are designed to be very general). Next, draw a graph that has one good on the vertical axis and the other good on the horizontal axis (again, it doesn't matter which one goes where). The distance along the axis from the origin will measure the units of the good consumed (candy bars, slices of pizza, hours on Facebook, etc.).

The next step is to pick some bundle of these two goods that has a moderate amount of both goods, for instance, 12 pieces of candy and 3 slices of pizza. Put a dot at that point in your graph. Now carry out the following thought experiment. First, imagine taking a few pieces of candy out of the bundle and

ask yourself how many additional slices of pizza you would need to leave you as well off as you are with 12 pieces of candy and 3 slices of pizza. Put a dot at that bundle. Then, suppose a couple of more candy pieces are taken away, and figure out how much more pizza you would need to be "made whole." Put another dot there. Next, imagine taking away some pizza from the original 12-piece, 3-slice bundle, and determine how many extra candy pieces you would have to be given to be as well off as with the original bundle. That new bundle is another point. All those points are on the same indifference curve. Connect the dots, and you've drawn an indifference curve.

Now try starting with a different initial bundle, say, one with twice as many of both goods as the first bundle you chose. Redo the same thought experiment of figuring out the tradeoffs of some of one good for a certain number of units of the other good, and you will have traced out a second indifference curve. You can start with still other bundles, either with more or less of both goods, figure out the same types of tradeoffs, and draw additional indifference curves.

There is no "right" answer as to exactly what your indifference curves will look like. It depends on your preferences. However, their shapes should have the basic properties that we have discussed: downward-sloping, never crossing, and convex to the origin.

Figure 4.4 : Tradeoffs Along an Indifference Curve

At point *A*, Michaela is willing to give up a lot of friends to get just a few more square feet, because she already has a lot of friends in the building but little space. At point *C*, Michaela has a large apartment but few friends around, so she now would require a large amount of space in return for a small reduction in friends to be left equally satisfied.

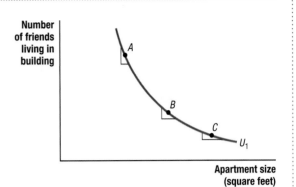

4.3 The Marginal Rate of Substitution

Indifference curves are all about tradeoffs: how much of one good a consumer will give up to get a little bit more of another good. The slope of the indifference curve captures this tradeoff idea exactly. Figure 4.5 shows two points on an indifference curve that reflects Sarah's preferences for t-shirts and socks. At point *A*, the indifference curve is very steep, meaning Sarah will give up multiple t-shirts to get one more pair of socks. The reverse is true at point *B*. At that point, Sarah will trade

---

Figure 4.5 : The Slope of an Indifference Curve Is the Marginal Rate of Substitution

The marginal rate of substitution measures the willingness of a consumer to trade one good for the other. It is measured as the negative of the slope of the indifference curve at any point. At point *A*, the slope of the curve is −2, meaning that the *MRS* is 2. This implies that, for that given bundle, Sarah is willing to trade 2 t-shirts to receive 1 more pair of socks. At point *B*, the slope is −0.5 and the *MRS* is 0.5. At this point, Sarah is only willing to give up 0.5 t-shirt to get another pair of socks.

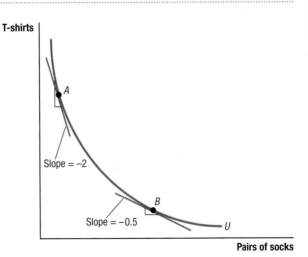

multiple pairs of socks for just one more t-shirt. As a result of this change in Sarah's willingness to trade as we move along the indifference curve, the indifference curve is convex to the origin.

This shift in the willingness to substitute one good for another along an indifference curve might be a little confusing to you initially. You might be more familiar with thinking about the slope of a straight line (which is constant) than the slope of a curve (which varies at different points along the curve). Also, you might find it odd that preferences differ along an indifference curve. After all, a consumer isn't supposed to prefer one point on an indifference curve over another, but now we're saying the consumer's relative tradeoffs between the two goods change as one moves along the curve. Let's address each of these issues in turn.

First, the slope of a curve, unlike a straight line, depends on where on the curve you are measuring the slope. To measure the slope of a curve at any point, draw a straight line that just touches the curve (but does not pass through it) at that point but nowhere else. This point where the line (called a tangent) touches the curve is called a tangency point. The slope of the line is the slope of the curve at the tangency point. The tangents that have points A and B as tangency points are shown in Figure 4.5. The slopes of those tangents are the slopes of the indifference curve at those points. At point A, the slope is -2, indicating that at this point Sarah would require 2 more t-shirts to give up 1 pair of socks. At point B, the slope is -0.5, indicating that at this point Sarah would require only half of a t-shirt to give up a pair of socks.

Second, although it's true that a consumer is indifferent between any two points on an indifference curve, that doesn't mean her relative preference for one good versus another is constant along the line. As we discussed above, Sarah's relative preference changes with the number of units of each good she already has.

marginal rate of substitution of *X* for *Y* (MRS_{XY})
The rate at which a consumer is willing to trade off one good (the good on the horizontal axis *X*) for another (the good on the vertical axis *Y*) and still be left equally well off.

Economists have a particular name for the slope of an indifference curve: the **marginal rate of substitution of *X* for *Y*** (MRS_{XY}). This is the rate at which a consumer is willing to trade off or substitute one good (the good on the vertical axis) for another (the good on the horizontal axis) and still be left equally well off:

$$MRS_{XY} = -\frac{\Delta Y}{\Delta X}$$

(A technical note: Because the slopes of indifference curves are negative, economists use the negative of the slope to make the MRS_{XY} a positive number.) The word "marginal" indicates that we are talking about the tradeoffs associated with small changes in the composition of the bundle of goods—that is, changes at the margin. It makes sense to focus on marginal changes because the willingness to substitute between two goods depends on where the consumer is located on her indifference curve.

Despite the intimidating name, the marginal rate of substitution is an intuitive concept. It tells us the relative value that a consumer places on obtaining a little more of the good on the horizontal axis, in terms of the good on the vertical axis. You make this kind of decision all the time. Whenever you order something off a menu at a restaurant, choose whether to ride a bicycle or drive, or decide on what brand of jeans to buy, you're evaluating relative values. As we see later in this chapter, when prices are attached to goods, the consumer's decision about what to consume boils down to a comparison of the relative value she places on two goods and the goods' relative prices.

freakonomics

Do Minnesotans Bleed Purple?

AP Photo/Paul Spinelli

People from Minnesota *love* their football team, the Minnesota Vikings. You can't go anywhere in the state without seeing people dressed in purple and yellow, especially during football season. If there is ever a lull in a conversation with a Minnesotan, just bring up the Vikings and you can be certain the conversation will spring to life. What are the Vikings "worth" to their fans? The answer to that question is obvious: The Vikings are priceless. Or are they?

There has often been discussion that the Vikings would leave the state because the owners were unhappy with the existing stadium. Two economists carried out a study to try to measure how much Minnesota residents cared about the Vikings.[*] The authors looked at the results of a survey that asked hundreds of Minnesotans how much their household would be willing to pay in extra taxes for a new stadium for the team. Every extra tax dollar for the stadium would be one less the household could spend on other goods, so the survey was in essence asking for the households' marginal rate of substitution of all other goods (as a composite unit) for a new Vikings stadium. Because it was widely perceived at the time that there was a realistic chance the Vikings would leave Minnesota if they didn't get a taxpayer-funded stadium, these answers were also viewed as being informative about Minnesotans' marginal rate of substitution between all other goods and the Minnesota Vikings.[†]

It turns out that fan loyalty does know some limits. The average household in Minnesota was willing to pay $571.60 to keep the Vikings in Minnesota. Multiplying that value by the roughly 1.3 million households in Minnesota gives a total marginal value of about $750 million. In other words, Minnesotans were estimated to be willing to give up $750 million of consumption of other goods in order to keep the Vikings. That's a lot of money—imagine how much people might pay if the Vikings could actually win a Super Bowl.

Alas, stadiums aren't cheap. Team officials estimate that a new stadium will cost about $1 billion. Not surprisingly in light of the analysis above, citizen response to taxpayer funding of the stadium has been lukewarm.

The Los Angeles Vikings? Don't even bring up this possibility in conversation with a Minnesotan, unless, of course, you have a check for $571.60 that you're ready to hand over.

---

[*] John R. Crooker and Aju J. Fenn, "Estimating Local Welfare Generated by an NFL Team under Credible Threat of Relocation." *Southern Economic Journal* 76, no. 1 (2009): 198–223.

[†] An interesting feature of this study is that it measures consumers' utility functions using data on hypothetical rather than actual purchases. That is, no Minnesotan had to actually give up consuming something else to keep the Vikings around. They were only answering a question about how much they would pay *if* it came time to actually make that choice. While economists prefer to measure consumers' preferences from their actual choices (believing actual choices to be a more reliable reflection of consumers' preferences), prospective choices are sometimes the only way to measure preferences for certain goods. An example of this is when economists try to measure the value of abstract environmental goods, such as species diversity.

The Marginal Rate of Substitution and Marginal Utility

Consider point A in Figure 4.5. The marginal rate of substitution at point A is equal to 2 because the slope of the indifference curve at that point is -2:

$$MRS_{XY} = -\frac{\Delta Y}{\Delta X} = -\frac{\Delta Q_{\text{t-shirts}}}{\Delta Q_{\text{socks}}} = 2$$

Literally, this means that in return for 1 more pair of socks, Sarah is willing to give up 2 t-shirts. At point B, the marginal rate of substitution is 0.5, which implies that Sarah will sacrifice only half of a t-shirt for 1 more pair of socks (or equivalently, will sacrifice 1 t-shirt for 2 pair of socks).

This change in the willingness to substitute between goods at the margin occurs because the benefit a consumer gets from another unit of a good tends to fall with the number of units she already has. If you already have all the bananas you can eat and hardly any kiwis, you might be willing to give up more bananas to get one additional kiwi.

Another way to see all this is to think about the change in utility (ΔU) created by starting at some point on an indifference curve and moving just a little bit along it. Suppose we start at point A and then move just a bit down and to the right along the curve. We can write the change in utility created by that move as the marginal utility of socks (the extra utility the consumer gets from a small increase in the number of socks consumed, MU_{socks}) times the increase in the number of socks due to the move (ΔQ_{socks}), plus the marginal utility of t-shirts ($MU_{\text{t-shirts}}$) times the decrease in the number of t-shirts ($\Delta Q_{\text{t-shirts}}$) due to the move. The change in utility is

$$\Delta U = MU_{\text{socks}} \times \Delta Q_{\text{socks}} + MU_{\text{t-shirts}} \times \Delta Q_{\text{t-shirts}}$$

where MU_{socks} and $MU_{\text{t-shirts}}$ are the marginal utilities of socks and t-shirts at point A, respectively. Here's the key: Because we're moving along an indifference curve (along which utility is constant), *the total change in utility from the move must be zero.* If we set the equation equal to zero, we get

$$0 = \Delta U = MU_{\text{socks}} \times \Delta Q_{\text{socks}} + MU_{\text{t-shirts}} \times \Delta Q_{\text{t-shirts}}$$

Rearranging the terms a bit will allow us to see an important relationship:

$$-MU_{\text{t-shirts}} \times \Delta Q_{\text{t-shirts}} = MU_{\text{socks}} \times \Delta Q_{\text{socks}}$$

$$-\frac{\Delta Q_{\text{t-shirts}}}{\Delta Q_{\text{socks}}} = \frac{MU_{\text{socks}}}{MU_{\text{t-shirts}}}$$

Notice that the left-hand side of this equation is equal to the negative of the slope of the indifference curve, or MRS_{XY}. We now can see a very significant connection: *The MRS_{XY} between two goods at any point on an indifference curve equals the inverse ratio of those two goods' marginal utilities:*

$$MRS_{XY} = -\frac{\Delta[Q_{\text{t-shirts}}]}{\Delta[Q_{\text{socks}}]} = \frac{MU_{\text{socks}}}{MU_{\text{t-shirts}}}$$

In more basic terms, MRS_{XY} shows the point we emphasized from the beginning: You can tell how much people value something by their choices of what they would be willing to give up to get it. The rate at which they give things up tells you the marginal utility of the goods.

This equation gives us a key insight into understanding why indifference curves are convex to the origin. Let's go back to the example above. At point A in Figure 4.5,

$MRS_{XY} = 2$. That means the marginal utility of socks is twice as high as the marginal utility of t-shirts. That's why Sarah is so willing to give up t-shirts for socks at that point—she will gain more utility from receiving a few more socks than she will lose from having fewer t-shirts. At point B, on the other hand, $MRS_{XY} = 0.5$, so the marginal utility of t-shirts is twice as high as that of socks. At this point, she's willing to give up many more socks for a small number of t-shirts.

As we see throughout the rest of this chapter, the marginal rate of substitution and its link to the marginal utilities of the goods play a key role in driving consumer behavior.

4.1 figure it out

Mariah consumes music downloads (M) and concert tickets (C). Her utility function is given by $U = 0.5M^2 + 2C^2$, where $MU_M = M$ and $MU_C = 4C$.

a. Write an equation for MRS_{MC}

b. Would bundles of ($M = 4$ and $C = 1$) and ($M = 2$ and $C = 2$) be on the same indifference curve? How do you know?

c. Calculate MRS_{MC} when $M = 4$ and $C = 1$ and when $M = 2$ and $C = 2$.

d. Based on your answers to question b, are Mariah's indifference curves convex? (*Hint:* Does MRS_{MC} fall as M rises?)

Solution:

a. We know that the marginal rate of substitution MRS_{MC} equals MU_M/MU_C
We are told that $MU_M = M$ and that $MU_C = 4C$. Thus, $MRS_{MC} = \dfrac{MU_M}{MU_C} = \dfrac{M}{4C}$.

b. For bundles to lie on the same indifference curve, they must provide the same level of utility to the consumer. Therefore we need to calculate Mariah's level of utility for the bundles of ($M = 4$ and $C = 1$) and ($M = 2$ and $C = 2$):

When $M = 4$ and $C = 1$, $U = 0.5(4)^2 + 2(1)^2 = 0.5(16) + 2(1) = 8 + 2 = 10$

When $M = 2$ and $C = 2$, $U = 0.5(2)^2 + 2(2)^2 = 0.5(4) + 2(4) = 2 + 8 = 10$

Each bundle provides Mariah with the same level of utility, so they must lie on the same indifference curve.

c. and d. To determine if Mariah's indifference curve is convex, we need to calculate MRS_{MC} at both bundles. Then we can see if MRS_{MC} falls as we move down along the indifference curve (i.e., as M increases and C decreases).

When $M = 2$ and $C = 2$, $MRS_{MC} = \dfrac{2}{(4)(2)} = \dfrac{2}{8} = \dfrac{1}{4} = 0.25$

When $M = 4$ and $C = 1$, $MRS_{MC} = \dfrac{4}{(4)(1)} = \dfrac{4}{4} = 1$

These calculations reveal that, holding utility constant, when music downloads rise from 2 to 4, the MRS_{MC} rises from 0.25 to 1. This means that as Mariah consumes more music downloads and fewer concert tickets, she actually becomes *more* willing to trade concert tickets for additional music downloads! Most consumers would not behave in this way. This means that the indifference curve becomes steeper as M rises, not flatter. In other words, this indifference curve will be concave to the origin rather than convex, violating the fourth characteristic of indifference curves listed above.

4.4 The Shape of Indifference Curves, Perfect Substitutes, and Perfect Complements

We've now established the connection between a consumer's preferences for two goods and the slope of her indifference curves (the MRS_{XY}). We have found that the slope of an indifference curve reveals a consumer's willingness to trade one good for another, or each good's relative marginal utility. We can flip this relationship on its head to see what the shapes of indifference curves tell us about consumers' utility functions. In this section, we discuss the two key characteristics of an indifference curve: how steep it is, and how curved it is.

Steepness

Figure 4.6 presents two sets of indifference curves reflecting two different sets of preferences for concert tickets and MP3s. In panel a, the indifference curves are steep, while in panel b they are flat. (These two sets of indifference curves have the same degree of curvature so we don't confuse steepness with curvature.)

When indifference curves are steep, consumers are willing to give up a lot of the good on the vertical axis to get a small additional amount of the good on the horizontal axis. So a consumer with the preferences reflected in the steep indifference curve in panel a would part with many concert tickets for some more MP3s. The opposite is true in panel b, which shows flatter indifference curves. A consumer with such preferences would give up a lot of MP3s for one additional concert ticket. These relationships are just another way of restating the concept of the MRS_{XY} that we introduced earlier.

Figure 4.6   The Steepness of Indifference Curves

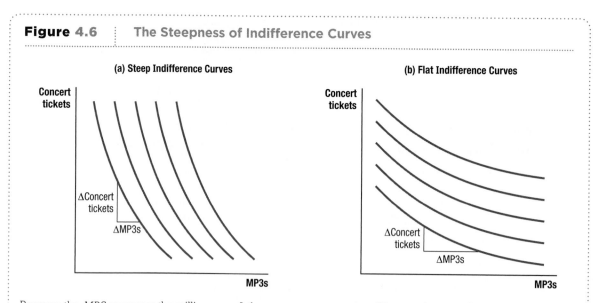

(a) Steep Indifference Curves

(b) Flat Indifference Curves

Because the *MRS* measures the willingness of the consumer to trade one good for another, we can tell a great deal about preferences by examining the shapes of indifference curves. (a) Indifference curves that are relatively steep indicate that the consumer is willing to give up a large quantity of the good on the vertical axis to get another unit of the good on the horizontal axis. Here, the consumer is willing to give up a lot of concert tickets for some additional MP3s. (b) Relatively flat indifference curves imply that the consumer would require a large increase in the good on the horizontal axis to give up a unit of the good on the vertical axis. The consumer with flat indifference curves will give up a lot of MP3s for one additional concert ticket.

Curvature

The steepness of an indifference curve tells us the rate at which a consumer is willing to trade one good for another. The curvature of an indifference curves also has a meaning. Suppose indifferences curves are almost straight, as in Figure 4.7a. In this case, a consumer (let's call him Evan) is willing to trade about the same amount of the first good (in this case, pairs of black socks) to get the same amount of the second good (pairs of blue socks), regardless of whether he has a lot of black socks relative to blue socks or vice versa. Stated in terms of the marginal rates of substitution, the *MRS* of black socks for blue ones doesn't change much as we move along the indifference curve. In practical terms, it means that the two goods are close substitutes for one another in Evan's utility function. That is, the relative value a consumer places on two substitute goods will typically not be very responsive to the amounts he has of one good versus the other. (It's no coincidence that we use in this example two goods, such as socks of two different colors, that many consumers would consider to be close substitutes for one another.)

On the other hand, for goods such as shirts and pants that are poor substitutes (Figure 4.7b) the relative value of one more pair of pants will be much greater when you have 10 shirts and no (or very few) pants than if you have 10 pairs of pants but no (or very few) shirts. In these types of cases, indifference curves are sharply curved, as shown. The *MRS* of shirts for pants is very high on the far left part of the indifference curve (where the consumer has few pants) and very low on the far right (when the consumer is awash in pants).

Figure 4.7 | The Curvature of Indifference Curves

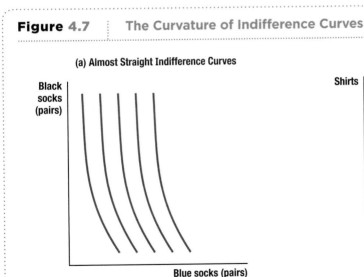

(a) Almost Straight Indifference Curves

Black socks (pairs)

Blue socks (pairs)

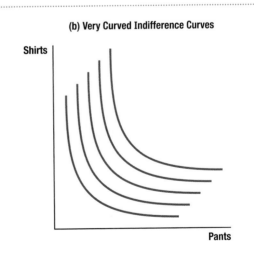

(b) Very Curved Indifference Curves

Shirts

Pants

The curvature of indifference curves reflects information about the consumer's preferences between two goods, just as its steepness does. (a) Goods that are highly substitutable (such as pairs of black socks and blue socks) are likely to produce indifference curves that are relatively straight. This means that the *MRS* does not change much as the consumer moves from one point to another along the indifference curve. (b) Goods that are complementary will generally have indifference curves with more curvature. For example, if Evan has many shirts and few pants, he will be willing to trade many shirts to get a pair of pants. If a consumer has many pants and few shirts, he will be less willing to trade a shirt for pants.

theory and data

Indifference Curves of Phone Service Buyers

Harken back to ancient times—1999–2003—when broadband was still a novelty. Most households that wanted to connect to the Internet had to use something known as a dial-up connection. The way it worked was that you hooked your computer up to the phone line in your house, and when you wanted to connect to the Internet, your computer would dial the number of your local Internet service provider (ISP). Then you had to wait, often for a very long time, listening to your computer making a screeching, fingernails-on-a-blackboard sound as it attempted to make the connection. This call to your ISP tied up your phone line (you couldn't talk on the phone while you were connected to the Internet) and was charged just like any other call on your phone bill.

A study by economists Nicholas Economides, Katja Seim, and Brian Viard used data on New York consumers' choices of land-line phone services during 1999–2003 to measure consumer utility functions and indifference curves over two related goods: local and regional phone calls.[*] Their study gives us a clear example of how different types of consumers can have different marginal rates of substitution for the same set of goods. One of their key results is sketched out in the figure shown. The indifference curves of households with Internet access Figure A (a), when drawn with local calls on the horizontal axis and regional calls on the vertical axis, are much steeper than the indifference curves of households without Internet access Figure A (b). For example, they found that a typical household in their data (one of average size and income, owning at least one mobile phone, and making the average number of local and regional calls) had an *MRS* of local for regional calls of about 1.0 if the household had Internet access and 0.5 if it didn't. That means the Internet household would be willing to give up 1 regional call to get another local call and be no worse off. The non-Internet household, on the other hand, would have to get 2 extra local calls to be no worse off for giving up 1 regional call. (Note that there is nothing special about our choice to put local calls as the good on the horizontal axis and regional calls on the vertical axis. We could have swapped the goods and redrawn the graph.)

Figure A

New Yorkers' Preferences for Local and Regional Phone Calls, 1999–2003

Households with dial-up Internet service (a) have a greater *MRS* (and steeper indifference curves) than households without Internet service (b). Accordingly, households with Internet service are more likely to use local minutes to purchase Internet usage, so they are less willing to trade local minutes for regional minutes.

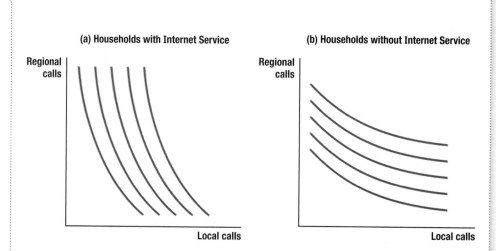

(a) Households with Internet Service   **(b) Households without Internet Service**

Regional calls   Local calls

Regional calls   Local calls

[*] Nicholas Economides, Katja Seim, and V. Brian Viard, "Quantifying the Benefits of Entry into Local Phone Service." *RAND Journal of Economics* 39, no. 3 (2008): 699–730.

Can you guess why having Internet access raised households' *MRS* of local for regional calls? Remember that the *MRS* is the ratio of the household's marginal utility of local calls to the marginal utility of regional calls, or

$$MRS_{LR} = \frac{MU_{local}}{MU_{regional}}$$

If Internet households have higher *MRS* values, their marginal utility of local calls is larger relative to their marginal utility from regional calls. In other words, they obtain greater utility on the margin from consuming local calls than do non-Internet households. This difference in relative marginal utilities most likely reflected that most of these households connected to the Internet using dial-up connections. Every time they went online, they were making a billable local call to their ISP. Their desire to browse the Internet or send e-mails therefore raised the marginal utilities they received from making local calls, which explains the patterns Economides, Seim, and Viard found.

The intuition behind the meaning of the curvature of indifference curves may be easier to grasp if we focus on the most extreme cases, **perfect substitutes** and **perfect complements.**

Perfect Substitutes   Figure 4.8 shows an example of two goods that might be perfect substitutes: 12-ounce bags of potato chips and 3-ounce bags of potato chips. If all the consumer cares about is the total amount of chips, then she is just as well off trading 4 small bags of chips for each large bag, regardless of how many of either she already has. These kinds of preferences produce linear indifference curves, and utility functions for perfect substitutes take on the general form $U = aX + bY$, where a and b are numbers that respectively indicate the marginal utility of consuming one more unit of X and Y. This is precisely the situation shown in Figure 4.8. The indifference curves are straight lines with a constant slope equal to $-1/4$, which means that the MRS_{XY} is also constant and equal to $1/4$. We can't actually say what values a and b take here, only that their ratio is 1 to 4—that is, $a/b = 1/4$. The indifference curves in the figure would be the same if $a = 1$ and $b = 4$ or if $a = 40$ and $b = 160$, for instance. This is another demonstration of the point we made above: A transformation of a utility function that does not change the order of which goods the consumer prefers implies the same preference choices.

Different-sized packages of the same good are just one example of why two goods would be perfect substitutes.[4] Another way perfect substitutes might arise is if there are attributes of a product that a particular consumer does not care at all about. For instance, some people might not care about the color of their toothbrush, or whether a bottle of water is branded Aquafina or Dasani. Their indifference curves when comparing red and green toothbrushes or Aquafina and Dasani water would therefore be straight lines. On the other hand, other consumers who *do* care about

perfect substitute
A good that a consumer can trade for another good, in fixed units, and receive the same level of utility.

perfect complement
A good whose utility level depends on its being used in a fixed proportion with another good.

---

[4] You could think of reasons why the different-sized bags might not be perfect substitutes—maybe there's a convenience factor involved with the smaller ones because there's no need to worry about storing open, partially eaten bags. But even allowing for these small differences, they're fairly close to perfect substitutes.

Figure 4.8 : **Indifference Curves for Perfect Substitutes**

Two goods that are perfect substitutes have indifference curves that are straight lines. In this case, the consumer is willing to trade one 12-ounce bag of chips for four 3-ounce bags of chips no matter how many of each she currently has and the consumer's preference for chips does not change along the indifference curve. The *MRS* is constant in this case.

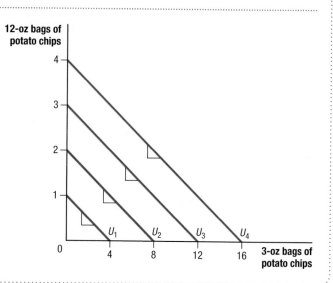

---

such features would not view the goods as perfect substitutes, and their indifference curves would be curved.

It is crucial to understand that two goods being perfect substitutes does *not* necessarily imply that the consumer is indifferent between single items of the goods. In our potato chip example above, for instance, the consumer likes a big bag a lot more than a small bag. That's why the consumer would have to be given 4 small bags, not just 1, to be willing to trade away 1 large bag. The idea behind perfect substitutes is only that the tradeoff the consumer is willing to make between the two goods—that is, the marginal rate of substitution—doesn't depend on how much or little she already has of each but is instead constant at every point along an indifference curve.

Perfect Complements When the utility a consumer receives from a good depends on its being used in fixed proportion with another good, the two goods are perfect complements. Figure 4.9 shows indifference curves for right and left shoes, which are an example of perfect complements (or at least something very close to it). Compare point *A* (2 right shoes and 2 left shoes) and point *B* (3 right shoes and 2 left shoes). Although the consumer has one extra shoe at point *B*, there is no matching shoe for the other foot, so the extra shoe is useless to her. She is therefore indifferent between these two bundles, and the bundles are on the same indifference curve. Similarly, comparing points *A* and *C* in the figure, we see that an extra left-footed shoe provides no additional utility if it isn't paired with a right-footed shoe, so *A* and *C* must also lie on the same indifference curve. However, if you add an extra left shoe *and* an extra right shoe (point *D* compared to point *A*), then the consumer is better off. That's why *D* is on a higher indifference curve.

Perfect complements lead to distinctive L-shaped indifference curves. Mathematically, this can be represented as $U = \min\{aX, bY\}$, where *a* and *b* are again numbers reflecting how consuming more units of *X* and *Y* affects utility. This mathematical structure means a consumer reaches a given utility level by consuming a minimum

---

Figure 4.9 : **Indifference Curves for Perfect Complements**

When goods are perfect complements, they have L-shaped indifference curves. For example, at point A, the consumer has 2 left shoes and 2 right shoes. Adding another right shoe while keeping left shoes constant does not increase the consumer's utility, so point B is on the same indifference curve as point A. In like manner, adding another left shoe will not increase the consumer's utility without an additional right shoe, so point C is on the same indifference curve as points A and B. Because shoes are always consumed together, 1 right shoe and 1 left shoe, the consumer's utility rises only when she has more of both goods (a move from point A to point D).

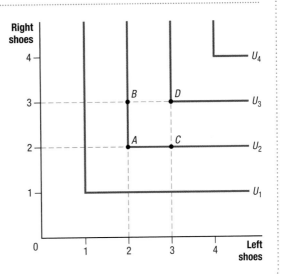

amount of each good X and Y. To be on the indifference curve U_2, for instance, the consumer must have *at least* 2 left shoes and 2 right shoes. The kink in the indifference curve is the point at which she is consuming the minimum amount of each good at that utility level.

This L-shape is the most extreme case of curvature of indifference curves. It is at the other extreme from the straight-line indifference curves that arise with perfect substitutes, and its shape produces interesting results for MRS_{XY}. The horizontal part of the indifference curve has MRS_{XY} equal to zero, while on the vertical portion, the marginal rate of substitution is infinite. As we've noted, indifference curves more generally will fall somewhere in between the shapes of the indifference curves for perfect substitutes and perfect complements, with some intermediate amount of curvature.

4.2 figure it out

Jasmine can watch hours of baseball (B) or hours of reality shows (R) on TV. Watching more baseball makes Jasmine happier, but she really doesn't care about reality shows—good or bad. Draw a diagram showing a set of Jasmine's indifference curves for hours of baseball and hours of reality shows. (Put reality shows on the horizontal axis.) What is Jasmine's MRS_{RB} when she is consuming one unit of each good?

Solution:

The easiest way to diagram Jasmine's preferences is to consider various bundles of reality shows and baseball and determine whether they lie on the same or different indifference curves. For example, suppose she watches 1 hour of reality TV and 1 hour of baseball. Plot this in Figure A as point A. Now, suppose she watches 1 hour of reality TV and 2 hours of baseball. Plot this as point B. Because watching more hours of baseball makes Jasmine happier, point B must lie on a higher indifference curve than point A.

Now, try another point with 2 hours of reality TV and 1 hour of baseball. Call this point C. Now, compare point A with point C. Point C has the same number of hours of baseball as point A, but provides Jasmine with more reality TV. Jasmine neither likes nor dislikes reality TV, however, so her utility is unchanged by having more reality TV. Points A and C must therefore lie on the same indifference curve. This would also be true of points D and E. Economists often refer to a good that has no impact on utility as a "neutral good."

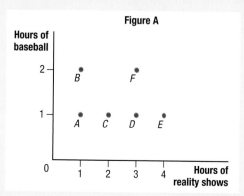

Looking at Figure A, we see that there will be an indifference curve that is a horizontal line going through points A, C, D, and E. Will all of the indifference curves be horizontal lines? Let's consider another bundle to make sure. Suppose that Jasmine watches 3 hours of reality TV and 2 hours of baseball, as at point F. It is clear that Jasmine will prefer point F to point D because she gets more baseball. It should also be clear that Jasmine will be equally happy between points B and F; she has the same hours of baseball, and reality shows have no effect on her utility. As shown in Figure B, points B and F lie on the same indifference curve (U_2) and provide a greater level of utility than the bundles on the indifference curve below (U_1).

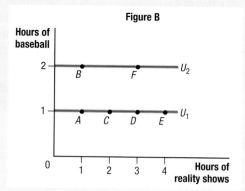

To calculate the marginal rate of substitution when Jasmine is consuming one unit of each good, we need to calculate the slope of U_1 at point A. Because the indifference curve is a horizontal line, the slope is zero. Therefore, MRS_{RB} is zero. This makes sense; Jasmine is not willing to give up any baseball to watch more reality TV because reality TV has no impact on her utility. Remember that MRS_{RB} equals MU_R/MU_B. Because MU_R is zero, MRS_{RB} will also equal zero.

The proportion in which perfect complements are consumed need not be one-for-one, as in the case of our left- and right-shoe example. Chopsticks and Chinese buffet lunches might be perfect complements for some consumers, for example, but it's likely that they will be consumed in a proportion of 2 chopsticks to 1 buffet. It's hard to eat with just one chopstick.

Different Shapes for a Particular Consumer   One final point to make about the curvature of indifference curves is that even for a particular consumer, indifference curves may take on a variety of shapes depending on the utility level. They don't all have to look the same.

For instance, indifference curve U_A in Figure 4.10 is almost a straight line. This means that at low levels of utility, this consumer considers bananas and strawberries almost perfect substitutes. Her marginal rate of substitution barely changes whether she starts with a relatively high number of bananas to strawberries, or a relatively small number. If all she is worried about is surviving (which might be the case at really low utility levels like that represented by U_A), how something tastes won't matter much to her. She's not going to be picky about the mix of fruit she eats. This leads the indifference curve to be fairly straight, like U_A.

Indifference curve U_B, on the other hand, is very sharply curved. This means that at higher utility levels, the two goods are closer to perfect complements. When this consumer has plenty of fruit, she is more concerned with enjoying variety when she eats. This leads her to prefer some of each fruit rather than a lot of one or the other. If she already has a lot of one good, she will have to be given a very large additional amount of that good to make her willing to give up a unit of the good she has less of. This leads to the more curved indifference curve. Remember, though, that even as the shapes of a consumer's indifference curves vary with her utility levels, the indifference curves will never intersect.

Figure 4.10   **The Same Consumer Can Have Indifference Curves with Different Shapes**

Indifference curves for a consumer can take on a variety of shapes, depending on the utility level. For example, at low levels of utility, bananas and strawberries may be substitutes and the consumer may just want to buy fruit, not caring whether it is a banana or a strawberry. This means that the indifference curve will be fairly linear, as is the case of U_A. But, at higher levels of utility, the consumer may prefer to have a variety of fruit. This means that she will be willing to give up many bananas for another strawberry when she has a lot of bananas, but is not willing to do so when she only has only a few bananas. Here, the consumer's indifference curve will have more curvature, such as U_B.

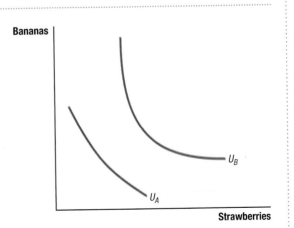

 **application**

Indifference curves for "bads"

All of the indifference curves we've drawn are for goods that a consumer likes and wants to consume. But sometimes we want to analyze consumer behavior with regard to things that a consumer doesn't want to consume—like air pollution, illness, commute time, or rutabagas. Instead of goods, these things are **bads,** things that would reduce a consumer's utility if she consumed more of them.

bad
A good or service that provides a consumer with negative utility.

Let's go back to Michaela and her apartment from Figure 4.2 and replace apartment size with distance to work. Greater distance to work is a bad because Michaela's commute time increases. Michaela's indifference curves between commute time (a bad) and the number of friends living in the building (a good) are shown in Figure 4.11.

Figure 4.11 Indifference Curves for a "Bad"

An economic "bad" is a product that reduces a consumer's utility. The consumer's (Michaela's) utility falls as commute time increases. Therefore, to keep Michaela's utility constant, we must provide her with more friends in the building if we increase her commute time. This leads to upward-sloping indifference curves. Indifference curve U_2 provides more utility than U_1, because (holding friends constant) bundle B has more commute time than bundle C, making Michaela worse off. Alternatively, points A and C provide her with a constant amount of commute time, but she has more friends at point C. Thus, Michaela is better off at point C (on U_2) than at point A (on U_1).

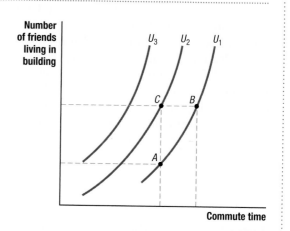

Figure 4.12 Indifference Curves for the Absence of a "Bad"

An economic "bad" can be converted into a "good." By changing the economic bad of "commute time" into the economic good of "saved commute time," we can have two goods that Michaela desires and produce typical downward-sloping, convex indifference curves. Michaela's utility increases with either an increase in the number of friends in the building or an increase in the amount of saved commute time.

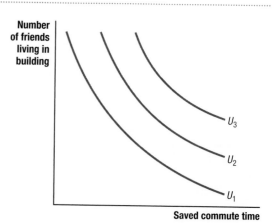

We see that the result is that indifference curves now slope upward, not downward. Why? Let's first consider bundles A and B, which lie on the same indifference curve, U_1. Notice how bundle B has more commute time than A. Michaela doesn't like to commute, so she has to be given more friends at B to be as well off as she was at point A (in other words, to keep her on the same indifference curve). Thus, Michaela receives the same level of utility from bundles A and B even though B has more of both products (we use the term "product" loosely). Bundle C has more friends than bundle A but the same commute time, so C must be preferred to A. Indifference curves that lie higher (more friends) and to the left (less commute time) indicate greater levels of utility. So do bads violate our assumption that more is better? Not really. We can keep all of our original assumptions by defining a particular good as an absence or reduction of a bad. In the case of commute time, "saved commute time" is a good. Graphing Michaela's indifference curves in terms of saved commute time—the opposite of a bad—produces the standard, downward-sloping indifference curves we've been working with, as in Figure 4.12. ■

4.5 The Consumer's Income and the Budget Constraint

In the preceding sections, we analyzed how a consumer's preferences can be described by a utility function, why indifference curves are a convenient way to think about utility, and how the slope of the indifference curve—known as the marginal rate of substitution—captures the relative utility that a consumer derives from different goods at the margin. Our ultimate goal in this chapter is to understand how consumers maximize their utility by choosing a bundle of goods to consume. Because consumers do not have an infinite amount of money and because goods are not free, consumers must make tradeoffs when deciding how much of each good to consume. That decision depends not only on the utility consumers get from each good, but also on how much money they have to spend and on the prices of the goods. We have to analyze the interaction among all of these factors.

We start looking at the interactions of utility, income, and prices by making some assumptions. To keep things simple, we continue to focus on a model with only two goods.

1. Each good has a fixed price, and any consumer can buy as much of a good as she wants at that price if she has the income to pay for it. We can make this assumption because each consumer is only a small part of the market for a good, so her consumption decision will not affect the equilibrium market price.

2. The consumer has some fixed amount of income to spend.

3. For now, the consumer cannot save or borrow. Without borrowing, she can't spend more than her income in any given period. With no saving, it means that unspent money is lost forever, so it's use it or lose it.

To incorporate prices and the consumer's income into our model of consumer behavior, we use a **budget constraint.** This constraint describes the entire set of consumption bundles that a consumer can purchase by spending all of her money. For instance, let's go back to the example of Sarah and her t-shirts and socks. Suppose

budget constraint
A curve that describes the entire set of consumption bundles a consumer can purchase when spending all income.

Sarah has an income of $50 to spend on t-shirts (which cost $10 each) and socks ($5 a pair). Figure 4.13 shows the budget constraint corresponding to this example. The number of pairs of socks is on the horizontal axis; the number of t-shirts is on the vertical axis. If Sarah spends her whole income on socks, then she can consume 10 pairs (10 pairs at $5 each is $50) and no t-shirts. This combination is point A in the figure. If instead Sarah spends all her money on t-shirts, she can buy 5 shirts and no socks, a combination shown at point B. Sarah can purchase any combination of t-shirts and socks that lies on the straight line connecting these two points. For example, she could buy 3 t-shirts and 4 pairs of socks. This is point C.

The mathematical formula for a budget constraint is

$$\text{Income} = P_X Q_X + P_Y Q_Y$$

where P_X and P_Y are the prices for one unit of goods X and Y (pairs of socks and t-shirts in our example) and Q_X and Q_Y are the quantities of the two goods. The equation simply says that the total expenditure on the two goods (the per-unit price of each good multiplied by the number of units purchased) equals the consumer's total income.

Any combination of goods on or below the budget constraint (i.e., any point between the origin and the budget constraint, including those on the constraint itself) is **feasible,** meaning that the consumer can afford to buy the bundle with her income. Any points above and to the right of the budget line are **infeasible.** These bundles are beyond the reach of the consumer's current income. Figure 4.13 shows the feasible and infeasible bundles for the budget constraint $50 = 5Q_{socks} + 10Q_{t-shirts}$.

The budget constraint in Figure 4.13 is straight, not curved, because we assumed Sarah can buy as much as she wants of a good at a set price per unit. Whether buying the first pair of socks or the tenth, the price is assumed to be the same. As we'll see later, if the goods' prices change with the number of units purchased, the budget line will change shape depending on the amount of the goods purchased.

feasible bundle
A bundle that the consumer has the ability to purchase; lies on or below the consumer's budget constraint.

infeasible bundle
A bundle that the consumer cannot afford to purchase; lies to the right and above a consumer's budget constraint.

Figure 4.13   The Budget Constraint

The budget constraint demonstrates the options available to a consumer given her income and the prices of the two goods. The horizontal intercept is the quantity of socks the consumer could afford if she spent all of her income (I) on socks, I/P_{socks}. The vertical intercept is the quantity of t-shirts she could afford if she spent all of her income on t-shirts, $I/P_{t-shirts}$. Given this, the slope of the budget constraint is the negative of the ratio of the two prices, $-P_{socks}/P_{t-shirts}$.

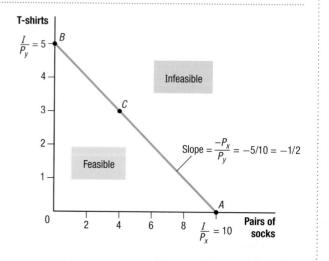

The Slope of the Budget Constraint

The relative prices of the two goods determine the slope of the budget constraint. Because the consumer spends all her money when she is on the budget constraint, if she wants to buy more of one good and stay on the constraint, she has to buy less of the other. Relative prices pin down the rate at which purchases of the two goods can be traded off between one another. If she wants to buy 1 more t-shirt (a cost of $10), for example, she'll have to buy 2 fewer pairs of socks at $5.

We can see the equivalence between relative prices and the slope of the budget constraint by rearranging the budget constraint:

$$\text{Income} = P_X Q_X + P_Y Q_Y$$

$$P_Y Q_Y = \text{Income} - P_X Q_X$$

$$Q_Y = \frac{\text{Income}}{P_Y} - \frac{P_X}{P_Y} Q_X$$

The equation shows if Q_X—the quantity purchased of good X—increases by one unit, the quantity of good Y or Q_Y that can be bought falls by P_X/P_Y. This ratio of the price of good X relative to the price of good Y is the negative of the slope of the budget constraint. It makes sense that this price ratio determines the slope of the constraint. If good X is expensive relative to good Y (i.e., P_X/P_Y is large), then buying additional units of X will mean you must give up a lot of good Y. In this case, the budget constraint will be steep. If on the other hand, good X is relatively inexpensive, you don't have to give up a lot of Y to buy more X, and the constraint will be flat.

We can use the equation for the budget constraint (Income = $P_X Q_X + P_Y Q_Y$) to find its slope and intercepts. Using the budget constraint ($50 = 5Q_{\text{socks}} + 10Q_{\text{t-shirts}}$) shown in Figure 4.13, we get

$$50 = 5Q_X + 10Q_Y$$

$$10Q_Y = 50 - 5Q_X$$

Dividing each side by 10—the price of Q_Y—yields a slope of $-1/2$:

$$Q_Y = 5 - \frac{1}{2}Q_X$$

As we noted earlier, if Sarah spends all her income on socks, she will buy 10 pairs of socks (the *x*-intercept), while she can purchase 5 t-shirts (the *y*-intercept) using all of her income. These relative prices and intercepts are shown in Figure 4.13.

As will become clear when we combine indifference curves and budget constraints in the next section, the slope of the budget constraint turns out to play an incredibly important role in determining what consumption bundles maximize consumers' utility levels.

Factors That Affect the Budget Constraint's Position

Because relative prices determine the slope of the budget constraint, changes in relative prices will change its slope. Figure 4.14a demonstrates what happens to our example budget constraint if the price of socks doubles to $10 per pair. The budget constraint rotates clockwise around the vertical axis, becoming twice as steep. That's because P_X/P_Y doubles (because P_X doubles). If Sarah spends all her money on socks, then the doubling of the price of socks means she can buy only half as many with the same income (the 5 pairs shown at A', rather than 10 pairs as before). If, on the other hand, she spends all her money on t-shirts (point B), then the change in socks' prices doesn't affect the bundle she can consume. That's because the price of t-shirts is still the same ($10). Notice that after the price increase, the set of feasible consumption bundles is smaller: There are now fewer combinations of goods that Sarah can afford with her income.

If instead the price of a t-shirt doubles to $20, but pairs of socks remain at their original $5 price (as in Figure 4.14b), then the budget constraint's movement is reversed: The budget constraint rotates counterclockwise around the horizontal axis, becoming half as steep. Someone who wants to buy only socks is unaffected, whereas someone who only wants t-shifts can obtain only half as many (if you could buy a half a t-shirt, that is; we'll assume you can for now), at bundle B'. Notice that this price increase also shrinks the feasible set of bundles just as the socks' price increase did. Always remember that when the price *rises,* the budget constraint rotates toward the origin, and when the price *falls,* it rotates away from the origin.

Now suppose Sarah's income falls by half (to $25) and prices stay at their original levels. With only half the income, Sarah can buy only half as many pairs of socks and t-shirts as she could before. If she spends everything on socks, she can now only buy 5 pairs. If she buys only t-shirts, she can afford 2.5. But because relative prices

---

Figure 4.14 : **The Effects of Price or Income Changes on the Budget Constraint**

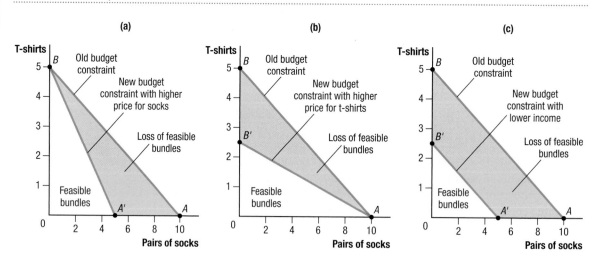

(a) When the price of socks increases, the horizontal intercept (I/P_{socks}) falls, the slope ($-P_{\text{socks}}/P_{\text{t-shirts}}$) gets steeper, the budget constraint rotates toward the origin, and the consumer (Sarah) has a smaller set of socks and t-shirt combinations from which to choose. The higher price for socks means that she can buy fewer socks, or if she purchases the same number of socks, she has less money remaining to buy t-shirts.

(b) When the price of t-shirts increases, the vertical intercept ($I/P_{\text{t-shirts}}$) falls, the slope ($-P_{\text{socks}}/P_{\text{t-shirts}}$) gets flatter, the budget constraint rotates toward the origin, and again, Sarah has a smaller choice set. The higher price for t-shirts means that

she can buy fewer t-shirts and, for a given purchase of t-shirts, she has less money available to buy socks.

(c) When Sarah's income is reduced, both the horizontal and vertical intercepts fall and the budget constraint shifts in. The horizontal intercept is lower because income I falls; thus, (I/P_{socks}) falls. The same holds for the vertical axis. Because the movement along both axes is caused by the change in income (the reduction in I is the same along both axes), the new budget constraint is parallel to the initial budget constraint. Given a reduction in income, Sarah's choice set is reduced.

haven't changed, the tradeoffs between the goods haven't changed. To buy 1 more t-shirt, Sarah still has to give up 2 pairs of socks. Thus, the slope of the budget constraint remains the same. This new budget constraint is shown in Figure 4.14c.

Note that had both prices doubled while income stayed the same, the budget constraint would be identical to the new one shown in Figure 4.14c. We can see this more clearly if we plug in $2P_X$ and $2P_Y$ for the prices in the slope-intercept format of the budget constraint:

$$Q_Y = \frac{\text{Income}}{2P_Y} - \frac{2P_X}{2P_Y}Q_X$$

$$Q_Y = \frac{1}{2}\frac{\text{Income}}{P_Y} - \frac{P_X}{P_Y}Q_X$$

In both the figure and the equation, this type of change in prices decreases the purchasing power of the consumer's income, shifting the budget constraint inward. The same set of consumption bundles is feasible in either case. If Sarah's income had increased rather than decreased as in our example (or the prices of both goods had fallen in the same proportion), the budget constraint would have shifted out rather than in. Its slope would remain the same, though, because the relative prices of t-shirts and socks have not changed.

We've now considered what happens to the budget constraint in two situations: when income changes while prices stay constant and when prices change, holding income constant. What happens when prices and income both go up proportionally (e.g., all prices double and income doubles)? The budget constraint doesn't change at all. You have double the money, but because everything costs twice as much, you can only achieve the same bundles you could before the change in price and income. You can see this mathematically in the equation for the budget constraint above: If you multiply all prices and income by whatever positive constant you want (call this constant k), all the k's will cancel out, leaving you with the original equation.

4.3 figure it out

Braden has $20 per week that he can spend on video game rentals (R), priced at $5 per game, and candy bars (C), priced at $1 each.

a. Write an equation for Braden's budget constraint and draw it on a graph that has video game rentals on the horizontal axis. Be sure to show both intercepts and the slope of the budget constraint.

b. Assuming he spends all of his allowance, how many candy bars does Braden purchase if he chooses to rent 3 video games?

c. Suppose that the price of a video game rental falls from $5 to $4. Draw Braden's new budget line (indicating intercepts and the slope).

Solution:

a. The budget constraint represents the feasible combinations of video game rentals (R) and candy bars (C) that Braden can purchase given the current prices and his income. The general form of the budget constraint would be $\text{Income} = P_R R + P_C C$. Substituting in the actual prices and income, we get $20 = 5R + 1C$.

To diagram the budget constraint, first find the horizontal and vertical intercepts. The horizontal intercept is the point on Braden's budget constraint where he spends all of his $20 on video game rentals. The x-intercept is at 4 rentals ($20/$5), point A on his budget constraint. The vertical intercept represents the point where Braden has used his entire budget to purchase candy bars. He could purchase 20 candy bars ($20/$1) as shown at point B. Because the prices of candy bars and video game rentals are the same no matter how many Braden buys, the budget constraint is a straight line that connects these two points.

The slope of the budget constraint can be measured by the rise over the run. Therefore, it is equal to $\frac{\Delta C}{\Delta R} = -\frac{20}{4} = -5$. We can check our work by recalling that the slope of the budget constraint is equal to the negative of the ratio of the two prices or $-\frac{P_R}{P_C} = -\frac{5}{1} = -5$. Remember that the slope of the budget constraint shows the rate at which Braden is able to exchange candy bars for video game rentals.

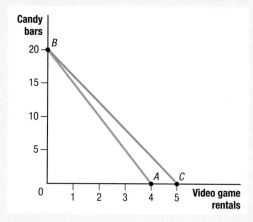

b. If Braden currently purchases 3 video game rentals, that means he spends $15 (= $5 × 3) on them. This leaves $5 (= $20 − $15) for purchasing candy bars. At a price of $1 each, Braden purchases 5 candy bars.

c. When the price of a video game rental falls to $4, the vertical intercept is unaffected. If Braden chooses to spend his $20 on candy bars, at a price of $1, he can still afford to buy 20 of them. Thus, point B will also be on his new budget constraint. However, the horizontal intercept increases from 4 to 5. At a price of $4 per rental, Braden can now afford 5 rentals if he chooses to allocate his entire budget to rentals (point C). His new budget constraint joins points B and C.

The slope of the budget constraint is $\frac{\Delta C}{\Delta R} = -\frac{20}{5} = -4$. Note that this equals the inverse price ratio of the two goods $\left(-\frac{P_R}{P_C} = -\frac{4}{1} = -4\right)$.

Nonstandard Budget Constraints

In all the examples so far, the budget constraint has been a straight line. There are some cases in which the budget constraint would be kinked instead.

Quantity Discounts   Suppose Alex spends his $100 income on pizzas and phone calls. A pizza costs $10; if he spends everything on pizzas, he can buy 10. If the price of phone minutes is constant at 10 cents per minute, he can buy as many as 1,000 minutes of phone time. Figure 4.15 portrays this example graphically. The budget constraint in the case where minutes are priced at a constant 10 cents is given by the solid section of the line running from zero minutes and 10 pizzas up to 1,000 minutes and zero pizzas.

Phone plans often offer quantity discounts on goods such as phone minutes. With a quantity discount, the price the consumer pays per unit of the good depends on the number of units purchased. If Alex's calling plan charges 10 cents per minute for the first 600 minutes per month and 5 cents per minute after that, his budget constraint will have a kink. In particular, because phone minutes become cheaper above 600 minutes, the actual budget constraint has a kink at 600 minutes and 4 pizzas. Because the price of the good on the *y*-axis (phone minutes) becomes relatively cheaper, the constraint rotates clockwise at that quantity, becoming steeper. To find where the budget constraint intercepts the vertical axis, we have to figure out how many minutes Alex can buy if he buys only cell phone time. This total is 1,400 minutes [(600 × $0.10) + (800 × $0.05) = $100]. In Figure 4.15, the resulting budget constraint runs from 10 pizzas and zero minutes to 4 pizzas and 600 minutes (part of the solid line) and then continues up to zero pizzas and 1,400 minutes (the dashed line). It's clear from the figure that the lower price for phone time above the 600-minute threshold means that Alex can afford a set of phone minute and pizza combinations (the triangle above the initial budget constraint and below the dashed line) that he could not afford when phone minutes had a constant price of 10 cents.

Quantity Limits   Another way a budget constraint can be kinked is if there is a limit on how much of one good can be consumed. For example, during World War II in the United States, certain goods like sugar and butter were rationed. Each

---

Figure 4.15   **Quantity Discounts and the Budget Constraint**

When the price of phone minutes is constant at 10 cents per minute, Alex's budget constraint for phone minutes and pizza has a constant slope, as represented by the solid line. If the phone company offers a quantity discount on phone minutes, however, Alex's budget constraint will be kinked. Here, Alex's calling plan charges 10 cents per minute for the first 600 minutes per month and 5 cents per minute after that, resulting in the kink at 600 phone minutes shown by the dashed line. The triangle above the initial budget constraint and below the dashed line represents the set of phone minute and pizza combinations Alex can afford under the new pricing scheme that he could not have purchased at a constant price of 10 cents per minute.

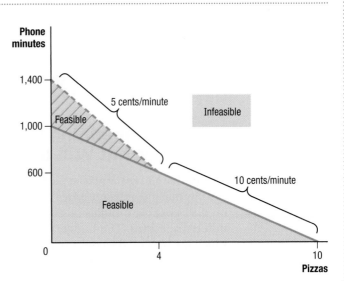

Figure 4.16   :   **Quantity Limits and the Budget Constraint**

When there is a limit on how much of a good a person can consume, a budget constraint will be kinked. When Alex is limited to 600 minutes on the phone per month, his budget constraint is horizontal at that quantity. The triangle above the horizontal section of the budget constraint and below the dashed line represents the set of phone minutes and pizzas that are now infeasible for Alex to buy. Note that Alex can still afford these sets since his income and the prices have not changed, but the restrictions on how much he can purchase dictate that he cannot buy them.

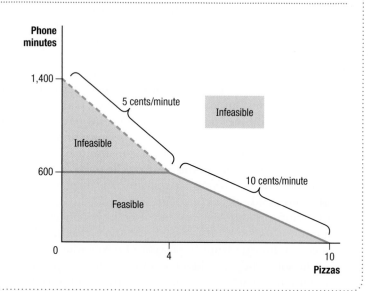

---

family could buy only a limited quantity. During the oil price spikes of the 1970s, gas stations often limited the amount of gasoline people could buy. These limits have the effect of creating a kinked budget constraint.[5]

Suppose that the government (or maybe his parents, if he lives at home) dictates that Alex can talk on the phone for no more than 600 minutes per month. In that case, the part of the budget constraint beyond 600 minutes becomes infeasible, and the constraint becomes horizontal at 600 minutes, as shown by the solid line in Figure 4.16. Note that neither Alex's income nor any prices have changed in this example. He still has enough money to reach any part in the area below the dashed section of the budget constraint that is labeled infeasible. He just isn't allowed to spend it. Consequently, for the flat part of the budget constraint, he will have unspent money left over. As we see in the next section, you will never actually want to consume a bundle on the flat part of the budget constraint. (You might want to see if you can figure out why yourself, before we tell you the answer.)

4.6 Combining Utility, Income, and Prices: What Will the Consumer Consume?

We now have in place all the pieces necessary to determine how much of each good a utility-maximizing consumer will consume. We know the consumer's preferences over all possible bundles of goods from the utility function and its associated indifference curves. The budget constraint shows us which bundles are feasible and which are beyond the consumer's reach given her income and the goods' prices. It's just a matter of combining this information in the right way.

---

[5] Note that limits on how much a consumer can purchase are a lot like the quotas we learned about in Chapter 3, except now they apply to a single consumer, rather than to the market as a whole.

Solving the Consumer's Optimization Problem

As we mentioned in the introduction to this chapter, the choice of how much to consume (like so many economic decisions) is a *constrained optimization* problem. There is something you want to maximize (utility, in this case), and there is something that limits how much of the good thing you can get (the budget constraint, in this case). And as we will see in the next chapter, the constrained optimization problem forms the basis of the demand curve.

Before we try to solve this constrained optimization problem, let's think for a minute about what makes it a tricky problem: It requires us to make comparisons between things (e.g., income and prices) measured in dollars and things (e.g., consumer utility)measured in imaginary units that we can't directly translate into dollars. How can you know whether or not you're willing to pay $3 to get some extra units of utility? Well, you can't, really. What you can figure out, however, is whether spending an extra dollar on, say, golf balls gives you more or less utility than spending an extra dollar on something else, like AAA batteries. It turns out that in figuring out this choice, you and other consumers use your indifference curves and budget constraints in such a way that solving the consumer's optimization problem becomes straightforward.

Maybe you didn't take much note of it earlier when we introduced indifference curves and the budget constraint, but look now at the axes we use to depict these two different concepts. They are the same: The quantity of some good is on the vertical axis, and the quantity of some other good is on the horizontal axis. This arrangement is extremely important, because it means we can display indifference curves and the budget constraint for two goods in the same graph, making the consumer's problem easier to solve.

Figure 4.17 presents an example that shows a combination of indifference curves and a budget constraint. Remember, the consumer wants to get as much utility as possible from consuming the goods, subject to the limits imposed by her budget

---

Figure 4.17   :   The Consumer's Optimal Choice

The consumer's optimal consumption bundle occurs at the point of tangency between her budget constraint and her indifference curve, shown here at point *A*. The consumer can afford the consumption bundles represented by points *B, C,* and *D,* but these are on a lower indifference curve (U_1) than is point *A* (U_2). Point *E* is on a higher indifference curve (U_3), but it lies outside the consumer's budget constraint and is thus infeasible.

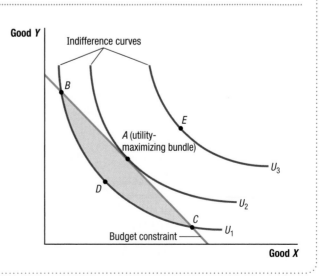

constraint. What bundle will she choose? The bundle at point *A*. That's the highest indifference curve she can reach given her budget line.

Why is *A* the utility-maximizing consumption bundle? Compare point *A* to another feasible bundle, such as *B*. Point *B* is on the budget constraint, so the consumer can afford it with her income. However, because *B* is on a lower indifference curve (U_1) than *A* is (U_2), bundle *B* provides less utility than *A*. Bundles *C* and *D* are feasible too, but also leave the consumer worse off. The consumer would love to consume a bundle like *E* because it's on an indifference curve (U_3) that corresponds to a higher utility level than U_2. Unfortunately, the consumer can't afford *E*: It's outside her budget constraint.

A look at the consumer's optimal consumption bundle *A* in Figure 4.17 shows that it has a special feature: The indifference curve running through it, U_2, touches the budget constraint once and only once, exactly at *A*. Mathematically speaking, U_2 and the budget constraint are tangent at point *A*. As long as the assumptions about utility we established earlier hold, no other indifference curve we can draw will have this feature. Any other indifference curve will not be tangent, and therefore will cross the budget constraint twice or not at all. If you can draw another indifference curve that is tangent, it will cross the indifference curve shown in Figure 4.17, violating the transitivity assumption. (Give it a try—it is a useful exercise.)

This single tangency is not a coincidence. It is, in fact, a requirement of utility maximization. To see why, suppose an indifference curve and the budget constraint never touched. Then no point on the indifference curve is feasible, and by definition, no bundle on that indifference curve can be the way for a consumer to maximize his utility given his income. Now suppose the indifference curve instead crosses the budget constraint twice. This implies there must be a bundle that offers the consumer higher utility than any on this indifference curve and that the consumer can afford. For example, the shaded region between indifference curve U_1 and the budget constraint in Figure 4.17 reflects all of the bundles that are feasible and provide higher utility than bundles *B, C, D,* or any other point on U_1.That means no bundle on U_1 could be utility-maximizing; there are other bundles that are both affordable and offer higher utility. By similar reasoning, this outcome will be generally true not just for indifference curve U_1, but for any indifference curve that crosses the budget constraint twice.

This means that only at a point of tangency are there no other bundles that are both (1) feasible and (2) offer a higher utility level. This tangency is the utility-maximizing bundle for the consumer.

Mathematically, the tangency of the indifference curve and budget constraint means that they have the same slope at the optimal consumption bundle. This has a very important economic interpretation that is key to understanding why the optimal bundle is where it is. In Section 4.3, we defined the negative of the slope of the indifference curve as the marginal rate of substitution, and we discussed how the MRS_{XY} reflects the ratio of the *marginal utilities* of the two goods. In Section 4.5, we saw that the slope of the budget constraint equals the negative of the ratio of the *prices* of the two goods. Therefore, the fact that the consumer's utility-maximizing bundle is at a tangency between an indifference curve and the budget constraint (and that it's on the budget constraint rather than inside it) gives us this key insight: *When the consumer spends all her income, her optimal consumption bundle is the one at which the ratio of the goods' marginal utilities exactly equals the ratio of their prices.*

This economic idea behind utility maximization can be expressed mathematically. At the point of tangency,

$$\text{Slope of indifference curve} = \text{Slope of budget constraint}$$

$$-MRS_{XY} = -MU_X/MU_Y = -P_X/P_Y$$

$$MU_X/MU_Y = P_X/P_Y$$

Why are the marginal utility and price ratios equal when the consumer maximizes her utility level? If they were not equal, she could do better by shifting consumption from one good to the other. To see why, let's say Meredith is maximizing her utility over bottles of Gatorade and protein bars. Suppose bottles of Gatorade are twice as expensive as protein bars, but she is considering a bundle in which her marginal utilities from the two goods *are not* 2 to 1 as the price ratio is. Say she gets the same amount of utility at the margin from another bottle of Gatorade as from another protein bar, so that the ratio of the goods' marginal utilities is 1. Given the relative prices, she could give up 1 bottle of Gatorade and buy 2 more protein bars and doing so would let her reach a higher utility level. Why? Because those 2 extra protein bars are worth twice as much in utility terms as the lost bottle of Gatorade.

Now suppose that a bottle of Gatorade offers Meredith four times the utility at the margin as a protein bar. In this case, the ratio of Meredith's marginal utilities for Gatorade and protein bars (4 to 1) is higher than the price ratio (2 to 1), so Meredith could buy 2 fewer protein bars in exchange for 1 more bottle of Gatorade. Because the Gatorade delivers twice the utility lost from the 2 protein bars, she will be better off buying fewer protein bars and more Gatorade.

It is often helpful to rewrite this optimization condition in terms of the consumer's marginal utility per dollar spent:

$$\frac{MU_X}{MU_Y} = \frac{P_X}{P_Y} \Rightarrow \frac{MU_X}{P_X} = \frac{MU_Y}{P_Y}$$

Here, the utility-maximation problem can be restated as finding the consumption bundle that gives the consumer the most bang for her buck. This occurs when the marginal utility per dollar spent (MU/P) is equal across all goods. If this is not the case, the consumer is able to adjust her consumption of Good X and Good Y to improve her utility.

4.4 figure it out

Suppose Antonio gets utility from consuming two goods, burgers and fries. His utility function is given by

$$U = \sqrt{BF} = B^{0.5}F^{0.5}$$

where B is the amount of burgers he eats and F the servings of fries. Antonio's marginal utility of a burger MU_B equals $0.5B^{-0.5}F^{0.5}$, and his marginal utility of an order of fries MU_F equals $0.5B^{0.5}F^{-0.5}$. Antonio's income is $20, and the prices of burgers and fries are $5 and $2, respectively. What are Antonio's utility-maximizing quantities of burgers and fries?

Solution:

We know that the optimal solution to the consumer's maximization problem sets the marginal rate of substitution—the ratio of the goods' marginal utilities—equal to the goods' price ratio:

$$MRS_{BF} = \frac{MU_B}{MU_F} = \frac{P_B}{P_F}$$

where MU_B and MU_F are the marginal utilities of burgers and fries, respectively. P_B and P_F are the goods' prices. Therefore, to find the utility-maximizing quantities of burgers and fries, we set the ratio of marginal utilities equal to the goods' price ratio and simplify:

$$\frac{MU_B}{MU_F} = \frac{P_B}{P_F}$$

$$\frac{0.5B^{-0.5}F^{0.5}}{0.5B^{0.5}F^{-0.5}} = \frac{5}{2}$$

$$\frac{0.5F^{0.5}F^{0.5}}{0.5B^{0.5}B^{0.5}} = \frac{5}{2}$$

$$\frac{F}{B} = \frac{5}{2}$$

$$2F = 5B$$

$$F = 2.5B$$

This condition tells us that Antonio maximizes his utility when he consumes fries to burgers at a 5 to 2 ratio. We now know the ratio of the optimal quantities, but do not yet know exactly what quantities Antonio will choose to consume. To figure that out, we can use the budget constraint, which pins down the total amount Antonio can spend, and therefore the total quantities of each good he can consume.

Antonio's budget constraint can be written as

$$\text{Income} = P_F F + P_B B, \text{ or}$$

$$B = \frac{\text{Income}}{P_B} - \frac{P_F}{P_B}F$$

Substituting in the values from the problem gives

$$B = \frac{20}{5} - \frac{2}{5}F$$

$$B = 4 - 0.4F$$

Now, we can substitute the utility-maximization condition $F = 2.5B$ into the budget constraint to find the quantity of burgers Antonio will consume:

$$B = 4 - 0.4F$$

$$B = 4 - 0.4(2.5B)$$

$$B = 4 - B$$

$$B = 2$$

And because $F = 2.5B$, then $F = 5$.

Therefore, given his budget constraint, Antonio maximizes his utility by consuming 2 burgers and 5 servings of fries.

Implications of Utility Maximization

The marginal-utility-ratio-equals-price-ratio result has another implication for the economy as a whole that can initially be quite surprising. Even if two consumers have very different preferences between two goods, they will have the *same* ratio of marginal utilities for the two goods, because utility maximization implies that *MRS* equals the ratio of the prices.[6]

This might seem odd. If Jack has consumed 9 packs of gum and 1 iTunes download, while Meg consumed 9 downloads and only 1 pack of gum, it seems that Jack likes gum a lot and would therefore be willing to pay more for another pack of gum (and a lot less for iTunes) than Meg. This assertion would be true *if both Jack and Meg had to consume the same bundle,* but they don't have to. They can choose how much of each good they want to consume. Because Jack likes gum a lot, he will consume so much of it that he drives down his marginal utility until, by the time he and Meg both reach their utility-maximizing consumption bundles, they both place the same relative marginal utilities on the two goods. Ultimately, the relative value they place on any two goods (on the margin) is dictated by the relative prices. Because Meg and Jack face the same prices, they have the same marginal values.

This situation is shown in Figure 4.18. To keep things simple, we assume Jack and Meg have the same incomes. Because they also face the same relative prices, their budget constraints are the same. Jack really likes gum relative to iTunes downloads, so his indifference curves tend to be flat: He has to be given a lot of iTunes to make up for any loss of gum. Meg has the opposite tastes. She has to be given a lot of gum to make her no worse off for giving up an iTunes download. Her indifference curves are therefore steep. Nevertheless, both Jack and Meg's utility-maximizing bundles are on the same budget line, and their marginal rates of substitution at those bundles are the same. We've drawn the indifference curves for Jack (U_J) and Meg (U_M) so that they are tangent to the budget line and therefore contain the utility-maximizing bundle.

Figure 4.18 | **Two Consumers' Optimal Choices**

Although they have the same budget constraint, Jack and Meg have different relative preferences and, therefore, different optimal consumption bundles. Because Jack likes gum relative to iTunes downloads, his indifference curve (U_J) is flat and he consumes much more gum than iTunes at his optimal consumption bundle at point *J*. Meg's indifference curve (U_M) is much steeper and reflects her relative preference for iTunes downloads over gum; her utility-maximizing bundle is shown at point *M*. Although their consumption bundles are different, the *MRS* is the same at these points.

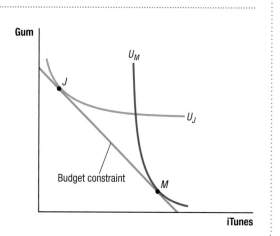

---

[6] Technically, this is true only of consumers who are consuming a positive amount of both goods, or who are at "interior" solutions in economists' lingo. We'll discuss this issue in the next section.

theory and data

Indifference Curves of Phone Service Buyers Revisited

From the Economides, Seim, and Viard study we discussed earlier, we learned that households with Internet access had higher relative marginal utilities for local phone calls than did non-Internet homes. Because the marginal utilities of regional calls were lower for Internet households, their *MRS* was higher than that for non-Internet households. Using the logic we just discussed, we can see that if the two types of households had the same budget constraint, the outcome would look something like Figure A. Just like Jack and Meg above, consumers with different tastes end up consuming different bundles. Because households with the Internet had steeper indifference curves than those without Internet access, they ended up consuming a larger amount of local calls, shown at bundle *I*. (U_{Internet} is the indifference curve tangent to the budget constraint.) Non-Internet households' phone use was relatively heavy in regional calls instead, as seen in their optimal bundle *NI*. However, because we've assumed all households face the same budget constraint (and therefore the same relative prices), they will all have the same *MRS* at their optimal bundles.

Figure A

Optimal Choices of Internet and Non-Internet Households

Non-Internet households and Internet households have the same budget constraint but different optimal bundles. Non-Internet households consume more regional calls than local calls at their utility-maximizing point (*NI*) because at any given level of local calls, they get higher marginal utility from regional calls. Internet households, on the other hand, consume more local calls than regional calls (point *I*) because they favor local calls on the margin more.

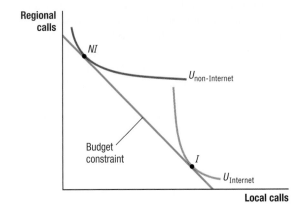

An interesting additional aspect of this market is that households actually have some choice in the relative prices they face. This is because they choose a specific calling plan from the many offered by the various competing phone companies. These menus typically let households trade off higher fixed monthly fees to face lower prices for additional calls on the margin. So, for example, a household could sign up for a billing plan that has a high fixed fee and a low marginal price for local phone service, but a low fixed fee with a high marginal price for regional service. Or vice versa.

How would these sorts of choices show up in our analysis? We know that the impact of different marginal prices would show up as a steeper or shallower budget constraint, depending on whether local or regional calls become relatively more expensive. How would a fixed fee affect the households' choices depicted in the figure drawn? You can think of paying a fixed fee as a reduction in the household's income. It doesn't affect relative prices on the margin, so in and of itself, it doesn't change the slope of the budget constraint. However, it does leave the household with less income to allocate between local and regional calls. Thus, if a household opts to pay a higher fixed fee, its budget constraint shifts in toward the origin.

A household might be willing to pay a higher fee and suffer the related income loss *if* the calling plan significantly lowers the price of the good it expects to consume a lot of. This is because the combination of these income and price changes would both shift (the result of the income change) and rotate (the result of the price change) the budget constraint, so that the household could still reach a higher utility level than before the shift.

An example of this is shown in Figure B. An Internet household's original optimal bundle I from Figure A is shown (now labeled I_1), along with the original budget constraint (BC_1) and tangent indifference curve (now labeled $U_{Internet,1}$). When the household pays a fee to reduce the price of local calls on the margin, the budget constraint shifts in and rotates counterclockwise, as shown. Notice that the household has suffered a loss in income—it can't even afford its old optimal bundle I_1 anymore; that point is now infeasible. Nevertheless, the new optimal bundle I_2 is on an indifference curve ($U_{Internet,2}$) that corresponds to a higher utility level than the household received before.

By reducing the price of the good it has stronger relative preferences for, the household is actually able to make itself better off by paying a fee and, in effect, reducing its income. (In the next chapter, we spend a lot of time looking at how consumers respond to simultaneous changes in income and relative prices.)

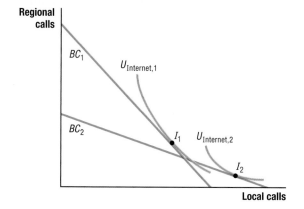

Figure B

Paying a Fixed Fee to Reduce the Price of Local Calls

By paying a fee, the Internet household can reduce the price of local calls on the margin, rotating the household's budget constraint from BC_1 to BC_2, due to the now lower relative price for local calls. The household has suffered a loss of income, but the new optimal bundle (I_2) is on an indifference curve ($U_{Internet,2}$) with a higher utility level than the original bundle (I_1 on indifference curve $U_{Internet,1}$).

While they have the same MRS_{XY}, what *is* different is the amount of each good they consume in their respective bundles. Jack, the gum lover, maximizes his utility by choosing a bundle (J) with a lot of gum and not many iTunes. Meg's optimal consumption bundle (M), on the other hand, has a lot of iTunes and little gum. Again, the idea is that the way both consumers end up with the same MRS in their utility-maximizing bundles is that each consumes a large amount of the good for which he or she has the stronger preference. By behaving in this way, Jack and Meg drive down the relative marginal utility of the good they prefer until their marginal utility ratio equals the price ratio.

Note that these two indifference curves cross, although earlier we learned that indifference curves can never cross. If a consumer's indifference curves did cross, her preferences wouldn't have the transitivity property, and the bundle located where the indifference curves crossed would supposedly deliver two different utility levels. However, the "no crossing" rule applies only to the indifference curves of one individual. Figure 4.18 shows indifference curves for two different people with different preferences. Transitivity doesn't have to hold across people. If you like gum more than iTunes, and your friend likes iTunes more than, say, coffee, that doesn't imply you have to like gum more than coffee. So the same consumption bundle (say, 3 packs of gum and 5 iTunes downloads) can offer different utility levels to different people.

A Special Case: Corner Solutions

Up to this point, we have been analyzing situations in which the consumer optimally consumes some of both goods. This assumption usually makes sense if we think that utility functions have the property that the more you have of a good, the less you are willing to give up of something else to get more. Because the first little bit of a good provides the most marginal utility in this situation, a consumer will typically want at least *some* amount of a good.

Depending on the consumer's preferences and relative prices, however, in some cases a consumer will want to spend all her money on one good. When consuming all of one good and none of the other maximizes a consumer's utility given the budget constraint, this is called a **corner solution.** (Its name comes from the fact that the optimal consumption bundle is at the "corner" of the budget line, where it meets the axis.) If the utility-maximizing bundle has positive quantities of both goods, like all the cases we've looked at to this point, this is referred to as an **interior solution.**

corner solution
A utility-maximizing bundle located at the "corner" of the budget constraint where the consumer purchases only one of two goods.

interior solution
A utility-maximizing bundle that contains positive quantities of both goods.

Figure 4.19 depicts a corner solution. Greg, our consumer, has an income of \$240 and is choosing his consumption levels of romance novels and economics textbooks. Let's say a hardcover romance novel costs \$20, and an economics text costs \$120. Because econ texts are more expensive than romance novels, Greg can afford up to 12 romance novels, but only 2 econ texts. Nonetheless, the highest utility that Greg can obtain given his income is bundle A, where he consumes all economics textbooks and no romance novels.

How do we know A is the optimal bundle? Consider another feasible bundle, such as B. Greg can afford it, but it is on an indifference curve U_1 that corresponds to a lower utility level than U_2. The same logic would apply to bundles on any indifference curve between U_1 and U_2. Furthermore, any bundle that offers higher utility than U_2 (i.e., above and to the right of U_2) isn't feasible given Greg's income. So U_2 must be the highest utility level Greg can achieve, and he can do so

Figure 4.19 : **A Corner Solution**

A corner solution occurs when the consumer spends all his money on one good. Given Greg's income and the relative prices of romance novels and economics textbooks, Greg is going to consume 2 economics textbooks and zero romance novels at his optimal consumption bundle (*A*). All other feasible consumption bundles, such as point *B*, correspond to indifference curves with lower utility levels than the indifference curve U_2 at point *A*. Greg cannot afford consumption bundles at a higher utility level, such as U_3, with his current income.

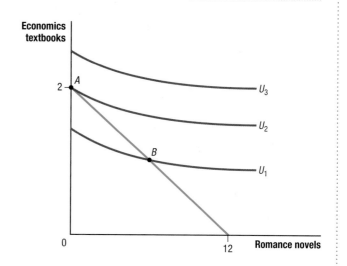

only by consuming bundle *A*, because that's the only bundle he can afford on that indifference curve.

In a corner solution, then, the highest indifference curve touches the budget constraint exactly once, just as with the interior solutions we discussed earlier. The only difference with a corner solution is that bundle *A* is not a point of tangency. The indifference curve is flatter than the budget constraint at that point (and everywhere else). That means Greg's *MRS*—the ratio of his marginal utility from romance novels relative to his marginal utility from textbooks—is *less* than the price ratio of the two goods rather than equal to it. In other words, even when he's consuming no romance novels, his marginal utility from them is so low, it's not worth paying the price of a novel to be able to consume one. The marginal utility he'd have to give up due to reduced textbook consumption would not be made up for by the fact that he could spend some of his textbook money on novels. In fact, if Greg were allowed to consume a negative quantity of romance novels (that would be kind of like Greg producing some romance novels to sell to other consumers), he would want to.

4.5 figure it out

A pizza chain recently offered the following special promotion: "Buy one pizza at full price and get your next three pizzas for just $5 each!" Assume that the full price of a pizza is $10, your daily income $40, and the price of all other goods $1 per unit.

a. Draw budget constraints for pizza and all other goods that reflect your situations both before and during the special promotion. (Put the quantity of pizzas on the horizontal axis.) Indicate the horizontal and vertical intercepts and the slope of the budget constraint.

b. How is this special offer likely to alter your buying behavior?

c. How might your answer to (b) depend on the shape of your indifference curves?

Solution:

a. To draw your budget constraint, you need to find the combinations of pizza and all other goods that are available to you before and during the promotion. The starting place for drawing your budget constraint is to find its x- and y-intercepts.

Before the promotion, you could afford 4 pizzas a day ($40/$10) if you spent all of your income on pizza. This is the x-intercept (Figure A). Likewise, you could afford 40 units of all other goods per day ($40/$1) if you purchased no pizza. This is the y-intercept. The budget constraint, shown in the diagram below, connects these two points and has a slope of $-40/4 = -10$. This slope measures the amount of other goods you must give up to have an additional pizza. Note that this is also equal to $-P_x/P_y = -\$10/\$1 = -10$.

Once the promotion begins, you can still afford 40 units of all other goods if you buy no pizza. The promotion has an effect only if you buy some pizza. This means the y-intercept of the budget constraint is unchanged by the promotion. Now suppose you buy 1 pizza. In that case, you must pay $10 for the pizza, leaving you $30 for purchasing all other goods. This bundle is point A on the diagram. If you were to buy a second pizza, its price would be only $5. Spending $15 on 2 pizzas would allow you to purchase $25 ($40 − $15) worth of other goods. This corresponds to bundle B. The third and fourth pizzas also cost $5 each. After 3 pizzas, you have $20 left to spend on other goods, and after 4 pizzas, you are left with $15 for other goods. These are points C and D on the diagram.

A fifth pizza will cost you $10 (the full price) because the promotion limits the $5 price to the next 3 pizzas you buy. That means if you choose to buy 5 pizzas, you will spend $35 on pizza and only $5 on other goods, as at bundle E. Now that you have again purchased a pizza at full price, you are eligible to receive the next 3 at the reduced price of $5. Unfortunately, you only have enough income for one more $5 pizza. Therefore, if you would like to spend all of your income on pizza, you can buy 6 pizzas instead of just 4.

As a result of the promotion, then, your x-intercept has moved out to 6, and your budget line has pivoted out (in a somewhat irregular way because of all the relative price changes corresponding to purchasing different numbers of pizzas) to reflect the increase in your purchasing power due to the promotion.

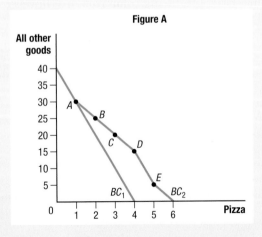

Figure A

b. It is likely that the promotion will increase how much pizza you consume. Most of the new budget constraint lies to the right of the initial budget constraint, increasing the number of feasible bundles available to you. Because more is preferred to less, it is likely that your optimal consumption bundle will include more pizza than before.

c. If your indifference curves are very flat, you have a strong preference for other goods relative to pizza. For example, look at U_A (Figure B). The slope of this indifference curve is relatively small (in absolute value). This means that the marginal rate of substitution of other goods for pizza is small. If your indifference curves look like this, you are not very willing to trade other goods for more pizza, and your optimal consumption bundle will likely lie on the section of the new budget constraint that coincides with the initial budget constraint. The promotion would cause no change in your consumption behavior; pizza is not a high priority for you, as indicated by your flat indifference curve.

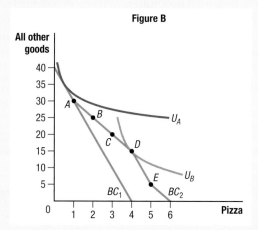

Figure B

On the other hand, if your indifference curves are steeper, like U_B, your marginal rate of substitution is relatively large, indicating that you are willing to forgo a large amount of other goods to consume an additional pizza. This promotion will more than likely cause you to purchase additional pizzas.

4.7 An Alternative Approach to Solving the Consumer's Problem: Expenditure Minimization

Up to this point, our strategy for determining what bundle of goods the consumer will consume has involved maximizing utility subject to the constraint that expenditure cannot exceed the consumer's income. As we discussed above, this is an example of a *constrained maximization* problem.

While this approach is natural and intuitive, any constrained maximization problem can also be solved by reversing the roles played by the constraint and the function being maximized. That is, we can also look at how a consumer decides what bundle to consume as a "constrained minimization" problem: The consumer minimizes expenditure (reflected in the budget constraint) subject to the constraint that she must achieve a given level of utility from this expenditure. Graphically speaking, utility maximization is about finding the highest indifference curve that is tangent to the budget constraint, while expenditure minimization is about finding the lowest budget constraint that is tangent to a given indifference curve.

Economists call this expenditure-minimization setup the "dual" to the utility-maximization problem. They're sort of mathematical mirror images.

Figure 4.20 shows these two approaches graphically. Panel a on the left is an example of the standard utility-maximization approach. The consumer has a fixed income reflected in the budget constraint BC^* and various levels of utility as reflected by the three indifference curves shown. Bundle A, which is at the point of tangency between the budget constraint and the indifference curve labeled U^*, represents the utility-maximizing feasible bundle.

Panel b solves the same problem using the expenditure-minimization approach. In this case, we start with a level of utility that the consumer wants to achieve. Specifically, we start with a given level of utility U^*, which is the same utility level that the consumer has in panel a. Then, we search over different levels of income (or equivalently, expenditure) for the smallest amount of income or expenditure necessary to achieve U^*. Each expenditure level is associated with a different budget line. These budget *lines* are just like the budget *constraints* we have seen earlier—they are straight lines with the slope determined by the relative prices of the two goods. We call them budget *lines* not budget *constraints* because now it is the indifference curve U^* that is the constraint.

Figure 4.20 : **Utility Maximization Versus Expenditure Minimization**

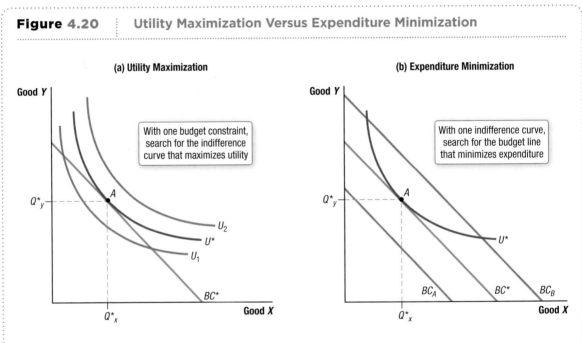

(a) Using the utility-maximization approach, the consumer chooses the bundle with the highest utility level that she can afford given her budget constraint. This occurs at the point of tangency (bundle A) between the indifference curve U^* and the budget constraint BC^*.

(b) Using the expenditure-maximization approach, the consumer begins with an indifference curve of a given utility level, U^*. She then chooses the budget line, BC^*, tangent to U^*. As in panel a, the consumer chooses bundle A, where she consumes quantities Q^*_x and Q^*_y.

In panel b, we've drawn in a few budget lines. We know from before that budget lines further from the origin reflect higher levels of income. Because the consumer wants to achieve his chosen level of utility with the least amount of income/expenditure, he must find the budget line *closest* to the origin that touches U^*. The answer, as in our original approach, boils down to finding the point of tangency between the indifference curve and the budget line. And, as shown in panel b, that point is bundle A, the same bundle from the utility-maximization problem in panel a.

It is no coincidence that the optimal solution in the two panels is the same. The utility-maximization and expenditure-minimization approaches are just two different ways of solving the same problem. Either we fix a budget constraint and try to find the highest indifference curve that is tangent to it (utility maximization), or we fix an indifference curve and try to find the lowest budget line that is tangent to it (expenditure minimization). The reason that the optimal solution in the two panels is the same consumption bundle is that when we set up the utility constraint in panel b's expenditure-minimization problem, we picked the same utility level reached in panel a's utility-maximization problem. If we had chosen any other utility level for our analysis, the minimum-expenditure budget line would be something other than BC^*, and the optimal consumption bundle would not be bundle A.

4.8 Conclusion

This chapter has looked at how consumers decide what to consume. This decision combines two characteristics of consumers, their preferences (embodied in their utility function) and their income, and one characteristic of the market, the goods' prices.

We saw that a consumer will maximize her utility from consumption when she chooses a bundle of goods such that the marginal rate of substitution between the goods equals their relative prices. That is, in this bundle the ratio of the goods' utilities equals their price ratio. Equivalently, the marginal utilities per dollar spent of all goods are equal. If this property didn't hold, a consumer could make herself better off by consuming more of the goods with high marginal utilities per dollar and less of the goods with low marginal utilities per dollar.

There is another way to think about the consumer's problem of what and how much to consume. Rather than thinking of consumers as trying to maximize utility subject to a budget constraint, we could think of them as trying to minimize the expenditure necessary for them to reach a given level of utility. This is called the expenditure-minimization problem. We saw how it turns out that this delivers the same rule for optimal consumption behavior: The *MRS* of the goods should equal their price ratio.

Summary

1. Utility is the economic concept of consumers' happiness or well-being, and the utility function is the construct that relates the amount of goods consumed (the inputs) to the consumer's utility level (the output). There are properties that we expect almost all utility functions to share: the completeness, rankability, and transitivity of utility bundles, that having more of a good is better than having less, and that the more a consumer has of a particular good, the less willing she is to give up something else to get more of that good.

2. Consumers' preferences are reflected in their indifference curves, which show all the combinations of goods over which a consumer receives equal utility. The set of properties imposed on utility functions imply some restrictions on the shapes of indifference curves. Namely, indifference curves slope downward, never cross for a given individual, and are convex to the origin.

3. The negative of the slope of the indifference curve is the marginal rate of substitution of good X for good Y (MRS_{XY}). The MRS is the ratio of the marginal utilities of the goods in the utility function.

4. Consumer preferences lead to differences in the steepness and curvature of indifference curves. If a consumer views two goods as perfect substitutes or perfect complements, their indifference curves will be shaped like straight lines and right angles, respectively.

5. The consumer's decision about how much of each good to consume depends not only on utility, but also on how much money that person has to spend (her income) and on the prices of the goods. In analyzing the role of income in consumption decisions, we assume the following: Each good has a fixed price, and any consumer can buy as much of a good as she wants at that price if the consumer has sufficient income to pay for it; the consumer has some fixed amount of income to spend; and the consumer cannot save or borrow.

The budget constraint captures both a consumer's income and the relative prices of goods. The constraint shows which consumption bundles are feasible (i.e., affordable given the consumer's income) and which are infeasible. The slope of the budget constraint is the negative of the ratio of the prices of the two goods ($-P_X/P_Y$).

6. The consumer's decision is a constrained-optimization problem: to maximize utility while staying within her budget constraint. The utility-maximizing solution is generally to consume the bundle of goods located where an indifference curve is tangent to the budget constraint. At this optimal point, the consumer's marginal rate of substitution—the ratio of the consumer's marginal utilities from the goods—equals the goods' relative price ratio.

A corner solution, where the optimal quantity consumed of one good is zero, can occur when a consumer's marginal utility of a good is so low compared to that good's relative price that she is better off not consuming any of that good at all. In such cases, the MRS does not equal the price ratio even though the consumer is at the utility-maximizing consumption bundle.

7. The consumer's problem of what and how much to consume can be recast as an expenditure-minimization problem. That is, rather than thinking of consumers as trying to maximize utility subject to a budget constraint, we could think of them as trying to minimize the expenditure necessary for them to reach a given level of utility. The optimal choices for both problems result in the same criterion: The MRS of the goods should equal their price ratio.

Review Questions

1. We make four assumptions about preferences: completeness and rankability, "more is better," transitivity, and consumers want variety. Briefly describe each assumption.

2. What does the term "utility" mean? How does utility relate to a utility function?

3. Define "indifference curve." What does an indifference curve tell us about the consumer?

4. We learned that the slope of the indifference curve is called the marginal rate of substitution of X for Y. What does the MRS_{XY} tell us about a consumer's preferences between two goods?

5. Why does the slope of the indifference curve vary along the curve? What does this variability tell us about consumers' preferences?

6. What does a steep indifference curve indicate about a consumer's preferences? What does a flat indifference curve say?

7. When are two goods perfect substitutes? What does the indifference curve look like, or what is its *curvature*?

8. When are two goods perfect complements? What does the indifference curve look like?

9. In addition to utility, what other factors determine how much of a good to buy?

10. Describe the three assumptions we make when incorporating income into our model of consumer behavior.

11. What is a budget constraint?

12. What determines the slope of a budget constraint? What situation would change the slope of a budget constraint?

13. What do we call the bundle represented by the point of tangency between the consumer's indifference curve and her budget constraint?

14. At the point of tangency, what is true about the ratio of the goods' marginal utilities and the ratio of their prices?

15. What is the difference between these approaches: utility maximization and expenditure minimization?

Problems

1. Which assumption about consumer preferences does each of the following individuals violate?
   a. Randy likes basketball more than football; football more than baseball; and baseball more than basketball.
   b. Paula prefers prune juice to orange juice but cannot decide how she feels about grapefruit juice.
   c. Simon likes superhero comic books but prefers 5 comic books to 10 comic books.

2. By assumption, individual preferences must be transitive so that if A is preferred to B, and B is preferred to C, then A is preferred to C. Suppose that Marsha, Jan, and Cindy individually have transitive preferences over three goods: oranges, apples, and pears. If Marsha, Jan, and Cindy were to vote on whether to name oranges, apples, or pears the "fruit of the month," show that it is possible the preferences for the *group* might *not* be transitive.

3. In Arbitrageville, 1 orange can be exchanged for 4 apples, and 4 apples for 1 orange. The mayor of Arbitrageville likes oranges a lot. He buys 100 oranges and 1 apple at the grocery store. As the mayor piles oranges onto the checkout counter, he tells the clerk, "I just love these oranges. In fact, I think you'd need to offer me three apples to pry one orange from my hands."
   a. Explain why the clerk, a sharp entrepreneur, immediately reaches under the counter and offers the mayor 3 apples.
   b. What should the mayor have said about how many apples the clerk would need to offer him for 1 orange, assuming that the mayor was maximizing his utility? What equation tells us how the mayor's preferences relate to prices?
   c. If the mayor maintained his preferences, how could the clerk wind up with all of the mayor's

oranges and the mayor (eventually) without a penny to his name?

4. Draw two indifference curves for each the following pairs of goods. Put the quantity of the first good on the horizontal axis and the quantity of the second good on the vertical axis.
   a. Paul likes pencils and pens.
   b. Rhonda likes carrots and dislikes broccoli.
   c. Emily likes hip-hop iTunes downloads and doesn't care about heavy metal downloads.
   d. Michael only likes dress shirts and cufflinks in 1 to 2 proportions.

5. Suppose that John is indifferent between consuming bundle A, which consists of 4 apples and 1 peach, and bundle B, which consists of 4 peaches and 1 apple. If John were given the choice between bundle A and bundle C, which contained 3 peaches and 2 apples, which should he pick? (*Hint:* Draw an indifference curve or two.)

6. The table below displays the total utility $U(X)$ that corresponds to the number of units of X consumed by three different consumers (Abe, Barbara, and Chuck), holding everything else constant:

Abe		Barbara		Chuck	
$U(X)$	X	$U(X)$	X	$U(X)$	X
10	2	10	2	10	2
14	3	10	3	12	3
16	4	10	4	15	4
17	5	9	5	19	5
17.5	6	8	6	24	6

a. Compute the marginal utility of X for each of the three consumers at each level of X.
b. Based on the data in the table, can you tell whether any of these consumers are violating any of the standard assumptions about preferences?
c. Is it possible that any of these three consumers have the exact same preferences, and that columns for the three consumers differ only because of the arbitrary units that are used to measure utility? Explain.

7. A consumer's utility function is given by $U = XY$, where $MU_X = Y$ and $MU_Y = X$.
a. What is the utility derived from 1 unit of X and 2 units of Y? What is the utility derived from 2 units of X and 1 unit of Y? What is the utility derived from 5 units of X and 2 units of Y?
b. How does the consumer rank the following bundles?

Bundle	Quantity of X	Quantity of Y
A	2	2
B	10	0
C	1	5
D	3	2
E	2	3

c. Graph an indifference curve that shows the bundles of X and Y for which $U = 6$ and $U = 8$. Is the "more is better" assumption satisfied for X and Y?

d. What are MU_X and MU_Y for the following bundles?

Bundle	Quantity of X	Quantity of Y
F	1	2
G	2	2
H	1	3

e. Does MU_X diminish, stay constant, or increase as X increases? (*Hint:* You must keep the values of all other variables fixed.)

8. Kelly's utility function is given by $U = 5X + 2Y$, where $MU_X = 5$ and $MU_Y = 2$.

a. What is MRS_{XY}?
b. What is MRS_{XY} when $X = 1$ and $Y = 5$? When $X = 2$ and $Y = 2.5$?
c. Draw a sample indifference curve.

9. Andrea loves to eat burritos with hot sauce. In fact, she cannot enjoy a burrito (B) unless it has three servings of hot sauce (H). She gets no additional enjoyment from more than three servings per burrito. Thus, her utility function is $U = \min\{B, \frac{1}{3}H\}$. Graph Andrea's indifference curves for $U = 1$ and $U = 2$.

10. If Harry considers Cubs tickets a "good" and White Sox tickets a "bad," draw a set of indifference curves for Harry.

11. Josie gets satisfaction from both music and fireworks. Josie's income is $240 per week. Music costs $12 per CD, and fireworks cost $8 per bag.
a. Graph the budget constraint Josie faces, with music on the vertical axis and fireworks on the horizontal axis.
b. If Josie spends all her income on music, how much music can she afford? Plot a point that illustrates this scenario.
c. If Josie spends all her income on fireworks, how many bags of fireworks can she afford? Plot a point that illustrates this scenario.
d. If Josie spends half her income on fireworks and half her income on music, how much of each can she afford? Plot a point that illustrates this scenario.
e. Connect the dots to create Josie's budget constraint. What is the slope of the budget constraint?
f. Divide the price of fireworks by the price of music. Have you seen this number before, and if so, where?
g. Suppose that a holiday bonus raises Josie's income temporarily to $360. Draw Josie's new budget constraint.
h. Indicate the new bundles of music and fireworks that are feasible, given Josie's new income.

12. Suppose that only one person in the world sells ice cream. He employs a strange pricing policy: You can buy 1 ice cream cone for $1, but if you buy 2 cones, you have to pay $2 each. If you buy 3, you have to pay $3 each, etc., so that if you buy 10, you have to pay $10 each. You have $100 dollars to spend on ice cream cones and chocolate milk, and chocolate milk costs $1 per unit. Draw your budget constraint. This strange ice cream pricing, where buying more costs you more, is called a quantity surcharge.

13. Matthew is redecorating his apartment. The amount of utility he gets from chairs and couch-

es is listed in the table below, where each number represents how much utility (in utils) he receives from the combination of chairs and couches:

	1 chair	2 chairs	3 chairs	4 chairs
1 couch	5	6	8	20
2 couches	6	7	10	21
3 couches	9	12	16	30

a. What is the marginal utility from buying an additional chair if Matthew has 2 chairs and 2 couches?

b. What is the marginal utility from buying an additional couch if Matthew has 2 chairs and 2 couches?

c. If couches are the same price as chairs, and Matthew wants one more piece of furniture but already has 2 couches and 2 chairs, will he buy a couch or a chair? Explain.

14. Good X sells for $4, and good Y sells for $2. At your current level of consumption, the marginal rate of substitution between X and Y is 4.

a. Are you maximizing your utility?

b. If not, are you buying too much X or too much Y? Explain.

15. For Mitzi, shampoo and conditioner are perfect complements. She likes to use 1 squirt of shampoo and 1 squirt of conditioner each time she washes her hair.

a. Draw a set of indifference curves for Mitzi that illustrate the utility she derives from using shampoo and conditioner.

b. Assume that shampoo costs $4 and conditioner costs $2. Construct a budget constraint for Mitzi and describe her purchasing habits. What is her optimal bundle likely to look like? (*Hint:* Assume some level of income for Mitzi.)

c. Suppose that prices change so that shampoo costs $2 and conditioner costs $4. What is likely to happen to Mitzi's optimal bundle as a result? Explain.

d. How would your answer to (c) change if Mitzi used 2 squirts of shampoo and 1 squirt of conditioner each time she washed her hair?

16. Suppose that there are only two goods, books and coffee. Wally gets utility from both books and coffee, but his indifference curves between them are concave rather than convex to the origin.

a. Draw a set of indifference curves for Wally.

b. What do these particular indifference curves

tell you about Wally's marginal rate of substitution between books and coffee?

c. What will Wally's utility-maximizing bundle look like? (*Hint:* Assume some level of income for Wally, and some prices for books and coffee; then draw a budget constraint.)

d. Compare your answer to (b) to real-world behaviors. Does the comparison shed any light on why economists generally assume convex preferences?

17. Anthony spends his income on fishing lures (L) and guitar picks (G). Lures are priced at $2, while a package of guitar picks cost $1. Assume that Anthony has $30 to spend and his utility function can be represented as $U(L,G) = L^{0.5}G^{0.5}$. For this utility function, $MU_L = 0.5L^{-0.5}G^{0.5}$ and $MU_G = 0.5L^{0.5}G^{-0.5}$.

a. What is the optimal number of lures and guitar picks for Anthony to purchase? How much utility does this combination bring him?

b. If the price of guitar picks doubles to $2, how much income must Anthony have to maintain the same level of utility?

18. A prominent online movie rental service mails rental DVDs to consumers. The service offers two pricing plans. Under the first plan, consumers face a flat $10 fee each month and can rent as many DVDs as they wish for free. Under the second plan, consumers can rent DVDs for an à la carte price of $2. Assume that a consumer has an income of $20 and uses it to purchase DVD rentals and a "composite good" that costs $1 per unit.

a. Draw a set of indifference curves for a representative consumer, putting DVD rentals on the horizontal axis.

b. Draw the budget constraint for the à la carte movie rental plan, making sure to indicate the horizontal and vertical intercepts. Find the consumer's optimum quantity of movie rentals. Label this point A.

c. Draw the budget constraint for the flat-fee plan, making sure to indicate the horizontal and vertical intercepts. Find the consumer's optimum quantity of movie rentals. Label this point B.

d. Under which plan does the consumer rent more movies?

e. Under which plan does the consumer end up with a lower marginal rate of substitution between movies and the composite good?

f. Under which plan is the consumer more likely to end up viewing *The Perils of Gwendoline in the Land of the Yik Yak*, widely acknowledged to be one of the worst movies of all time?

19. Suppose that doctors' visits cost $20, and the typical consumer has an income of $100. Consumers spend all of their incomes on doctors' visits and a "composite good" that costs $1 per unit.
    a. Draw a graph that illustrates the consumer's budget constraint, putting doctor's visits on the horizontal axis. Make sure you indicate the horizontal and vertical intercepts.

    Now, suppose the local government is considering two health plans. Under plan A, the government will give out vouchers worth 2 free visits to the doctor. Under plan B, the government will give out four 50% coupons to be used at the doctor's office.
    b. Draw the new budget constraint the consumer faces under plan A.
    c. Draw the new budget constraint the consumer faces under plan B.
    d. For whom is the choice of plan A or plan B not likely to matter—those who are quite well, or those who are quite sick? (*Hint:* Superimpose some indifference curves on your budget constraints.)
    e. Which plan would someone who is generally well be likely to choose, if offered a choice?

20. Elaine loves receiving flowers and has a particular fondness for daisies and daffodils. Her relative preferences for the two flowers are illustrated by the set of utility curves in the diagram. The number at the bottom of each indifference curve indicates the amount of happiness she receives from the various combinations of daisies and daffodils on the curve. Elaine's boyfriend Jerry would like to give her enough flowers to provide her with 200 units of happiness, but would like to do so as inexpensively as possible.
    a. If daisies sell for $3 and daffodils sell for $6, what is the minimum amount Jerry will have to spend?
    b. Suppose that Jerry fails to make it to the flower store on time, so he quickly tucks the money he was planning to spend on flowers [as you determined in part (a)] in a card and gives it to Elaine. If Elaine spends the money on flowers, how much happiness will she receive from her purchase?

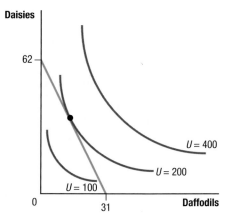

Individual and Market Demand

5

I
n Chapter 4, we learned the basics of how consumers make choices: Preferences (embodied in the consumer's utility function and its associated indifference curves) and income and market prices (both embodied in the consumer's budget constraint) combine to pin down the consumer's utility-maximizing bundle of goods. Variations in preferences are reflected in the shapes of indifference curves, and variations in income and prices are reflected in the location and slope of the budget constraint.

Now that we've built our consumer choice framework, we can show how it forms the basis of the demand curves in Chapters 2 and 3. We'll see exactly where demand curves come from, when they shift, and how to add up individual consumers' demands to get market demand curves.

The importance of a deeper understanding of the determinants of demand is clear: Demand is half the story in any market. Knowing what drives consumer demand is crucial to understanding a number of issues, including:

- why shifts in tastes affect prices,

- the benefits that products offer consumers,

■ what happens to purchase patterns as consumers (or even entire countries) become wealthier,

■ how changes in the price of one good affect the demand for other goods, and

■ what factors determine consumers' responses to price changes.

We start this chapter by looking at what happens to a consumer's choices when prices stay fixed and his income goes up or down. This analysis involves finding the consumer's optimal bundle not just once for a particular income level (as we did in Chapter 4), but over and over for every possible amount of income.

Next, we determine how the bundle a given consumer chooses changes as the price of one good in the bundle changes, holding constant income and the price of the other good. Once again, this analysis involves finding the utility-maximizing optimal consumption bundle not just once, but for every possible price of the good in the bundle. By analyzing how the quantity desired of a good changes as the price of that good changes (holding everything else constant), we can map out an individual consumer's demand curve for that good. We'll see that consumers' responses to price changes have two components: the change in relative prices caused by the price change and the change in the purchasing power of the consumer's income caused by the price change.

We then see how changes in the price of *other* goods affect the consumer's decision about how much of a particular good to consume. This effect can increase or decrease the quantity of a good demanded, depending on whether one good is a substitute for the other or if the two goods are consumed together.

After we explore all these features of an *individual's* choices, we show how total *market* demand responds to the same changes. Once this is done, we'll have a full understanding of what determines the same market demand that we took as given in Chapters 2 and 3.

5.1 How Income Changes Affect an Individual's Consumption Choices

In Section 4.5, we learned how changes in income affect the position of a consumer's budget constraint. Lower incomes shift the constraint toward the origin; higher incomes shift it out. In this section, we look at how a change in income affects a consumer's utility-maximizing consumption decisions. This is known as the **income effect.** To isolate this effect, we hold everything else constant during our analysis. Specifically, we assume that the consumer's preferences (reflected in the utility function and its associated indifference curves) and the prices of the goods stay the same.

Figure 5.1 shows the effect of an increase in income on consumption for Evan, a consumer who allocates his income between vacations and fancy gourmet restaurant meals. Initially, Evan's budget constraint is BC_1 and the utility-maximizing consumption bundle is at point *A,* where indifference curve U_1 is tangent to BC_1. If the prices of vacations and gourmet meals remain unchanged, an increase in Evan's income means that he can afford more of both goods. As a result, the increase in income induces a parallel, outward shift in the budget constraint from BC_1 to BC_2. Note that, because we hold prices fixed, the slope of the budget constraint (the ratio of the goods' prices) remains fixed. The new optimal consump-

income effect
The change in a consumer's consumption choices that results from a change in the purchasing power of the consumer's income.

Figure 5.1	A Consumer's Response to an Increase in Income When Both Goods Are Normal

Evan allocates his income between two normal goods, vacations and gourmet restaurant meals. His initial budget constraint BC_1 is tangent to the utility curve U_1 at the optimal consumption bundle A. An increase in Evan's income is represented by the outward parallel shift of BC_1 to BC_2. Since the prices of the goods are unchanged, Evan can now afford to buy more vacations and meals, and his new utility-maximizing bundle is B, where utility curve U_2 is tangent to BC_2. At bundle B, Evan's consumption of vacations and restaurant meals rises from Q_v to Q'_v and Q_m to Q'_m, respectively.

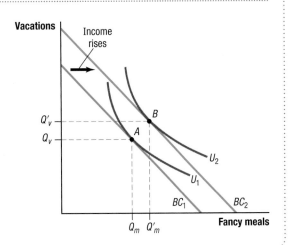

tion bundle at this higher income level is B, the point where indifference curve U_2 is tangent to BC_2.

Because U_2 shows bundles of goods that offer a higher utility level than those on U_1, the increase in income allows Evan to achieve a higher utility level. Note that when we analyze the effect of changes in income on consumer behavior, we hold preferences (as well as prices) constant. Thus, indifference curve U_2 does not appear because of some income-driven shift in preferences. U_2 was always there even when Evan's income was lower. At the lower income, however, point B and all other bundles on U_2 (and any other higher indifference curves) were infeasible because Evan could not afford them.

Normal and Inferior Goods

Notice how the new optimum in Figure 5.1 involves higher levels of consumption for both goods. The number of vacations Evan takes rises from Q_v to Q'_v, and the number of gourmet meals increases from Q_m to Q'_m. This result isn't that surprising; Evan was spending money on both vacations and gourmet meals before his income went up, so we might expect that he'd spend some of his extra income on both goods. Economists call a good whose consumption rises when income rises—that is, a good for which the income effect is positive—a **normal good.** Vacations and gourmet meals are normal goods for Evan. As "normal" suggests, most goods have positive income effects.

It is possible that an increase in income can lead to a consumer optimally consuming a smaller quantity of a good. As we indicated in Chapter 2, economists refer to such goods as **inferior goods.** Figure 5.2 presents an example in which one of the goods is inferior. An increase in the consumer's income from BC_1 to BC_2 leads to more steak being consumed, but less macaroni and cheese. Note that it isn't just that the quantity of mac and cheese *relative to* the quantity of steak falls. This

normal good
A good for which consumption rises when income rises.

inferior good
A good for which consumption decreases when income rises.

Figure 5.2 | A Consumer's Response to an Increase in Income When One Good Is Inferior

When a good is inferior, an increase in a consumer's income decreases the consumer's consumption of that good. Here, mac and cheese is an inferior good, while steak is a normal good. When the consumer's income increases, shifting the budget constraint outward from BC_1 to BC_2, she consumes less mac and cheese and more steak at the optimal consumption bundle. From initial optimal consumption bundle A to her new optimal consumption bundle B, the quantity of mac and cheese consumed decreases from Q_{mac} to Q'_{mac} while her consumption of the normal good steak increases from Q_s to Q'_s.

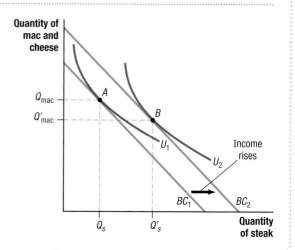

---

change can happen even when both goods are normal (i.e., they both rise, but steak rises more). Instead, it is the *absolute* quantity of macaroni and cheese consumed that drops in the move from A to B, because Q'_{mac} is less than Q_{mac}. Note also that this drop is optimal from the consumer's perspective—B is her utility-maximizing bundle given her budget constraint BC_2, and this bundle offers a higher utility level than A because indifference curve U_2 represents a higher utility level than U_1. The difference is the shape of the indifference curves for these goods (which comes from the utility function).

What kind of goods tend to be inferior? Usually, they are goods that are perceived to be low-quality or otherwise undesirable. Examples might include generic cereal brands, secondhand clothing, nights spent in youth hostels, and Spam. When we say Spam, we mean the kind you buy in the grocery store, not the kind you get via e-mail. Junk e-mail probably isn't a good at all, but rather a "bad."

We do know that *every* good can't be inferior, however. If a consumer were to consume a smaller quantity of everything when his income rises, he wouldn't be spending all his new, higher income. This outcome would be inconsistent with utility maximization, which states that a consumer always ends up buying a bundle on his budget constraint. (Remember there is no saving in this model.)

Whether the effect of an income change on a good's consumption is positive (consumption increases) or negative (consumption decreases) can often vary with the level of income. (We look at some of these special cases later in the chapter.) For instance, a good such as a used car is likely to be a normal good at low levels of income, and an inferior good at high levels of income. When someone's income is very low, owning a used car is prohibitively expensive and riding a bike or taking public transportation is necessary. As income increases from such low levels, a used car becomes increasingly likely to be purchased, making it a normal good. But once someone becomes rich enough, used cars are supplanted by new cars and his consumption of used cars falls. Over that higher income range, the used car is an inferior good.

Income Elasticities and Types of Goods

We've discussed how the income effect can be positive (as with normal goods) or negative (as with inferior goods). We can make further distinctions between types of goods by looking not just at the sign of the income effect, but at the **income elasticity** as well, which we discussed in Chapter 2. Remember that the income elasticity measures the *percentage* change in the quantity consumed of a good in response to a given *percentage* change in income. Formally, the income elasticity is

$$E_I^D = \frac{\%\Delta Q}{\%\Delta I} = \frac{\Delta Q/Q}{\Delta I/I} = \frac{\Delta Q}{\Delta I}\frac{I}{Q}$$

where Q is the quantity of the good consumed (ΔQ is the change in quantity), and I is income (ΔI is the change in income). As we noted in our earlier discussion, income elasticity is like the price elasticity of demand, except that we are now considering the responsiveness of consumption to income changes rather than to price changes.

The first ratio in the income elasticity definition is the income effect shown in the equations above: $\Delta Q/\Delta I$, the change in quantity consumed in response to a change in income. Therefore, the sign of the income elasticity is the same as the sign of the income effect. For normal goods, $\Delta Q/\Delta I > 0$, and the income elasticity is positive. For inferior goods, $\Delta Q/\Delta I < 0$, and the income elasticity is negative.

Within the class of normal goods, economists occasionally make a further distinction. The quantities of goods with an income elasticity between zero and 1 (sometimes called **necessity goods**) rise with income, but at a slower rate. Because prices are held constant when measuring income elasticities, the slower-than-income quantity growth implies the *share* of a consumer's budget devoted to the good *falls* as income grows. Many normal goods fit into this category, especially things that just about everyone uses or needs, like toothpaste, salt, socks, and electricity. Someone who earns $1 million a year may well consume more of these goods (or more expensive varieties) than an aspiring artist who earns $10,000 annually, but the millionaire, whose income is 100 times greater than the artist's, is unlikely to spend 100 times more on toothpaste (or salt, or socks. . .) than the artist spends.

Luxury goods have an income elasticity greater than 1. Because their quantities consumed grow faster than income does, these goods account for an increasing fraction of the consumer's expenditure as income rises. Luxury goods tend to be those that one does not need to live, but that improve the quality of life: first-class airline tickets, jewelry, fancy coffee drinks, beach homes, and so on.

The Income Expansion Path

Imagine repeating the analysis in the previous section for every possible income level. That is, for a given set of prices and a particular set of preferences, we can find the utility-maximizing bundle for every possible budget constraint, where each constraint corresponds to a different income level. Those optimal bundles will be located wherever an indifference curve is tangent to a budget line. In both of the examples above, they'll include bundles *A* and *B*.

income elasticity
The percentage change in the quantity consumed of a good in response to a 1% change in income.

necessity good
A normal good for which income elasticity is between zero and 1.

luxury good
A good with an income elasticity greater than 1.

Figure 5.3 demonstrates an example of such an exercise. In the figure, Meredith allocates her income between bus rides and bottled water. Points *A*, *B*, *C*, *D*, and *E* are the optimal consumption bundles at five different income levels that correspond to the budget constraints shown. Point *A* is Meredith's utility-maximizing bundle for the lowest of the five income levels, point *B* is the bundle for the second-lowest income, and so on. Note that the indifference curves themselves come from the individual's utility function. We have chosen various shapes here just to illustrate that these points can move around in different ways.

If we draw a line connecting all the optimal bundles (the five here plus all the others for budget constraints we don't show in the figure), it would trace out a curve known as the **income expansion path**. This curve always starts at the origin because when income is zero, the consumption of both goods must also be zero. We've drawn in Meredith's income expansion path for bus rides and bottled water in Figure 5.3.

When both goods are normal goods, the income expansion path will be positively sloped because consumption of both goods rises when income does. If the slope of the income expansion path is negative, then the quantity consumed of one of the goods falls with income while the other rises. The good whose quantity falls is therefore inferior. Remember that whether a given good is normal or inferior can depend on the consumer's income level. In the example in Figure 5.3, for example, both bus rides and bottled water are normal goods at incomes up to the level corresponding to the budget constraint containing bundle *D*. As income rises above that and the budget constraint continues to shift out, the income expansion path begins to curve downward. This outcome means that bus rides become an inferior good as Meredith's income rises beyond that level. We can also see from the income expansion path that bottled water is never inferior, because the path never curves back to the left. When there are only two goods, it's impossible for both goods to be inferior at a given income level. If they were both inferior, an increase in income would actually lead to lower expenditure on both goods, meaning that the consumer wouldn't be spending all of her income.

income expansion path
A curve that connects a consumer's optimal bundles at each income level.

Figure 5.3   ⋮   **The Income Expansion Path**

Meredith's income expansion path connects all of the optimal bundles of bottled water and bus rides for each income level. Points *A*, *B*, *C*, *D*, and *E* are optimal consumption bundles associated with budget constraints BC_1 through BC_5. Where both bottled water and bus rides are normal goods, the income expansion path is upward-sloping. At incomes higher than that shown at the budget constraint BC_4 and to the right of bundle *D*, bus rides become inferior goods, and the income expansion path slopes downward.

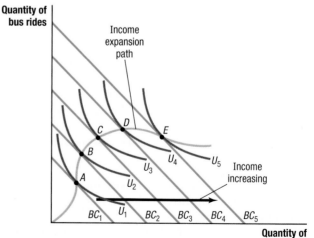

The Engel Curve

The income expansion path is a useful tool for examining how consumer behavior changes in response to changes in income, but it has two important weaknesses. First, because we have only two axes, we can only look at two goods at a time. Second, although we can easily see the consumption quantities of each good, we can't see directly the income level that a particular point on the curve corresponds to. The income level equals the sum of the quantities consumed of each good (which are easily seen in the figure) multiplied by their respective prices (which aren't easily seen). The basic problem is that when we talk about consumption and income, we care about three numbers—the quantities of each of the two goods and income—but we have only two dimensions on the graph in which to see them.

A better way to see how the quantity consumed of one good varies with income (as opposed to how the relative quantities of the two goods vary) is to take the information conveyed by the income expansion path and plot it on a graph with income on the vertical axis and the quantity of the good in question on the horizontal axis. Panel a of Figure 5.4 illustrates this for the relationship between income and the quantity of bus rides from our example in Figure 5.3. The five points mapped in panel a of Figure 5.4 are the same five consumption bundles represented by points *A*, *B*, *C*, *D*, and *E* in Figure 5.3; the only difference between the figures is in the variables measured by the axes.

The lines traced out in Figure 5.4 are known as **Engel curves,** named for the nineteenth-century German economist Ernst Engel who first presented the data

Engel curve
A curve that shows the relationship between the quantity of a good consumed and a consumer's income.

Figure 5.4   **An Engel Curve Shows How Consumption Varies with Income**

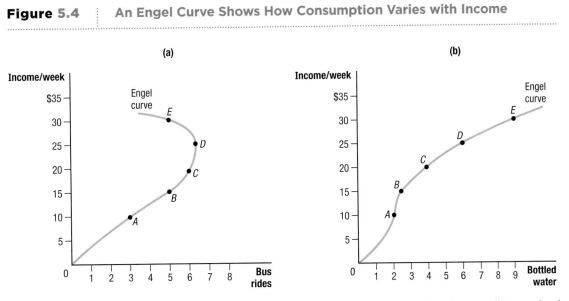

(a) In contrast to an income expansion path, an Engel curve compares the consumption of a single good to the consumer's income. As Meredith's income increases from $10/week to $25/week, her consumption of bus rides increases from 3 to a little over 6 bus rides. At income levels above $25/week, bus rides are inferior goods, and the number of bus rides she takes decreases.

(b) Bottled water is a normal good across all income levels shown here. At an income of $10/week at point *A*, Meredith consumes 2 bottles of water. At point *E*, Meredith's income is $30/week, and the number of bottles of water she buys increases to 9 per week.

in this manner. Engel curves tell you the quantities of goods—bus rides and bottled water, in this case—that are consumed at each income level. If the Engel curve has a positive slope, the good is a normal good at that income level. If the Engel curve has a negative slope, the good is an inferior good at that income. In Figure 5.4a, bus rides are initially a normal good, but become inferior after bundle *D*, just as we saw in Figure 5.3. In panel b, bottled water is a normal good at all income levels and the Engel curve is always positively sloped.

Whether the income expansion path or Engel curves are more useful for understanding the effect of income on consumption choices depends on the particular question we are trying to answer. If we care about how the relative quantities of the two goods change with income, the income expansion path is more useful because it shows both quantities at the same time. On the other hand, if we want to investigate the impact of income changes on the consumption of one particular good, the Engel curve isolates this relationship more clearly. The most important thing to remember is that the two curves contain the same information displayed in different ways due to the limitations imposed by having only two axes.

 ## application

Engel curves and house sizes

Houses in the United States have been getting larger for several decades. In 1950 newly built houses had an average of about 1,000 square feet (93 square meters) of floor area, a little less than one-fourth the size of a basketball court. By 2008 the average new house was well over twice as large, at 2,519 square feet. Recent debates about "McMansions" and tear-downs, still present even after the housing crash, have highlighted this trend and how it has affected discussions of public policies like zoning laws.

Explanations for this trend vary. Some have suggested homeowners' utility functions have changed in a way that favors more space. But another (not mutually exclusive) possibility is that space is a normal good, so homeowners demand more space as they become wealthier. It isn't necessary for homeowners' utility functions to have changed to see such effects. It could just be that an increase in income has moved them to a different part of their utility function where they demand more space.

The historical patterns are consistent with those that would arise from an income effect at work. Figure 5.5 plots the average size of newly built homes (in square feet) and average inflation-adjusted household income (in thousands of dollars) from 1975 to 2009. Both house sizes and income trended upward through this period. The sizes of the changes in these variables were similar too; for every 10% increase in average income, average house size rose by about 11%.[1]

These trends are consistent with income growth driving homeowners to buy larger homes. We should be careful in leaping to this interpretation, though. Many things can trend over time even though they aren't closely related. (For example, population also increased over the period, but it's hard to argue that simply having more people around makes everyone want larger homes.) And even if income ef-

---

[1] These data are collected from various U.S. Census Bureau publications.

Figure 5.5 Average New House Size and Household Income in the United States, 1975–2009

House sizes and income trended upward between 1975 and 2009, increasing at almost the same rate.

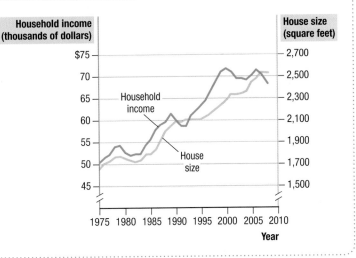

fects matter here, other factors that make larger homes more common, such as falling construction costs, could also be changing over time. It would therefore be nice to have additional evidence about the income–house size relationship that doesn't involve simple trends over time.

Such additional evidence does exist. The American Housing Survey (AHS) is conducted every two years and contains information on housing and demographics for thousands of households. Comparing home sizes to income levels across individual households at a given moment in time should complement our analysis of the average trends above.

Figure 5.6 An Engel Curve for House Size in the United States

The Engel curve for housing slopes upward, indicating that housing is a normal good. However, for incomes between approximately $175,000 and $250,000 per year, house size does not change much as income grows.

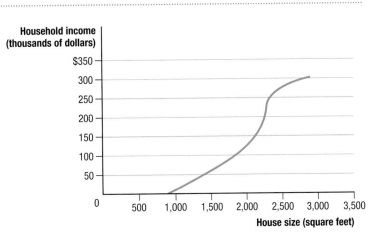

Time & Life Pictures/Getty Images

Then

Brendel/Wikimedia Commons

Now

We fit a curve relating home size and annual household income in the 2007 survey data (a survey containing about 35,000 households) in Figure 5.6. This is very similar to an Engel curve for home size: It shows how much a household's purchases of a good (square feet) varies with its income.[2]

We can see that this Engel curve always slopes up. That is, based on these data, house size is always a normal good. However, there is a considerable income range—from about $175,000 to $250,000 a year—where the size of the income effect is fairly small and home size does not change much as income grows. It's also interesting to compare the average slope of this Engel curve to the size-income correlation we saw in the time trend data. In the time trends in Figure 5.5, 10% income growth was tied to an 11% increase in house size. This relationship is smaller when we look across households in Figure 5.6: People with 10% more income have houses that are around 2% larger. One reason why the relationship across people might be smaller than across time is that the cross section of people includes all houses, not just newly built ones. If home sizes are trending upward over time (which they did from 1950 to 2005), and not just the highest income households are buying new houses, this will reduce the correlation between size and income in the cross section because some higher-income households will be in older, smaller houses. It could also be that factors in addition to income growth (such as preferences) are driving the trends of the past several decades. Nevertheless, it's clear from both sets of data that income changes are strongly related to the demand for house size. ■

5.1 figure it out

Annika spends all of her income on golf and pancakes. Greens fees at a local golf course are $10 per round. Pancake mix is $2 per box. When Annika's income is $100 per week, she buys 5 boxes of pancake mix and 9 rounds of golf. When Annika's income rises to $120 per week, she buys 10 boxes of pancake mix and 10 rounds of golf. Based on these figures, determine whether each of the following statements is true or false, and briefly explain your reasoning.

a. Golf is a normal good, and pancake mix is an inferior good.

b. Golf is a luxury good.

c. Pancakes are a luxury good.

[2] It's not exactly an Engel curve for a few reasons. For one, we aren't able to hold constant everything else about households' choices. To read Figure 5.6 as an Engel curve, we're assuming that every household is the same except for its income level. In reality, households might differ in their preferences and size as well as incomes. Furthermore, different households might face various prices for square footage depending on where they live. If these prices are related to income levels (say, because people who live in urban areas both have higher average incomes and face higher house prices per square foot), this could mix up price and income effects. Nevertheless, the relationship in Figure 5.6 is probably close to the true Engel curve for square footage.

Solution:

a. A normal good is one of which a consumer buys more when income rises. An inferior good is a good for which consumption falls when income rises. When Annika's income rises, she purchases more pancake mix and more rounds of golf. This means that both goods are normal goods for Annika. Therefore, the statement is *false*.

b. A luxury good has an income elasticity greater than 1. The income elasticity for a good is calculated by dividing the percentage change in quantity demanded by the percentage change in income. Annika's income rises from \$100 to \$120. Therefore, the percentage change in income is $\frac{\Delta I}{I} \times 100 = \frac{20}{100} \times 100 = 20$. When Annika's income rises, her consumption of golf changes from 9 rounds to 10. Thus, the percentage change in the quantity of rounds demanded is $\frac{\Delta Q}{Q} \times 100 = \frac{1}{9} \times 100 = 11.1$. To calculate the income elasticity, we divide the percentage change in quantity by the percentage change in price, $\frac{11.1}{20} = 0.555$. Golf cannot be a luxury good for Annika because the elasticity is not greater than 1. Therefore, the statement is *false*.

c. Again, we must calculate the income elasticity, this time for pancake mix. When Annika's income rises from \$100 to \$120 [a 20% rise as calculated in part (b)], Annika increases her purchases of pancake mix from 5 boxes to 10 boxes. Thus, the percentage change in the quantity of pancake mix demanded is $\frac{\Delta Q}{Q} \times 100 = \frac{5}{5} \times 100 = 100$.

This means that the income elasticity of demand is $\frac{\%\Delta Q}{\%\Delta I} = \frac{100}{20} = 5$. Because the income elasticity is greater than 1, pancake mix is a luxury good for Annika. Therefore, the statement is *true*.

5.2 How Price Changes Affect Consumption Choices

In the previous section, we looked at how a consumer's choices change when we vary income, holding prices and preferences constant. In this section, we see what happens when the price of a good changes, holding income, preferences, and the prices of all other goods constant. *This analysis tells us exactly where a demand curve comes from.*

At this point, it is useful to recall exactly what a demand curve is because it has been a few chapters since we discussed the concept. We learned in Chapter 2 that many factors influence the quantity that a consumer demands of a good. The demand curve isolates how one particular factor, a good's own price, affects the quantity demanded while holding everything else constant. Changes in any other factor that influences the quantity demanded (such as income, preferences, or the prices of other goods) shift the location of the demand curve.

Up to this point, we know that demand curves slope downward because diminishing marginal utility implies that consumers' willingness to pay falls as quantities rise. That explanation is correct, but it skips a step. A consumer's demand curve actually comes straight from the consumer's utility maximization. A demand curve answers the following question: As the price of a good changes while holding all else constant, how does the quantity of that good in the utility-maximizing bundle change? This is exactly the question we're going to answer here.

Deriving a Demand Curve

To see how a consumer's utility-maximizing behavior leads to a demand curve, let's look at a specific example. Suppose Caroline is deciding how to spend her income on two goods, 2-liter bottles of Mountain Dew and 1-liter bottles of grape juice, and we want to know her demand curve for grape juice. Caroline's income is $20, and the price of Mountain Dew is $2 per 2-liter bottle. We'll hold these factors (income and price of Mountain Dew) and Caroline's preferences constant throughout our analysis. If we didn't, we would not be mapping out a single demand curve (which, remember, shows the relationship between price of a good and the quantity demanded of that good), but would instead be shifting the demand curve around.

To build the demand curve, we start by figuring out the consumer's utility-maximizing consumption bundle at some price for grape juice. It doesn't actually matter what price we use to start because we will eventually compute the quantity demanded at all prices. Let's start with a price of $1 per liter bottle of grape juice. (It makes the math easy.)

The top half of Figure 5.7a shows Caroline's utility-maximization problem. Her budget constraint reflects the combinations of bottles of Mountain Dew and bottles of grape juice that she can afford at the current prices. With an income of $20, she can buy up to 10 bottles of Mountain Dew at $2 per bottle if that's all she spends

Figure 5.7   Building an Individual's Demand Curve

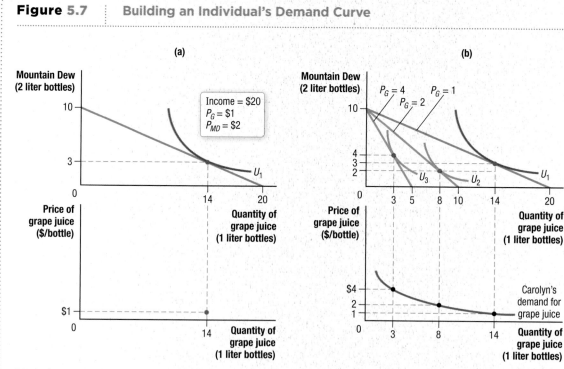

(a) At her optimal consumption bundle, Caroline purchases 14 bottles of grape juice when the price per bottle is $1 and her income is $20. The bottom panel plots this point on her demand curve, with the price of grape juice on the y-axis and the quantity of grape juice on the x-axis.

(b) A completed demand curve consists of many of these quantity-price points. Here, the optimal quantity of grape juice consumed is plotted for the prices $1, $2, and $4 per bottle. This creates Caroline's demand curve, as shown in the bottom panel.

her money on, or up to 20 bottles of grape juice at $1 per bottle if she restricts her purchases to grape juice. The slope of the budget constraint equals the negative of the price ratio P_{MD}/P_G, which is –0.5 in this case. Caroline's indifference curve that is tangent to this budget constraint is also shown in the figure. We know that the point of tangency shown is the utility-maximizing bundle. Given her income, her preferences, and the prices of the two juices, Caroline's optimal quantities to consume are 3 bottles of Mountain Dew and 14 bottles of grape juice.

We now have one point on Caroline's demand curve for grape juice: At a price of $1 per liter, her quantity demanded is 14 bottles. The only problem is that the top panel of Figure 5.7a does not have the correct axes for a demand curve. Remember that a demand curve for a good is drawn with the good's price on the vertical axis and its quantity demanded on the horizontal axis. When we graphically search for the tangency of indifference curves and budget constraints, however, we put the quantities of the two goods on the axes. So we'll make a new figure, shown in the bottom panel of Figure 5.7a, that plots the same quantity of grape juice as the figure's top panel, but with the price of grape juice on the vertical axis. Because the horizontal axis in the bottom panel is the same as that in the top—the quantity of grape juice—we can vertically transfer that dimension of the figure directly from the top to the bottom panel.

To finish building the demand curve, we need to repeat the process described above again and again for many different grape juice prices. When the price changes, the budget constraint's slope changes, which reflects the relative prices of the two goods. For each new budget constraint, we find the optimal consumption bundle by finding the indifference curve that is tangent to it. Because preferences are constant, the set of indifference curves corresponding to Caroline's utility function remains the same. It's just that the particular indifference curve that is tangent to the budget constraint will depend on where the constraint is. Each time we determine the optimal quantity consumed at a given price of grape juice, we have found another point on the demand curve.

Figure 5.7b shows this exercise for grape juice prices of $1, $2, and $4 per bottle. As the price of grape juice rises (holding fixed the price of Mountain Dew and Caroline's income), the budget constraint gets steeper, and the utility-maximizing quantity of grape juice falls. In our example, Caroline's optimal quantity of grape juice when it costs $2 per bottle is 8 bottles. When the price is $4, she consumes 3 bottles. These combinations of prices and quantities are plotted in the lower panel. These points are all on Caroline's demand curve for grape juice. Repeating this exercise for every possible grape juice price will trace out her whole demand curve, which we've drawn in the figure. Note that Caroline's quantity demanded falls as price rises.

Shifts in the Demand Curve

If a consumer's preferences or income change, or the prices of other goods change, then the demand curve shifts. But the process for tracing out the demand curve under these new conditions is exactly the same: We trace out the utility-maximizing quantity of the good under every possible price. It's just that we do so under the updated circumstances.

Let's look at an example where preferences change. Suppose that Caroline meets a scientist at a party who argues that the purported health benefits of grape juice are overstated and that it stains your teeth red. What happens to Caroline's demand

freakonomics

Even Animals Like Sales

If you think the laws of economics only apply to humans, think again. Monkeys, and even rats, behave in ways that would make you think they've taken intermediate micro.

Some of the most intensive testing of the economic behavior of animals was carried out by Yale economist Keith Chen and his co-authors on a group of Capuchin monkeys. As a first step, Chen introduced the monkeys to the concept of money. He gave them "money" in the form of metal washers that they could exchange for various types of foods including Jell-O, grapes, and Marshmallow Fluff (Capuchin monkeys *love* sweet foods).

Just Like Us?

After about six exasperating months, these monkeys finally figured out that the washers had value. Chen observed that individual monkeys tended to have stable preferences: Some liked grapes the best, others were fans of Jell-O. How did he learn this? He would give a particular monkey a coin and then offer that monkey a choice between a bowl of three Jell-O cubes and a bowl of six grapes and see which one the monkey chose.

Next, Chen did what any good economist would do: He subjected the monkeys to price changes! Instead of getting three Jell-O cubes for one washer, he would offer the monkey, say, the choice between a single Jell-O cube per washer and a bowl of six grapes per washer. Thus, the relative price of Jell-O became three times as high. The monkeys responded exactly the way economic theory would predict, shifting their consumption away from the goods whose prices had risen.[*]

Perhaps it is not that surprising that monkeys, one of our closest relatives in the animal kingdom, would be sophisticated consumers. But there is no way rats understand supply and demand, is there? It seems they do. Economists Raymond Battalio and John Kagel equipped rats' cages with two levers, each of which dispensed a different beverage.[†] One of these levers gave the rat a refreshing burst of root beer. Rats, it turns out, love root beer. The other lever released quinine water. Quinine is a bitter-tasting substance initially used to treat malaria, and now used primarily to give vodka tonics their distinctive flavor. Rats are far less fond of quinine than they are of root beer, and they made that quite clear to the researchers by pressing the root beer lever far more often. Battalio and Kagel, like Chen, then explored changes in "prices" (how much liquid came out per press of the lever) and in the rats' budget constraint (how many times they could press the levers each day). Like monkeys (and humans), the rats consumed less of a drink when its relative price increased. Even more interesting is that when the rats were made very poor (i.e., they got very few lever presses each day), they shifted their consumption away from root beer toward quinine water. The researchers found that root beer is a luxury good for rats, and quinine water is an inferior good! Wonder what rats would make of a vodka tonic. . . .

---

[*] That wasn't the only human-like behavior these monkeys exhibited when exposed to money—for the whole amusingly sordid story, see the epilogue to *SuperFreakonomics*.

[†] A description of the work by Battalio and Kagel may be found in: Tim Harford, *The Logic of Life: The Rational Economics of an Irrational World* (New York: Random House, 2008), pp. 18–21.

Courtesy M. Keith Chen

for grape juice? We wouldn't expect the market prices of Mountain Dew or grape juice to change based on this private conversation, nor will Caroline's income be affected by this information. Her preferences toward grape juice will change, however. She'll find it less desirable than before. This will show up as a flattening of Caroline's indifference curves, because now she'll have to be given more grape juice to be indifferent to a loss of Mountain Dew. Another way to think about it is that, because the marginal rate of substitution (*MRS*) equals $-MU_G/MU_{MD}$, this preference shift shrinks Caroline's marginal utility of grape juice at any quantity, reducing her *MRS*—that is, flattening her indifference curves.

Figure 5.8 repeats the demand-curve building exercise after the preference change. With the flatter indifference curves(labeled U'_1, U'_2, and U'_3), Caroline's utility-maximizing consumption bundles have changed. Now her optimal consumption levels of grape juice at prices of $1, $2, and $4 per bottle are 9, 6, and 2 bottles, respectively. The bottom half of Figure 5.8 plots these points on Caroline's new demand curve D_2.

We can see that because Caroline's preferences have changed, she now demands a smaller quantity of grape juice than before at every price. As a result, her demand curve for grape juice has shifted in from D_1 to D_2. This result demonstrates why and how preference changes shift the demand curve. Changes in Caroline's income or in the price of Mountain Dew also shift her demand curve. (We saw earlier how income shifts affect quantity demanded, and we investigate the effects of price changes in other goods in Section 5.4.) Remember, however, that for any given value of these nonprice influences on demand, the change in the quantity demanded of a good in response to changes in its own price results in a movement along a demand curve, not a shift in the curve.

Figure 5.8   Preference Changes and Shifts in the Demand Curve

(a) Caroline's indifference curves for grape juice flatten when her preference for grape juice decreases relative to her preference for Mountain Dew. At each price level, she now consumes fewer bottles of grape juice.

(b) Because she purchases fewer bottles of grape juice at each price point, Caroline's demand curve for grape juice shifts inward from D_1 to D_2.

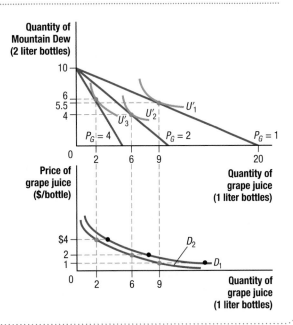

5.2 figure it out

Cooper allocates $200 of his weekly budget to entertainment. He spends all of this $200 on two goods: theater tickets (which cost $50 each) and movie tickets (which cost $10 each).

a. With theater tickets on the horizontal axis, draw Cooper's budget constraint, making sure to indicate the horizontal and vertical intercepts. What is the slope of the budget constraint?

b. Suppose that Cooper currently purchases 3 theater tickets per week. Indicate this choice on the budget constraint and mark it as point A. Draw an indifference curve tangent to the budget constraint at point A. How many movie tickets does Cooper buy?

c. Suppose that the price of a theater ticket rises to $80, and Cooper lowers his purchases of theater tickets to 2. Draw Cooper's new budget constraint, indicate his choice with a point B, and draw an indifference curve tangent to the new budget constraint at point B.

d. Once again, the price of a theater ticket rises to $100, and Cooper lowers his purchases of theater tickets to 1 per week. Draw his new budget constraint, show his choice on the budget constraint with a point C, and draw an indifference curve tangent to this new budget constraint at C.

e. Draw a new diagram below your indifference curve diagram. Use your answers to parts (b)–(d) to draw Cooper's demand for theater tickets. Indicate his quantities demanded at $50, $80, and $100. Is there an inverse relationship between price and quantity demanded?

Solution:

a. To start, we need to calculate the horizontal and vertical intercepts for Cooper's budget constraint. The horizontal intercept is the point at which Cooper spends all of his income on theater tickets and purchases no movie tickets. This occurs when he buys $200/$50 = 4 theater tickets (Figure A). The vertical intercept is the point at which Cooper spends his entire income on movie tickets and buys no theater tickets. This means that he is buying

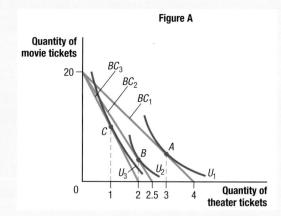

Figure A

$200/$10 = 20 movie tickets. The budget constraint connects these two intercepts. The slope of the budget constraint equals rise/run = −20/4 = −5.

Note that this slope is the negative of the ratio of the two prices $= -\dfrac{P_{\text{theater tickets}}}{P_{\text{movie tickets}}} = -\$50/\$10 = -5$.

b. Maximum utility occurs where the indifference curve is tangent to the budget constraint. Therefore, point A should be the point where this tangency takes place. If Cooper purchases 3 theater tickets a week, he will spend $50 × 3 = $150, leaving him $200 − $150 = $50 to spend on movie tickets. Since movie tickets cost $10 each, he purchases $50/$10 = 5 movie tickets.

c. Cooper's budget constraint will rotate in a clockwise direction. The vertical intercept is not affected because neither Cooper's income nor the price of movie tickets changes. However, the price of theater tickets has risen to $80, and now if Cooper were to allocate his entire budget to theater tickets, he could only afford $200/$80 = 2.5 of them. This is the new horizontal intercept. If Cooper chooses to buy 2 theater tickets, he will have an indifference curve tangent to this budget constraint at that point (B).

d. The budget constraint will again rotate clockwise and the vertical intercept will remain unchanged. The new horizontal intercept will be $200/$100 = 2. Point C will occur where Cooper's indifference curve is tangent to his new budget constraint at a quantity of 1 theater ticket.

e. The demand curve shows the relationship between the price of theater tickets and Cooper's quantity demanded. We can take the information from our indifference curve diagram to develop three points on Cooper's demand curve:

POINT	PRICE	QUANTITY OF THEATER TICKETS DEMANDED
A	$50	3
B	$80	2
C	$100	1

We can then plot points A, B, and C on a diagram with the quantity of theater tickets on the horizontal axis and the price of theater tickets on the vertical axis (Figure B). Connecting these points gives us Cooper's demand curve for theater tickets.

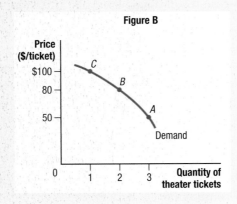

Figure B

5.3 Decomposing Consumer Responses to Price Changes into Income and Substitution Effects

When the price of a good changes, the demand curve for that good tells us how much consumption will change. This total change in quantity demanded, however, is a result of two distinct forces that affect consumers' decisions: the substitution effect and the income effect. Any change in quantity demanded can be decomposed into these two effects.

substitution effect
The change in a consumer's consumption choices that results from a change in the relative prices of two goods.

income effect
The change in a consumer's consumption choices that results from a change in the purchasing power of the consumer's income.

total effect
The total change (substitution effect + income effect) in a consumer's optimal consumption bundle as a result of a price change.

1. When the price of one good changes relative to the price of another good, consumers will want to buy more of the good that has become relatively cheaper and less of the good that is now relatively more expensive. Economists call this the **substitution effect.**

2. A price shift changes the purchasing power of consumers' incomes—the amount of goods they can buy with a given dollar-level expenditure. If a good gets cheaper, for example, consumers are effectively richer and can buy more of the cheaper good and other goods. If a good's price increases, the purchasing power of consumers' incomes is reduced, and they can buy fewer goods. Economists refer to consumption changes resulting from this shift in spending power as the **income effect.**

Any change in quantity demanded can be decomposed into these two effects. We introduce them in this book, but we are just scratching the surface. We're going to be upfront with you: The distinction between income and substitution effects is one of the most subtle concepts that you will come across in this entire book. If you go on to take more advanced economics courses, income and substitution effects will come up again and again.[3] There are two reasons why this topic is so difficult. First, we don't separately observe these two effects in the real world, only their combined effects. Their separation is an artificial analytical tool. Put another way, as a consumer you can (and do) figure out how much to consume without knowing or figuring out how much of the change is due to income effects and how much is due to substitution effects. Second, the income effect occurs even when the consumer's income as measured in dollars remains constant. How rich we feel is determined both by how much income we have and how much things cost. If your income stays at $1,000 but the prices of all goods fall by half, you are effectively a lot wealthier. The income effect refers to how rich you feel, not the number of dollar bills in your pocket.

In our overview, we demonstrate income and substitution effects using graphs. The appendix to this chapter describes these effects mathematically.

Figure 5.9 shows how a consumer, Carlos, who spends his income on rounds of golf and restaurant meals, reacts to a fall in the price of restaurant meals. This is just like the analysis we did in Section 5.2. Lower restaurant meal prices lead the budget constraint to rotate outward from BC_1 to BC_2 because Carlos can now purchase more restaurant meals with his income. As a result, the optimal consumption bundle shifts from A (the point of tangency between indifference curve U_1 and budget constraint BC_1) to B (the point of tangency between indifference curve U_2 and budget constraint BC_2). Because of the fall in the price of restaurant meals, the quantity of rounds of golf consumed increases from 5 to 6, and the number of restaurant meals Carlos purchases rises from 3 to 5. These overall changes in quantities consumed between bundles A and B are the **total effect** of the price change.

---

[3] For instance, it is much easier to describe the properties of a demand curve when there is no income effect, only a substitution effect. Demand curves that reflect only substitution effects are known as "Hicksian demand curves" in honor of the economist Sir John Hicks. The demand curves that combine both effects—the kind you're accustomed to working with, and the kind we'll continue to use throughout the text—are called "Marshallian demand curves" after economist Alfred Marshall. Because we stick with this standard demand curve throughout the book, we'll skip the modifier and just keep calling them demand curves.

Figure 5.9 | The Effects of a Fall in the Price of Restaurant Meals

When the price of restaurant meals decreases, Carlos's budget constraint rotates outward from BC_1 to BC_2. The total effect of the price change is shown by the increase in his optimal consumption bundle from point A to point B. In particular, the number of restaurant meals Carlos consumes increases from 3 to 5, and the number of rounds of golf he consumes increases from 5 to 6.

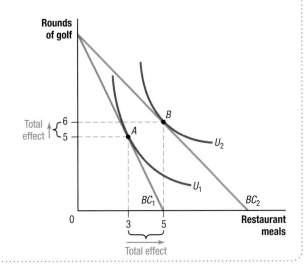

Note that just as in Section 5.2, we figured out the optimal bundle without any reference to income or substitution effects. In the next sections, we decompose the total effect into separate substitution and income effects. That is,

$$\text{Total Effect} = \text{Substitution Effect} + \text{Income Effect}$$

Breaking down the movement from A to B into income and substitution effects helps us understand how much of the total change in Carlos's quantity demanded occurs because Carlos switches what he purchases as a result of the reduction in the relative prices of the two goods (the substitution effect), and how much of the change is driven by the fact that the decrease in the price of restaurant meals gives Carlos more purchasing power (the income effect).

Note that all the examples we work through involve a drop in the price of a good. When the price of a good increases, the effects work in the opposite direction.

Isolating the Substitution Effect

Let's begin by isolating the substitution effect. This part of the change in quantities demanded is due to the change in relative prices, not to the change in Carlos's buying power. To isolate the substitution effect, we need to figure out how many rounds of golf and restaurant meals Carlos would want to consume if, after the price change, there was no income effect, that is, if he had the same purchasing power as before the price change and felt neither richer nor poorer.

For Carlos to feel neither richer nor poorer, *the bundle he consumes after the price change must provide him with the same utility he was receiving before the price change; that is, the new bundle must be on the initial indifference curve U_1.*

So where is this substitution-effect-only bundle on U_1? We know this bundle has to reflect the fact that the goods' relative prices have changed. Those new relative prices are embodied in the slope of the new budget line BC_2. The problem is that there isn't a point of tangency between U_1 and BC_2—as we can see in Figure 5.10. However, there *is* a point of tangency between U_1 and a budget line with the same slope (i.e., the same relative prices) as BC_2. The budget line we're talking about is BC', the dashed line in panel a of Figure 5.10, and the point of tangency is point A'.

Bundle A' is what Carlos would buy if the relative prices of rounds of golf and restaurant meals changed the way they did, but Carlos experienced no change in purchasing power. This is the definition of the substitution effect. Thus, the substitution effect in isolation moves Carlos's demanded bundle from A to A'. To find this effect, we have to shift the post-price-change budget line BC_2 back in parallel (to preserve the new relative prices) until it is tangent to the pre-price-change indifference curve U_1 (to keep the original utility level the same). *It's important to recognize that the budget line BC' is hypothetical—Carlos never actually faces it.* Instead, it is a conceptual device that lets us figure out what Carlos would do if he did face it; that is, if relative prices changed in the way they actually did while at the same time any income gains he enjoyed as a result were taken away from him.

There are a few things to notice about the change in quantities due to the substitution effect. First, the quantity of rounds of golf decreases (from 5 to 3), and the quantity of restaurant meals increases (from 3 to 4). The decrease in the quantity of rounds of golf demanded occurs because the price change has caused restaurant meals to become cheaper relative to rounds of golf, so Carlos wants to buy relatively more restaurant meals. Second, while points A and A' are on the same indifference

Figure 5.10   Substitution and Income Effects for Two Normal Goods

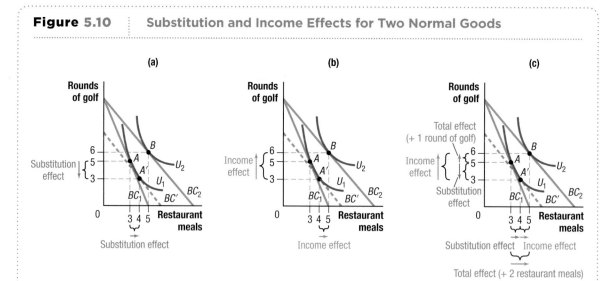

(a) The substitution effect is the change in quantities demanded due to the change in relative prices of restaurant meals and rounds of golf after the price of restaurant meals decreases. The budget constraint BC' is parallel to Carlos's new budget constraint BC_2 but tangent to his original utility level U_1. The point of tangency between BC' and U_1, consumption bundle A', is the bundle Carlos would purchase if relative prices changed but his purchasing power did not. The change from bundle A to bundle A' is the substitution effect.

(b) The income effect is the change in quantities demanded due to the change in the consumer's purchasing power after the change in prices. When the price of restaurant meals decreases, Carlos can afford to purchase a larger bundle than he could before the price change. The change in the quantity of goods consumed from bundle A' to B represents the income effect.

(c) The total effect is the sum of the substitution and income effects. In this case, Carlos consumes 1 more round of golf and 2 more restaurant meals.

curve (and Carlos therefore gets the same utility from either bundle), it costs Carlos less to buy bundle A' at the new prices than to buy A. We know this because point A is located above BC', and so is infeasible if the budget constraint is BC'. (A', however, being on BC', is feasible with this constraint.)

Carlos therefore responds to the decline in restaurant meal prices by substituting away from rounds of golf and toward restaurant meals. By moving down along U_1, Carlos has effectively made himself better off; he is getting the same utility (he's still on U_1) for less money (bundle A is no longer feasible even though A' is).

Isolating the Income Effect

The income effect is the part of the total change in quantities consumed that is due to the change in Carlos's buying power after the price change. Why is there an income effect even though only the price of a good changed, not the actual number of dollars that Carlos had to spend? The key to understanding this outcome is to recognize that when the price of a good falls, Carlos becomes richer overall. The reduction in a good's price means there's a whole new set of bundles Carlos can now buy that he couldn't afford before because he has more money left over. At the old prices, everything above and to the right of BC_1 was infeasible; at the new prices, only bundles outside BC_2 are infeasible (see panel b of Figure 5.10).

This increase in buying power allows Carlos to achieve a higher level of utility than he did before. The income effect is the change in Carlos's choices driven by this shift in buying power while holding relative prices fixed at their new level. Finding these income-effect consumption changes is fairly easy once we've isolated the substitution effect. Remember that to find bundle A', we shifted the new budget constraint back in parallel until it was tangent to the original indifference curve. Doing that shift in reverse reflects the income effect exactly: It is the shift in consumption quantities (from bundle A' to B in panel b of Figure 5.10) due to Carlos's ability to reach a higher indifference curve (U_2 instead of U_1) while holding relative prices fixed (BC_2 and BC' have the same slope).

Therefore, the income effect of the decline in the restaurant meal price is illustrated by the move from the substitution-effect bundle (point A') to the final

make the grade

Computing substitution and income effects from a price change

There are three basic steps to analyzing substitution and income effects. We start with the consumer at a point of maximum utility (Point A) where his indifference curve is tangent to his budget constraint.

1. When prices change, draw the new budget constraint (a price change rotates the budget constraint, altering its slope). Then find the optimal quantity at the point (Point B) where this new budget constraint is tangent to a new indifference curve.

2. Draw a new line that is parallel to the new budget constraint from Step 1 and tangent to the origi-

nal indifference curve at Point A'. The movement along the original indifference curve from Point A (the original, pre-price change bundle) to this new tangency (point A') is the substitution effect. This movement shows how quantities change when relative prices change, even when purchasing power of income is constant.

3. The income effect of the price change is seen in the movement from point A' to point B. Here, relative prices are held constant (the budget lines are parallel) but the purchasing power of income changes.

bundle, point B. Because the decline in restaurant meal prices has, in effect, made Carlos wealthier, he can reach a higher indifference curve U_2 and consume more of both goods. Due to the income effect, his desired quantity of rounds of golf increases by 3 from 3 (at A') to 6 (at B) and his desired quantity of restaurant meals increases by 1 from 4 (at A') to 5 (at B).

In this particular example, the income effect led to increases in the quantities of both rounds of golf and restaurant meals. That means both goods are normal goods. In the next section, we show an example in which one of the goods is inferior.

The Total Effects

The total effects of the decline in restaurant meal prices are shown in panel c of Figure 5.10:

1. The quantity of rounds of golf Carlos desires rises by 1 round of golf from 5 in the initial bundle at point A to 6 in the final bundle at point B. (A decline of 2 caused by the substitution effect is counteracted by a rise of 3 caused by the income effect for a net gain of 1 round of golf.)

2. The quantity of restaurant meals Carlos desires rises by 2 restaurant meals, from 3 in the initial bundle A to 5 in the final bundle B. (A rise of 1 caused by the substitution effect plus a rise of 1 caused by the income effect.)

What Determines the Size of the Substitution and Income Effects?

The size (and as we'll see shortly, sometimes the direction) of the total effect of a price change depends on the relative sizes of its substitution and income effects. So it's important to understand what factors influence how large substitution and income effects are. We discuss some of the more important factors below.

The Size of the Substitution Effect   The size of the substitution effect depends on the degree of curvature of the indifference curves. This can be seen in Figure 5.11. The figure's two panels show the substitution effects of the same change in the relative prices of rounds of golf and restaurant meals for two different indifference curve shapes. (We know it's the same relative price change because the budget constraints experience the same change in slope in both panels.) When indifference curves are highly curved, as in panel a, the *MRS* changes quickly as one moves along them. This means any given price change won't change consumption choices much, because one doesn't need to move far along the indifference curve to change the *MRS* to match the new relative prices. Thus, the substitution effect is small. This is unsurprising, because we learned in Chapter 4 that indifference curves have more curvature in cases where the two goods are not highly substitutable. In panel a, the relative price change causes a substitution from A to A', and the consumer moves from purchasing a bundle with 2 restaurant meals and 2 rounds of golf to a bundle containing 3 restaurant meals and 1.25 rounds of golf.

When indifference curves are less curved, as in panel b, the *MRS* doesn't change much along the curve, so the same relative price change causes a much greater substitution effect. The substitution from A to A' in panel b involves much larger changes in golf and meals consumption than that caused by the same relative price change in panel a.[4] In panel b, the quantity of restaurant meals purchased grows to 4 (rather than 3) and the quantity of rounds of golf purchased falls to 0.75 (rather than 1.25). Again, we can relate this to what we learned about the curvature of indifference curves in Chapter 4. Indifference curves with little curvature indicate that the two goods are close substitutes. Thus, it makes sense that a price change will lead to a much greater adjustment in the quantities in the consumer's preferred bundle.

The Size of the Income Effect   The size of the income effect is related to the quantity of each good the consumer purchases before the price change. The more the consumer was spending on the good before the price change, the greater the fraction of the consumer's budget affected by the price change. A price drop of a good that the consumer is initially buying a lot of will leave him with more income left over than a price drop of a good with a small budget share (and a price increase

Figure 5.11   **The Shape of Indifference Curves Determines the Size of the Substitution Effect**

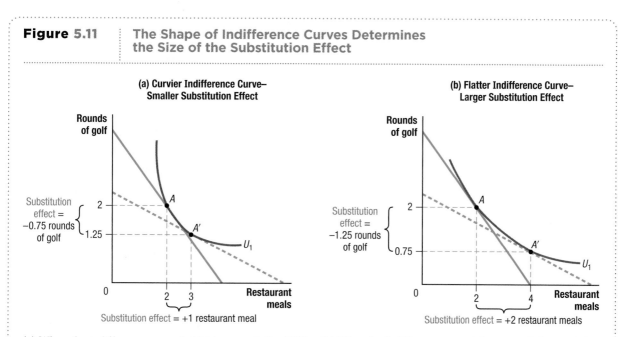

(a) When the indifference curve is highly curved, the *MRS* changes quickly along the curve. Thus, any given price change will not change consumption choices by much. Here, the original consumption bundle *A* is 2 restaurant meals and 2 rounds of golf. After a change in prices, the new optimal consumption bundle is *A'*, and the consumer now demands 1.25 rounds of golf and 3 restaurant meals.

(b) When the indifference curve is less curved, the *MRS* does not change quickly along the curve. Thus, any given price change affects consumption choices more strongly. At the new optimal consumption bundle *A'*, the consumer now demands 0.75 rounds of golf and 4 restaurant meals.

---

[4] This logic also explains why perfect substitutes, the special case we discussed in Chapter 4 with perfectly straight indifference curves, have the largest substitution effects. There, a small relative price change can lead the consumer to shift from one corner solution to another—that is, from consuming all of one good, *A*, and none of the other good, *B*, to consuming only *B* and no *A*. (To see this, suppose all a consumer cares about is the number of potato chips he consumes, and he views 3-ounce and 12-ounce bags of chips as perfect substitutes. If the price of 12-ounce bags is less than four times the price of 3-ounce bags, he will only buy 12-ounce bags. But if the price of 12-ounce bags is just a bit more than four times the price of 3-ounce bags, he will only buy 3-ounce bags.) It's also why perfect complements, with their right-angled indifference curves, have no substitution effect; they are always consumed in constant proportion regardless of relative prices.

will sap a greater share of the consumer's income). For example, consider the effects of a change in the prices of two goods homeowners deal with: electricity and pest control. A typical consumer spends much more of his budget on electricity. Therefore, a change in the price of electricity will affect his income and alter his purchases by more than a similar change in the price of pest control. (At the extreme, if the consumer currently purchases no pest control, a change in the price of pest control will have no income effect at all.)

5.3 figure it out

Pavlo eats cakes and pies. His income is $20, and when cakes and pies both cost $1, Pavlo consumes 4 cakes and 16 pies (point *A* on Figure A). But when the price of pies rises to $2, Pavlo consumes 12 cakes and 4 pies (point *B*).

a. Why does the budget constraint rotate as it does in response to the increase in the price of pies?

b. Trace the diagram on a piece of paper. On your diagram, separate the change in the consumption of pies into the substitution effect and the income effect. Which is larger?

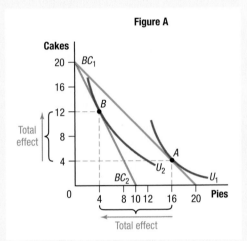

Figure A

c. Are pies a normal or inferior good? How do you know? Are cakes a normal or inferior good? How do you know?

Solution:

a. The price of cakes hasn't changed so Pavlo can still buy 20 cakes if he spends his $20 all on cakes (the *y*-intercept). However, at $2 per pie, Pavlo can now afford to buy only 10 pies instead of 20.

b. The substitution effect is measured by changing the ratio of the prices of the goods but holding utility constant (Figure B). Therefore, it must be measured along one indifference curve. To determine the substitution

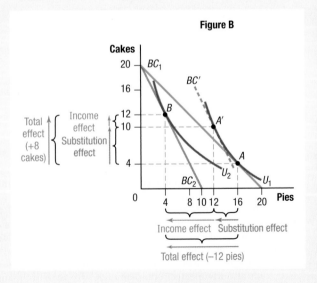

Figure B

effect of a price change in pies, you need to shift the post-price-change budget constraint BC_2 out until it is tangent to Pavlo's initial indifference curve U_1. The easiest way to do this is to draw a new budget line BC' that is parallel to the new budget constraint (thus changing the ratio of the cake and pie prices) but tangent to U_1 (thus holding utility constant). Label the point of tangency A'. Point A' is the bundle Pavlo would buy if the relative prices of cakes and pies changed as they did, but he experienced no change in purchasing power. When the price of pies rises, Pavlo would substitute away from buying pies and buy more cakes.

The income effect is the part of the total change in quantities consumed that is due to the change in Pavlo's buying power after the price of pies changes. This is reflected in the shift from point A' on budget constraint BC' to point B on budget constraint BC_2. (These budget constraints are parallel because the income effect is measured holding relative prices constant.)

For pies, the income effect is larger than the substitution effect. The substitution effect leads Pavlo to purchase 4 fewer pies (from 16 to 12), while the income effect further reduces his consumption by 8 pies (from 12 to 4).

c. Pies are a normal good because Pavlo purchases fewer pies (4 instead of 12) when the purchasing power of his income falls due to the price increase. However, cakes are an inferior good because the fall in purchasing power actually leads to a rise in cake consumption.

 ## application

Backward-bending labor supply and income effects in leisure

The relative sizes of substitution and income effects can create an interesting phenomenon sometimes observed in individuals' willingness to work. Think for a minute about leisure time (no jokes about skipping class). For just about everyone, leisure is a good, just like rounds of golf, restaurant meals, cakes, pies, electricity, pest control, and all the other examples we have worked with. Consuming more of it raises people's utility.

But if leisure is a good, what is its price? Well, consuming leisure involves using up time. The price of leisure is the value of what one could be doing with that time if she wasn't being leisurely. The main alternative use of leisure time is work. (Economists often consider any time a person spends not working as leisure, whether or not that individual is doing something we might think of as leisurely.) What's the value of working? Aside from any inherent pleasure someone might get from his job, its value is the income he earns from it—or more precisely, the utility he would obtain by consuming goods and services bought with his work income. What this means is that by choosing to take an extra unit of leisure, a person is giving up the income he could have earned had he worked during that period. That lost income equals his wage rate. So that is the price of leisure: a person's wage, and the goods and services that he could have bought with that income.

Based on these ideas, then, we can think of a person's willingness to work as involving a choice between consuming leisure and consuming the goods and services that can be bought with his work income. If we treat those other goods and services as a single good (call it "consumption," with its quantity measured in dollars), the relative price between leisure and consumption is the wage. If a person's wage is $30 per hour, for example, and she chooses to take one more hour of leisure (i.e., work one hour less), she is giving up $30 in consumption.

Economists call the choice of how much to work an individual's labor supply choice, because it involves how much time the person offers to supply to the labor market as a function of the wage level. We can describe the work-leisure choice using the set of tools we've been working with in this chapter: A person has a utility function (with its associated indifference curves) that depends on both the amount of leisure time she spends and the consumption she enjoys from her work income. She maximizes her utility subject to a budget constraint for which the relative price of leisure and consumption equals her wage rate. The only thing that's a bit different in this case is that we aren't taking her income—how much she has to spend on the two goods—as a fixed number, as we usually do. Instead, her income will depend on his choice of how much leisure to take and, therefore, how much work. That would complicate things some, but it turns out we don't need to deal with this explicitly to understand the basic economics underlying how changes in the wage rate affect someone's willingness to work.

Suppose a person's wage goes up. (Maybe she gets a raise.) One consequence of this is that leisure now has a higher price relative to consumption. Choosing to work one less hour has become more expensive in terms of forgone consumption. This change is going to tend to make her choose less leisure (more work) and consume more goods and services. This is a substitution effect applied to these two goods, leisure and consumption.

The substitution effect therefore tends to make people want to work more when their wage rises. (If the wage were to fall instead, it would make leisure relatively cheap and tend to make workers want to work less.) This makes a person's labor supply curve, which shows how much she is willing to work at any given wage level, slope up. That shape is how we usually think of supply curves for anything: The higher the price of the good (the wage here), the higher the quantity of the product (work hours) the producer (worker) is willing to supply.

But there's another effect of an increase in the wage that we hinted at before. For any given level of work—or equivalently, any given level of leisure time—it raises the person's income. This means there is also an income effect of a wage increase, not just a substitution effect. What impact will the income effect have on someone's leisure choice? For most people, leisure is a normal good; they consume more of it as their income rises. If this doesn't seem obvious to you, imagine that you win a $100 million lottery prize, but your job doesn't change. This scenario is a pure income effect: an increase in income without a change in the relative price of leisure, the wage. Would you take more vacation time and work less after winning the lottery? Most people would.

The bottom line of the income effect from an increase in the wage, then, is to make a person want to work less. This is exactly the opposite of the substitution effect. The net effect of a wage change on how much a person is willing to work is the difference between the two. In principle, at least, if the income effect is large enough, a person's labor supply curve will no longer have a positive slope. Instead, there will be a negative relationship between wages and how much an individual is willing to work. An example of this is shown in Figure 5.12. At wages below w^*, the substitution effect dominates; increases in the wage will make the person willing to work more. Above w^*, however, the income effect begins to dominate, and the

---

Figure 5.12 | **Backward-Bending Labor Supply**

When the income effect dominates, laborers choose to consume more leisure and work fewer hours, creating a backward-bending labor supply curve. At wages below w^*, the substitution effect is dominant, and the supply curve is upward-sloping. For any given increase in wages, laborers will choose to work more hours. At wages above w^*, the income effect dominates, and the supply curve is backward-bending. For any given increase in wages, laborers will choose to work fewer hours.

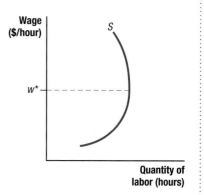

---

amount of work the person is willing to supply falls as wages rise. Economists call labor supply curves with this negative slope *backward-bending* labor supply curves.

Economists have found examples of backward-bending labor supply curves in certain markets. In one broad-ranging case, economic historian Dora Costa gathered surveys on the work habits of thousands of U.S. men working in the 1890s.[5] She found that low-wage workers spent more hours per day working than those earning high wages. Specifically, workers in the lowest wage decile (those being paid wages in the lowest 10% of all observed wage rates) averaged 11.1 hours of work per day, but those in the top wage decile (the top 10% of wage rates) only worked 8.9 hours per day. Workers in the highest wage group worked 5% fewer hours than those being paid the median wage, who in turn worked 14% less than those in the lowest wage group. In other words, the daily labor supply curve appeared to exhibit backward-bending patterns.

Interestingly, using other data, Costa also showed that the pattern had reversed itself by the 1990s. While workers in that period across the wage scale spent on average less time per day working than a century before, now those at the high end of the scale worked more than those at the low end. Those in the lowest wage decile averaged 7.6 hours per day, and those in the highest averaged 8.5 hours a day. Thus, over the course of the intervening century, the substitution effect became larger relative to the income effect, and eventually started to dominate in magnitude.

It's not clear what factors caused this shift. One possibility is that the overall decline in average daily hours for all workers (which may itself reflect an income effect that affected all workers as the country became wealthier over the twentieth century) meant workers had more free time during the day, reducing their willingness to pay on the margin for another hour of leisure when the wage rose. It might also be that higher-wage workers still want to take more leisure, but this shows up as an earlier retirement age in the later period rather than lower average daily hours. Thus, the income effect is still large in this case, but its effect on day-to-day work choice is smaller relative to its effect over a person's lifetime. ∎

---

[5] Dora Costa, "The Wage and the Length of the Work Day: From the 1890s to 1991," *Journal of Labor Economics* 18, no. 1 (2000): 156–181.

theory and data

Golfers' Backward-Bending Labor Supply Curves

Tiger Woods is perhaps the most recognizable face in professional golf. He's won 71 PGA tour events and picked up 14 Majors. He's lent his name to campaigns for Nike and Titleist—and taken home a cool $40 million and $20 million, respectively, for the work. But it's not just his athletic skill that separates him from the average American laborer: He's probably one of the few people facing wages on the backward-bending portion of his labor supply curve. In other words, as his wages increase, he actually decreases the number of tournaments in which he plays.

PGA rules allow each golfer to elect which and how many events to play in, meaning the athlete considers the labor–leisure tradeoff separately for each tournament event. With tournament payoffs in the millions of dollars for just four rounds of golf, you probably think it a no-brainer to play. Indeed, for most golfers, it is. Generally, around 100 players sign up for any given event. This doesn't even include the over 1,000 hopefuls who play in brutal qualifying rounds, vying for just 25 spots on the PGA Tour.

Given the opportunity, these hopefuls would gladly play every tournament, but as economists Otis Gilley and Marc Chopin discovered, players like Tiger Woods don't.* In a 2000 paper, Gilley and Chopin looked at how low- and middle-income PGA players in the 1990s responded to increases in their wages and compared this result to the effects of wage increases on high-income players. Whereas low-level players entered more events as their event winnings increased, golfers at the top of their game decreased their tournament play as their wages increased. Top golfers were actually operating on the backward-bending portion of their labor supply curve! In particular, for every $1,000 increase in expected per-event winnings, the number of tournaments entered in a season by high-income players decreases by 0.05 to 0.1. For these select players, the income effect dominated the substitution effect, and faced with the leisure–labor tradeoff, they elected to consume more leisure.

Workers in other fields—including many economists—often spend their leisure time on the golf course. But for a professional golfer, a day on the green is work, not leisure. So just what does a PGA player do on his day off? Gilley and Chopin found that married golfers took more days off than did single golfers. Drawing on their own experiences as family men, the two hard-working economists concluded that golfers must be taking off work to spend more quality time with their wives and kids. The example of Tiger Woods, however, shows that the predictions of economic theory don't always hold up in the real world.

* Otis W. Gilley and Marc C. Chopin, "Professional Golf: Labor or Leisure." *Managerial Finance* 26, no. 7 (2000): 33–45.

An Example of the Income Effect with an Inferior Good

Figure 5.13 provides another example of decomposing quantity changes into income and substitution effects. Here, however, one of the goods is inferior, at least over the price range explored in the example.

Figure 5.13 shows Judi's utility-maximizing bundles of steak and ramen noodles for two sets of prices. The optimal bundle at the original prices is shown at point A. The price of ramen noodles then drops, rotating the budget constraint outward. With the new budget constraint BC_2, Judi can reach a higher level of utility (U_2) and chooses bundle B to maximize her utility.

To decompose the shift from bundle A to bundle B into its substitution and income effects, we follow the steps we described in the previous section. To find the

---

Figure 5.13 : **A Fall in the Price of an Inferior Good**

When the price of ramen noodles decreases, Judi's budget constraint rotates outward from BC_1 to BC_2. The total effect of this price change is represented by the increase in quantities consumed from the original utility-maximizing bundle A to bundle B. Overall, Judi's consumption of both ramen noodles and steak increases.

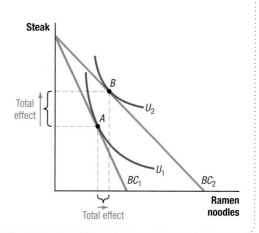

---

substitution effect, we shift in the budget constraint after the price change until it is tangent to the original indifference curve U_1. This is shown by the dashed line BC' in panel a of Figure 5.14. The point of tangency between BC' and U_1 is bundle A'.

Figure 5.14 : **Substitution and Income Effects for an Inferior Good**

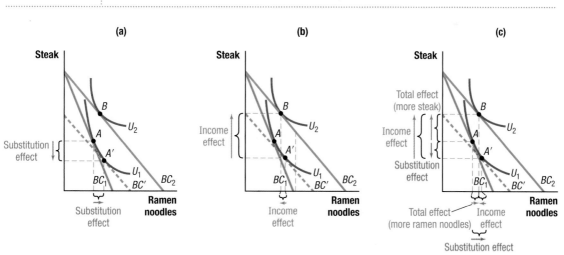

(a) BC' is the budget constraint parallel to BC_2, the budget constraint after the price change, and tangent to U_1, the consumer's utility before the price change. The point of tangency between BC' and U_1, consumption bundle A', is the bundle the consumer would purchase if relative prices changed but her purchasing power did not change. The change from bundle A to bundle A' is the substitution effect. As before, Judi chooses to purchase more of the good that has become relatively cheaper (ramen) and less of the other good (steak).

(b) The change in the quantity of goods consumed from bundle A' to B represents the income effect. Because ramen is an inferior good, the income effect leads Judi to decrease her consumption of ramen noodles, while her consumption of steak still increases.

(c) The change in the quantity of goods consumed from bundle A to B represents the total effect. Since the substitution effect increases the quantity demanded by more than the income effect decreases it, Judi consumes more ramen noodles in the new optimal bundle B than in the original optimal bundle A.

Because this is the bundle that provides the same utility as the original bundle *A* but with ramen noodles at their new, lower price, the shift from *A* to *A′* is the substitution effect. Just as before, the substitution effect leads Judi to consume more of the good that becomes relatively cheaper (ramen noodles) and less of the other good (steak).

The quantity shifts between bundle *A′* and bundle *B*, shown in panel b of Figure 5.14, are due to the income effect. As before, this is the change in quantities consumed due to the shift in the budget lines from *BC′* to *BC*₂: Judi's increase in buying power while holding relative prices constant. Notice that now the income effect actually *reduces* the quantity of ramen noodles consumed, even though the drop in their price makes Judi richer by expanding the set of bundles she can consume. This means ramen is an inferior good over this income range; an increase in income makes Judi want less of it.

Does the fact that a price drop leads to a reduction in the quantity consumed due to the income effect mean that the demand curve for ramen noodles slopes up? No, because the substitution effect increases the quantity demanded by more than the income effect decreases it. Thus, the quantity of ramen noodles demanded still rises when their price falls even though ramen noodles are an inferior good. We see this outcome in panel c of Figure 5.14 because the total effect on the quantity of ramen noodles is positive: The optimal bundle after ramen noodles become cheaper (bundle *B*) has a higher quantity of ramen than the optimal bundle before their price fell (bundle *A*). So the demand curve for ramen does indeed slope down. This is generally the case for inferior goods in the economy—while the income effect will make people want to consume less of them as their price falls, the substitution effect has a larger impact in the opposite direction, leading to a net increase in their consumption.

If the income effect is large enough, however, it is possible that a reduction in the price of an inferior good could actually lead to a net decrease in its consumption. A good that exhibits this trait is called a Giffen good.

Giffen Goods

Giffen good
A good for which price and quantity demanded are positively related.

Giffen goods are goods for which a fall in price leads the consumer to want *less* of the good. That is, an inverse relationship does not exist between price and quantity demanded and the demand curves of Giffen goods slope *up*! The more expensive a Giffen good is, the higher the quantity demanded.

This seemingly paradoxical effect arises because, for Giffen goods, the substitution effect of a price drop, which acts to increase the quantity a consumer demands of the good, is smaller than the reduction in the desired quantity caused by the income effect. Note that this means Giffen goods *must* be inferior goods. The income effect of a price drop can only reduce the desired quantity if the good is inferior; for all normal goods, the income effect of a price drop acts to increase the quantity demanded. Remember, though, that while all Giffen goods are inferior, not all inferior goods are Giffen goods—they are extremely rare. Typically, there will still be a net increase in the quantity demanded when price falls, just as we saw with the ramen noodles example before.

Figure 5.15 shows a graphical example. The two goods are potatoes and meat, and potatoes are the Giffen good. The utility-maximizing bundle at the original prices is shown at point *A*. When potatoes become cheaper, the budget constraint rotates out from *BC*₁ to *BC*₂ and the optimal bundle shifts from *A* to *B*. Notice that

---

Figure 5.15 : A Change in the Price of a Giffen Good

When the price of a Giffen good falls, the consumer consumes less of that good. Here, when the price of potatoes decreases, the consumer purchases fewer potatoes, as reflected in the change in quantities consumed from bundle A to bundle B.

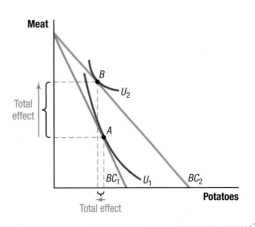

---

in this case, the quantity of potatoes consumed at point B is smaller than the quantity consumed at A even though potatoes are now cheaper.

The substitution and income effects underlying this change are shown in panels a and b of Figure 5.16. We isolate the substitution effect the same way as before: shifting the new budget constraint back in parallel until it is tangent to the original

---

Figure 5.16 : Substitution and Income Effects of a Giffen Good

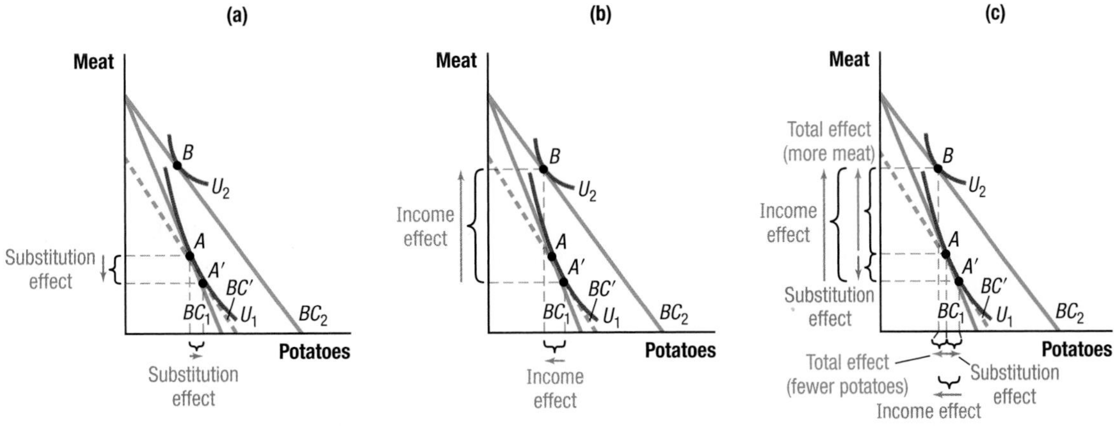

(a) The substitution effect is reflected in the change from consumption bundle A to bundle A'. The substitution effect leads the consumer to increase his consumption of potatoes while decreasing his consumption of steaks.

(b) The income effect is reflected in the change from consumption bundle A' to B. The income effect leads the consumer to decrease his consumption of potatoes while greatly increasing his consumption of steaks. Because this negative income effect on potatoes is of a larger magnitude than the positive substitution effect, the overall consumption of potatoes decreases, and potatoes are classified as a Giffen good.

(c) The total effect is reflected in the change from consumption bundle A to B. The negative income effect has a larger magnitude than the positive substitution effect, and the consumer thus consumes fewer potatoes in the new optimal bundle B than in the original optimal bundle A.

indifference curve. This creates changes in the quantity consumed corresponding to the shift from bundle *A* to bundle *A'*. As always, the substitution effect increases the quantity of the good that has become relatively cheaper, potatoes, and decreases the quantity of the relatively more expensive good, meat.

The income effect is the change in quantities associated with moving from bundle *A'* to *B*. Here, those changes are an increase in meat and a decrease in potatoes. Potatoes are therefore an inferior good, like ramen noodles in the previous example. But here, the negative income effect on potatoes has a larger magnitude than the positive substitution effect, so the net change in potatoes consumed from their drop in price is negative. This is what we saw in the shift from bundle *A* to *B*.

We discussed before that for a good to be a Giffen good, it must be an inferior good, and consumers' preferences for it must have an income effect that is larger in size than the substitution effect. When would we expect this? First, Giffen goods

make the grade

Simple rules to remember about income and substitution effects

It is easy to get tripped up when you're asked to identify income and substitution effects. First, remember to always start your analysis on the indifference curve associated with the consumption bundle *before* the price change. If you want to know why consumption changed going from one bundle to the other, you must start with the initial bundle. Next, keep in mind the key distinctions between the two effects listed in the table below.

SUBSTITUTION EFFECTS	INCOME EFFECTS
Involve comparisons of bundles that lie on the same indifference curve.	Involve comparisons of bundles that lie on two different indifference curves.
The direction of the effect on quantity consumed for a given change in the relative price of the good is unambiguous.	The direction of the effect on quantity consumed for a given change in the relative price of the good is ambiguous and depends on whether the good is normal or inferior.
If the good's relative price falls, the substitution effect causes the consumer to want more of it.	If the good is normal, then a fall in either its price or the price of the other good will cause the consumer to want more of it. (A drop in any price, even of another good, increases the effective income of the consumer.) If the good is inferior, then a price drop will cause the consumer to want less of it.
If the good's relative price rises, the substitution effect causes the consumer to want less of it.	If the good is normal, then a rise in either its price or the price of the other good will cause the consumer to want less of it. If the good is inferior, then a rise in either price will cause the consumer to want more of it.

Finally, remember that the total effect of a price change (for either good) on quantity consumed depends on the relative size of the substitution and income effects. If the price of one good falls, the quantities of both goods consumed may rise, or consumption of one good may rise and consumption of the other good may decline. But the quantities consumed of both goods cannot both decline, because this would mean the consumer would not be on her budget constraint.

would have to have limited substitutability with other goods; that is, the substitution effect would need to be small, and therefore the indifference curves would have to be highly curved. Second, the income effect needs to be large; this is more likely if, before the price change, a large fraction of the consumer's budget is spent on the good. This way, if the price of the good falls because the consumer is already spending most of her income on it, she's likely to feel a larger bump in effective buying power than if the good were only a small share of her budget.

 ## application

In search of Giffen goods

While Giffen goods are a theoretical possibility, they are extremely rare in practice. An often cited example of a Giffen good is the potato in Ireland during the Irish famine of the mid-1800s. The story is that the famine-driven increase in potato prices drastically reduced the purchasing power of Irish families' incomes, shrinking the bundles of goods that they could afford because potatoes already consumed a very large fraction of a typical Irish family's meager cash income. The resulting income effect led to a decrease in the demand for other foods such as meat that were normal goods for Irish families, and an increase in the demand for potatoes, an inferior good, that swamped any substitution effect. However, more recent reexaminations of the data by economists Gerald Dwyer and Cotton Lindsay, and later Sherwin Rosen in a separate study, found that even this canonical example proved not to be a Giffen good.[6]

These reexaminations differ in their explanations, but one common element between them is that the purported Giffen demand of Irish households just doesn't add up when confronted with what is known about the potato famine. Specifically, if potatoes were a Giffen good for individual households, then the total market demand curve for potatoes in Ireland should have also sloped up (quantity demanded would have increased as price increased). (We learn about how individuals' demand curves add up to total market demand later in this chapter.) But that would mean that the huge drop in supply due to the blight—about which there is no historical argument—should have led to lower potato prices. This is inconsistent with historical accounts reporting cases where no potatoes were available at any price, and when potatoes were available, they were sold at historically unprecedentedly high prices.

However, a recent policy experiment with extremely poor households in rural areas of China's Hunan province by Robert Jensen and Nolan Miller has produced what might be the most convincing documentation of a Giffen good to date.[7] Jensen and Miller subsidized the purchases of rice to a randomly selected set of such households, effectively lowering the price of rice that they faced. They then compared the change in rice consumption in the subsidized households to rice consumption in unsubsidized households of similar incomes and sizes.

Jensen and Miller found that the subsidy, even though it made rice cheaper, actually caused the households' rice consumption to fall. Rice was a Giffen good

---

[6] Gerald P. Dwyer, Jr. and Cotton M. Lindsay, "Robert Giffen and the Irish Potato," *American Economic Review* 74, no. 1 (1984): 188–192. Sherwin Rosen, "Potato Paradoxes." *Journal of Political Economy* 107, no. 6 (1999): S294–S313.

[7] Robert T. Jensen and Nolan H. Miller, "Giffen Behavior and Subsistence Consumption," *American Economic Review* 98, no. 4 (2008): 1553–1577.

for these households. (Jensen and Miller conducted a similar experiment subsidizing wheat purchases in Gansu province, and also found evidence that wheat was a Giffen good for some families, though the effect was weaker in this case.) The apparent mechanism behind this result is in accordance with our discussion above. Rice purchases took up so much of these households' incomes that the subsidy greatly increased the households' effective buying power. The resulting income effect made them want to consume less rice in place of other foods for the sake of dietary variety. This income effect was large enough to outweigh the substitution effect. To oversimplify things a little, the households were buying enough rice to meet their caloric needs and spending their leftover income on foods that added variety. When they could meet their caloric needs more cheaply, they used the now freed-up income to buy variety foods—enough to replace some of the calories formerly supplied by rice.

Interestingly, Jensen and Miller also found that while rice was a Giffen good for very poor households, it was not a Giffen good for the very poorest of the poor. Those extremely impoverished households basically ate only rice before the subsidy, and not really enough to meet their basic caloric needs at that. When rice became cheaper, they bought more in order to meet some basic level of healthy subsistence. Essentially, even the subsidy didn't raise their income enough to allow them to buy any other foods besides rice. ∎

5.4 The Impact of Changes in Another Good's Price: Substitutes and Complements

The two preceding sections showed how a change in the price of a good leads to a change in the quantity demanded of that same good. In this section, we look at the effects of a change in a good's price on the quantity demanded of *other* goods.

The approach to examining what happens when the price of another good changes is similar to that in the previous sections. We start with a fixed level of income, a set of indifference curves representing the consumer's preferences, and initial prices for the two goods. We compute the optimal consumption bundle under those conditions. Then, we vary one of the prices, holding everything else constant. The only difference is that as we vary that price, we focus on how the quantity demanded of the other good changes.

A Change in the Price of a Substitute Good

Figure 5.17 shows an example of the effects of a change in the price of a substitute good. Initially, the consumer's utility-maximizing bundle is 15 quarts of Pepsi and 5 quarts of Coke—the point labeled *A*. When the price of Pepsi doubles, the consumer can only afford a maximum of 10 quarts instead of 20. The maximum quantity of Coke the consumer can buy stays at 20 because the price of Coke has not changed. As a result, the budget constraint rotates inward to BC_2. In the new optimal consumption bundle *B*, the consumer demands more Coke (10 quarts) and less Pepsi (5 quarts).

As we learned in Chapter 2, when the quantity demanded of one good (Coke) rises when the price of another good (Pepsi) rises, the goods are **substitutes.** More generally, the quantity a consumer demands of a good moves in the same direction as the prices of its substitutes. The more alike two goods are, the more one can be substituted for the other, and the more responsive the increase in quantity demanded of one will be to price increases in the other. Pepsi and Coke are closer substitutes than milk and Coke, for instance.

substitute
A good that can be used in place of another good.

Figure 5.17   When the Price of a Substitute Rises, Demand Rises

At the original prices, the consumer consumes 15 quarts of Pepsi and 5 quarts of Coke at the utility-maximizing bundle *A*. When the price of Pepsi doubles, the consumer's budget constraint rotates inward from BC_1 to BC_2. At the new optimal consumption bundle *B*, the consumer decreases his consumption of Pepsi from 15 to 5 quarts and increases his consumption of Coke from 5 to 10 quarts. Since the quantity of Coke demanded rose while the price of Pepsi rose, Coke and Pepsi are considered substitutes.

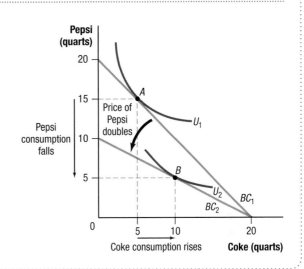

Changes in the prices of a good's substitutes lead to shifts in the good's demand curve. When a substitute for a good becomes more expensive, this raises the quantity demanded of that good at any given price level. As a result, the demand curve for the good shifts out (the demand for that good increases). When a good's substitutes become cheaper, the quantity demanded at any given price falls, and the good's demand curve shifts in.

When the quantity consumed of a good moves in the opposite direction of another good's price, they are **complements.** Complements are often goods that the consumer would use in tandem, like golf clubs and golf balls, pencils and paper, or home theater systems and installation services. Vanilla ice cream and hot fudge, for example, are complementary goods. Figure 5.18 shows how an increase in

complement
A good that is purchased and used in combination with another good.

Figure 5.18   When the Price of a Complement Rises, Demand Falls

At the original prices, the consumer consumes 20 gallons of ice cream and 30 quarts of hot fudge at the utility-maximizing bundle *A*. When the price of ice cream increases, the consumer's budget constraint rotates inward from BC_1 to BC_2. At the new optimal consumption bundle *B*, the consumer decreases his consumption of ice cream from 20 to 15 gallons and likewise decreases his consumption of hot fudge from 30 to 20 quarts. Since the quantities demanded of both ice cream and hot fudge decreased with an increase in price of only one of those goods, ice cream and hot fudge are considered complements.

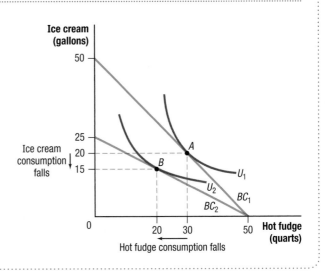

Figure 5.19 | **Changes in the Prices of Substitutes or Complements Shift the Demand Curve**

When the price of a substitute good rises or the price of a complement falls, the demand curve for good *X* shifts out. When the price of a substitute good falls or the price of a complement rises, the demand curve for good *X* shifts in.

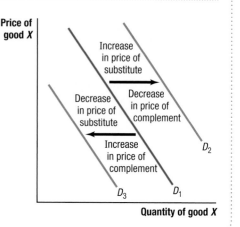

---

ice cream's price leads to a decrease in the quantity demanded of hot fudge. The higher ice cream price causes the budget constraint to rotate in, shifting the utility-maximizing bundle from *A* (30 quarts of hot fudge and 20 gallons of vanilla ice cream) to *B* (20 quarts of hot fudge and 15 gallons of vanilla ice cream). The quantity demanded of both goods falls; an increase in the price of ice cream not only causes the consumer to demand less ice cream (this is the own-price effect we've studied so far in this chapter), but less hot fudge, the complementary good, as well.

When the price of a complement of a good increases, the quantity demanded of that good at every price decreases and its demand curve shifts in. If the price of a complement of a good falls, the quantity demanded of that good rises at all prices and the demand curve shifts out. Changes in the price of a complementary good *shift* the demand curve for the other good. Changes in a good's own price cause a *move along* the same demand curve.

The effects of price changes in substitute and complementary goods on demand are summarized in Figure 5.19.

Indifference Curve Shapes, Revisited

As we touched on in Chapter 4, the shape of indifference curves is related to whether two goods are substitutes or complements. The more curved the indifference curve, the less substitutable (or, equivalently, the more complementary) are the goods.

In Section 5.3, we learned that the size of the substitution effect from a change in a good's *own* price was larger for goods with less-curved indifference curves (see Figure 5.11). The logic behind this is that, because the marginal rate of substitution (*MRS*) doesn't change much along straighter indifference curves, a given relative price change will cause the consumer to move a longer distance along his indifference curve to equate his *MRS* to the new price ratio. This logic holds true when it comes to the effects of changes in *other* goods' prices. All that matters to the substitution effect are the *relative* prices; whether it's Good *A*'s or Good *B*'s price that changes doesn't matter. Therefore, an increase (decrease) in a good's price will create a larger movement toward (away from) a substitute good when the indifference curves between the goods are less curved.

application

Movies in a theater and at home—substitutes or complements?

If you own a movie theater company, one of the most important issues you face for the long-run viability of your firm is whether watching a movie on a home theater system and seeing a film in your movie-plex are substitutes or complements. Improvements in home electronics like large-screen, high-definition TVs, Blu-ray disc players, downloadable digital movies, and compact surround sound audio systems have greatly reduced the price of having a high-quality movie-watching experience at home. A middle-class family today can buy a home theater system that a multi-millionaire could have only dreamed about a few decades ago. If movies at home are a substitute good for movies in a theater, this price reduction will reduce the number of people visiting their local movie-plex. This change will surely lead to some theaters going out of business sooner or later. If movies at home are instead a complement, theater-going will increase and bring new-found growth to the movie exhibition business.

Either case is plausible. On one hand, there is clear scope for substitution. If home electronics can better replicate the theater experience, people could find it less costly (either in terms of direct expenditures, convenience, or both) to watch a movie at home. On the other hand, if people become more interested in films in general because they now watch more at home—perhaps they develop a movie habit, or appreciate the art of film, or get caught up in following their favorite actors or watching their favorite movie again and again—then they might be more likely to see movies in theaters than they were before, particularly if theaters offer some component of the movie-watching experience that you can't get at home (audiences to laugh or be scared with, really big screens, super-greasy popcorn, etc.).

The data are not yet clear about the answer to this question. Figure 5.20 shows the trends in total U.S. box office receipts (inflation adjusted to 2010 dollars) and the

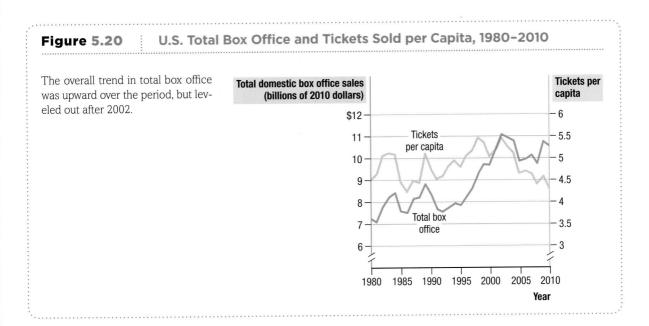

Figure 5.20   U.S. Total Box Office and Tickets Sold per Capita, 1980–2010

The overall trend in total box office was upward over the period, but leveled out after 2002.

number of tickets sold per capita since 1980.[8] The overall trend in total box office has been upward over the period, but it topped out in 2002 after a run-up in the 1990s. The decline between 2002 and 2010 was just under 5%, though this is mitigated some by the fact that 2009 and 2010 were good years. The data on the number of tickets sold per capita—you can think of this as the average number of times a person goes to see a movie during the year—are more volatile, but show a similar pattern of a run-up in the 1990s and then a drop after 2002. The drop is larger relative to that for the total box office, though, falling about 20% from 5.5 to 4.3 movies a year by 2010.

The decrease in theater-going after 2002 suggests that watching movies at home is a substitute, because it coincides with the period of the increased availability of big-screen HDTV and disc players. However, the data are fairly noisy: That is, there is a large amount of variation across the years, so it's not completely clear if these are long-run trends or just temporary blips due to the quality of movies or changes in the prices of other entertainment goods such as video game systems. Furthermore, the widespread diffusion of VCRs, DVD players, and early surround-sound systems in the 1980s and 1990s didn't scar the movie exhibition industry because revenues and tickets per capita both rose, indicating that they may have been complements to watching films in a theater.

So perhaps movie-plex owners will be helped by cheap, high-quality home theater systems. Then again, in 1946, before TVs were in most people's homes, over 4 billion tickets were sold in the United States when the population was about 140 million (compared to over 310 million today). That's an average of over 28 movies a year per person! By 1956 attendance was half that. It seems quite likely that movie houses and TVs were substitutes then. Time will tell whether the same holds for movie houses and home theaters. ■

5.5 Combining Individual Demand Curves to Obtain the Market Demand Curve

When studying consumer demand, we're often more interested in the combined demand of all consumers, rather than any one consumer's demand. For instance, if you are a company trying to figure out how many scooters to make and what to charge for them, what ultimately matters is the overall market demand for scooters.[9] Similarly, a government that wants to figure out how much revenue a tax or tariff on tires will raise needs to look at the market demand for tires.

The market demand for a good is the sum of all the individual demand curves for it. That is, the market quantity demanded for a good at a particular price is the sum of every individual consumer's quantity demanded at that price.

Figure 5.21 shows graphically how this adding up works. Suppose you and your cousin are the only two consumers in the market for Razor scooters. The total market demand curve is obtained by summing horizontally each of the individual demand curves. For instance, at a price of $40, you and your cousin each want 3 scooters, so the combined market quantity demanded is 6 scooters. When the price is $20, you want 4 scooters and your cousin wants 8, for a market quantity demanded of

---

[8] The data in this application are from www.boxofficemojo.com.

[9] An exception to this rule would be when the firm can charge different prices to different consumers (what economists call *price discrimination*). In that case, which we explore in Chapter 10, the firm can take advantage of individual consumers' demand curves rather than just the overall market demand. By charging different prices to different consumers depending on their individual demand, the firm can make higher profits.

Figure 5.21 : The Market Demand Curve

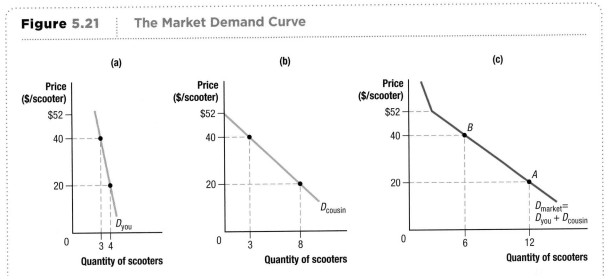

(a) Your market demand curve D_{you} shows the number of scooters you would demand at each price. At a price of $40 per scooter, you demand 3 scooters; at $20 per scooter, you demand 4 scooters.

(b) Your cousin's market demand curve D_{cousin} shows that he is more sensitive to price changes in scooters than you are. At a price of $40 per scooter, he similarly demands 3 scooters, but when the price of a scooter is $20, he demands 8 scooters.

(c) In a market consisting only of you and your cousin, the total market demand curve D_{market} is the sum of your de-

mand curve D_{you} and your cousin's demand curve D_{cousin}. At a price of $40 per scooter, you and your cousin each demand 3 scooters, summing to 6 scooters on D_{market}. When scooters cost $20 each, you demand 4 scooters and your cousin demands 8 scooters, summing to 12 scooters on D_{market}. At prices above $52, your cousin's quantity demanded is zero, so D_{market} overlaps with D_{you}, and therefore D_{market} is kinked at a price of $52. Market demand will always be flatter and to the right of the individual demand curves.

12 scooters. Adding up the individual consumers' quantities demanded at all possible prices gives the market demand curve.

The Market Demand Curve

There are a few things to notice about market demand curves. First, a market demand curve will always be to the right of any individual demand curve, because all consumers combined must consume at least as much of a good at a given price as any single consumer does. For a similar reason, the slope of the market demand curve must also be as flat as or flatter than any of the individual demand curves. That is, for a given change in price, the change in quantity demanded for the market as a whole must be at least as great as the change in quantity demanded by any individual consumer.[10] Finally, if the price is so high that only one consumer wants any of the good, the individual demand curve for that consumer will lie directly on top of the market demand curve at that price. At that point, the consumer *is* the market.

---

[10] Even though the *slope* of the market demand curve is always flatter than that of individual demand curves, it doesn't necessarily imply that the *elasticity* of the market demand curve is higher than that of individual demand curves (though this is often the case). This is because the elasticity doesn't just depend on the slope, but also on the level of demand. The percentage change in prices (the denominator in the elasticity equation) will be the same for both individuals and the market. While the change in quantity will be smaller for individuals, the level of demand will be lower too. If the level is small enough, the percentage change in quantities for the individual can be large enough to make individual demand as or more elastic than market demand.

Using Algebra to Move from Individual to Market Demand

We can move from individual to market demand algebraically as well as graphically. The formulas for the two demand curves in Figure 5.21 are

$$Q_{you} = 5 - 0.05P$$

$$Q_{cousin} = 13 - 0.25P$$

To find the market demand for the tickets, we start by adding up the two individual demand curves:

$$Q_{market} = Q_{you} + Q_{cousin} = (5 - 0.05P) + (13 - 0.25P)$$

$$Q_{market} = 18 - 0.3P$$

If we plug in the prices from Figure 5.21, they match the quantities in the figure as long as we are on the part of the curve labeled A in Figure 5.21 where both quantities demanded are above zero. According to the equation, market demand when $P = 40$ is $Q_{market} = 6$, which is what the figure shows, and when $P = 20$, $Q_{market} = 12$, just as on the figure.

  We're not quite done yet, though. The prices at which you and your cousin will consume no scooters—the demand choke prices—are different. Yours is $100; your cousin's is $52. (You can check this by plugging these prices into the demand curves and verifying that the quantities demanded equal zero.) That means at prices above $52, the market demand is only *your* demand because your cousin's quantity demanded is zero. There is no negative demand allowed. This isn't accounted for when we add together the two demand curves above, however, because at prices above $52, the part of the market demand curve coming from the formula for Q_{cousin} is less than zero. Therefore, market demand is your demand, $Q = 5 - 0.05P$, for prices between $52 and $100 (quantity demanded is zero at prices higher than $100), and is $Q = 18 - 0.3P$ (yours plus your cousin's) for prices below $52. That is, the market demand has a kink at $P = 52$.

make the grade

Adding demand curves horizontally, not vertically

Moving from individual demand curves to market demand is conceptually fairly simple. There's just one thing you have to be careful about. Market demand curves are derived by adding *quantities* of individual demand curves, not prices. That is, individual demands are graphically added horizontally, not vertically.

When you add horizontally, you are summing up all the individual quantities demanded, holding price fixed. This is exactly what you want to do because market demand is the total quantity demanded at any given price. If you add individual demand curves vertically, however, you are holding quantities demanded fixed while adding up the prices. That's a very different conceptual exercise and one that, in this case at least, doesn't really make any sense.

Likewise, if you are combining individual demand curves algebraically rather than graphically, make sure you've written out the individual demand curves as quantities demanded as a function of price. When you add those equations, you'll just be adding the quantities, which is again what you want to do. If you instead try to add equations where prices are a function of quantities (economists call these "inverse demand curves"), again you'll be doing the very different exercise of adding up prices across individuals while holding the quantities fixed.

5.4 figure it out

Suppose that at a rural gas station in Toby Acres, there are only two customers, Johnny (who drives a 4X4 pickup) and Olivia (who drives a Prius). Johnny's demand for gasoline is $Q_J = 32 - 8P$, while Olivia's demand is $Q_O = 20 - 4P$, where Q is measured in gallons and P is the price per gallon.

a. Solve for the market demand equation for gasoline at Toby Acres.

b. Draw a diagram showing the market demand curve for gasoline at Toby Acres.

Solution:

a. The market demand curve is the horizontal sum of the buyers' demand curves. Remember that summing horizontally means to add up quantities demanded at each price. This means that we can get the market demand by adding Q_J and Q_O:

$$Q_{market} = Q_J + Q_O$$
$$= (32 - 8P) + (20 - 4P)$$
$$= 52 - 12P$$

But there is more to the story than solving for the summation of the two demand curves. Johnny is not willing to buy any gas if the price is greater than or equal to $4 per gallon because that is his demand choke price:

$$Q_J = 32 - 8P$$
$$0 = 32 - 8P$$
$$8P = 32$$
$$P = 4$$

So, once the price hits $4, only Olivia will be in the market. Her demand choke price is $5:

$$Q_O = 20 - 4P$$
$$0 = 20 - 4P$$
$$4P = 20$$
$$P = 5$$

Thus, as long as the price is below $4 per gallon, the market demand for gasoline is the horizontal sum of the two buyers' demand curves. Between a price of $4 and $5, the market demand is simply the same as Olivia's demand. At a price greater than or equal to $5, quantity demanded is zero.

b. The figure here shows the market demand for gasoline in Toby Acres. Notice that the market demand curve is kinked as a result of the buyers' different choke prices. Segment A is the section of demand below the price of $4 and is the horizontal summation of Johnny's and Olivia's demand for gasoline.

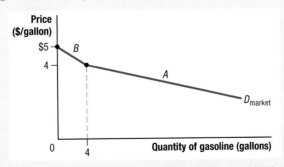

Segment B is the segment of market demand where Olivia is the only buyer (since the price is above Johnny's demand choke price). At a price of $5 or above, quantity demanded is zero.

5.6 Conclusion

In this chapter, we used the consumer choice model of Chapter 4 to see where demand curves come from and what factors shift them. We studied how changes in various factors that drive consumer demand for a good—their income, the good's price, and the prices of other goods—affect the consumer's utility-maximizing bundle and, through this, the demand curve.

We decomposed the response of a consumer's choices to a price change in a good into two components: the substitution effect and the income effect. The substitution effect reflects changes in quantities consumed due to the new relative prices of goods after the price change. The income effect reflects the fact that a price change affects a consumer's buying power, and this in turn changes the consumer's optimal consumption bundle.

We also saw how individuals' demand curves for a good are added up to create the market demand curve for that good.

This chapter ends our examination of the factors that determine consumer demand. In the next chapter, we move on to producer behavior and the supply side of markets.

Summary

1. Shifts in income holding prices constant are reflected in parallel shifts in the budget constraint and affect a consumer's demand curve. An Engel curve shows the relationship between income and the quantity of a good demanded. Whether an increase in income raises or reduces the quantity demanded of a good depends on the type of good. Normal goods are those for which demand increases with income. Inferior goods are those for which demand decreases with income. Within normal goods, goods with an income elasticity between zero and 1 (those whose share of expenditure rises more slowly than income rises) are called necessity goods. Goods with an income elasticity greater than 1 (those whose share of expenditure grows faster than income) are called luxury goods.

2. The way in which changes in the price of a good affect the quantity demanded of that good is what creates the shape of the demand curve. We construct a consumer's demand curve by examining what happens to a consumer's utility-maximizing bundle as the price of one good changes, holding the price of the other good, income, and preferences fixed. Changes in income, holding preferences and prices constant, can shift the demand curve. Changes in preferences, holding income and prices constant, can shift the demand curve.

3. The total effect on the quantity demanded of a good in response to a change in its own price can be broken down into two components.

   The substitution effect causes the consumer to shift toward the good that becomes relatively cheaper and away from the good that becomes relatively more expensive. This shows up as a movement along the consumer's initial indifference curve, driven by the change in relative prices.

   The income effect occurs because a change in the price of a good changes the purchasing power of the consumer; a price drop increases purchasing power and expands the set of bundles a consumer may choose from, while a rise in price decreases purchasing power and reduces the consumer's options. The income effect shows up as a move to a new indifference curve, reflecting a change in utility for the consumer. The direction of the income effect on quantity demanded depends on whether the good is normal (where demand rises when income rises) or inferior (demand falls when income rises). If the income effect is large enough for inferior goods, it is theoretically possible for the quantity demanded of a good to rise when its price rises. However, these types of goods, called Giffen goods, are exceedingly rare in the real world.

4. Changes in the prices of other goods shift the demand curve for a good. Which ways these

cross-price effects shift demand depends on the nature of the relationship between the goods. Goods are substitutes if a price increase in one leads to an increase in demand of the other, due to consumers switching away from the now more expensive good and toward the substitute. Goods are complements if an increase in one's price causes demand of the other to fall. Com-

plements are goods that are often consumed together.

5. Individuals' demand curves are aggregated to get total market demand. Market demand at a given price is the sum of all individual demands at that same price. Another way of saying this is that market demand is the horizontal (i.e., quantity) sum of individual demands.

Review Questions

1. Define the income effect. What variables do we hold constant in order to isolate the income effect?
2. What are the differences between normal goods, inferior goods, and luxury goods?
3. Both the income expansion path and the Engel curve show the effect of income on consumption choices. When might you choose to use the income expansion path? When might the Engel curve be more useful?
4. Describe how we can derive a consumer's demand curve from his indifference curves. Why would we expect the demand curve to slope downward?
5. Name at least three factors that can shift an individual's demand curve for pizza. Also describe the effect each factor has on demand (e.g., does it rise or fall?).
6. Define the substitution effect. How does it relate to the income effect?

7. Describe how to decompose the consumer's response to price changes into the substitution and income effects.
8. How do income and substitution effects differ between normal and inferior goods?
9. What is a Giffen good?
10. What are complements and substitutes?
11. When the cross-price elasticity of demand is positive, are the two goods complements or substitutes? What type of goods have a negative cross-price elasticity?
12. What can the shape of the indifference curve tell us about two goods?
13. How does the market demand relate to individual demand curves?
14. Why will a market demand curve always be at least as flat as a given individual demand curve?

Problems

1. A principles of microeconomics instructor regularly asks her class to give an example of an inferior good. "No matter how poor we might be," the students tell her, "ramen noodles are an inferior good." Explain why the students must be wrong in their reasoning.
2. Can you tell whether a good is normal or inferior by looking at the shape of a single indifference curve? Explain your answer.
3. Andrew has an income of $30 he spends on cupcakes and cakes. The price of a cupcake is $5. Suppose that Andrew has the following preferences depicted on the right:
   a. With this in mind, draw Andrew's demand curve for cake.
   b. When the price of cake changes, which effect is stronger, the substitution effect or the income effect? Give your answer for every price change depicted in the figure.

c. If Andrew's preferences shifted toward not distinguishing between cake and cupcakes (i.e., if they became closer substitutes), all his indifference curves would become flatter. How would Andrew's demand curve for cake change?

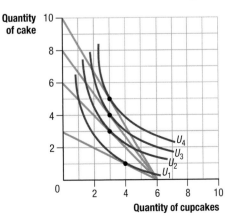

4. Suppose that, holding prices constant, Alice has preferences over the number of books she purchases that look like:

Income (thousands of dollars)	Optimal number of books purchased
5	5
10	6
15	20
20	25
25	26
30	10
35	9
40	8
45	7
50	6

  a. Draw a smooth approximation of Alice's Engle curve for books, indicating the ranges over which books are inferior goods and over which they are normal goods.
  b. A luxury good is a good that has an income elasticity greater than 1. Give the ranges in which books are luxury goods for Alice.

5. Suppose that Sonya faces an increase in the price of pasta, as depicted below, moving her from an optimum bundle of rice and pasta at A to an optimal bundle at B.
  a. Trace a copy of this diagram. Graphically depict the substitution and income effect.
  b. Which effect is strongest? How can you tell?

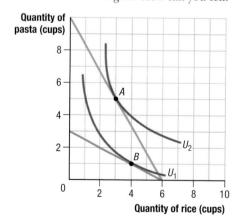

6. Kim's utility function is given by $U = 5X + 2Y$, where $MU_X = 5$ and $MU_Y = 2$.
  a. Suppose that at the prices P_X and P_Y of good X and good Y, respectively, Kim is consuming (optimally) some positive amount of good X and some positive amount of good Y. What is the price of good X in terms of the price of good Y?
  b. How will her consumption change if P_X doubles, while P_Y does not change?

7. You may have noticed that the market demand curve is always flatter than any individual demand curve. Is market price elasticity of demand also always lower than individual price elasticity of demand? Why or why not?

8. Indicate whether the following statements are true, false, or uncertain. If false or uncertain, explain why.
  a. The price of a watch increases by 10%, and you spend a larger fraction of your income on it. The watch is a Giffen good.
  b. Due to a flood, corn prices and soybean prices increase. If corn and soybeans are substitutes, the quantity of corn demanded falls.
  c. Goods 1 and 2 are substitutes, and goods 2 and 3 are substitutes. This must mean that goods 1 and 3 are substitutes.

9. Suppose that Grover consumes two goods, cookies and milk. Grover's income expansion path is shown in the diagram below. Use the information in the diagram to explain whether each of the statements below is true or false. Provide an explanation for each answer.
  a. At low levels of income, both cookies and milk are normal goods for Grover.
  b. As Grover's income grows, eventually cookies become an inferior good.
  c. Draw, intuitively, the Engel curve for Grover's consumption of milk at various incomes.
  d. Draw, intuitively, the Engel curve for Grover's consumption of cookies at various incomes.

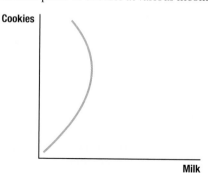

10. Josie gets great pleasure from eating flan. Her preferences for flan and tofu are given in the graph below:

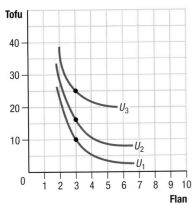

Suppose that Josie's income is $40, and that tofu costs $1.

a. Draw budget constraints for Josie given three different prices for flan: $5, $8, and $10.
b. Find the optimal consumption of flan at each of those prices.
c. Draw Josie's price-consumption curve. What shape does it have?
d. What will Josie's demand curve for flan look like? Describe it in terms of the elasticity of demand.
e. What can you say about the size of the income and substitution effects of a change in the price of flan?

11. Consider the following graph, which illustrates Tyler's preferences for DVD rentals and in-theater movie tickets:

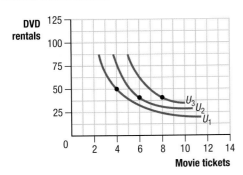

Suppose that DVD rentals always cost $1, and that Tyler's income is $100 per week.

a. If the price of a movie ticket is $10, draw Tyler's budget line. Be very careful to draw to scale. How many movies does he see in the theater?

b. In another graph, plot a point that reflects how many movies Tyler sees in the theater at a price of $10.
c. The movie theater changes the price of tickets to $12.50. Repeat your work in (a) and (b) using this new price.
d. Tyler's mother gives him a discount card that allows him to purchase movie tickets for $7.50. Repeat your work in (a) and (b) using this new price.
e. Connect the dots in your second graph to complete Tyler's demand curve for movie tickets.

12. Consider the following three graphs, which illustrate the preferences of three consumers (Bob, Carol, and Ted) regarding two goods, apples and peaches. Each consumer has an income of $30, and each consumer pays $2 for apples and $3 for peaches.

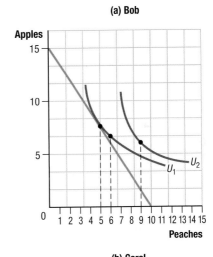

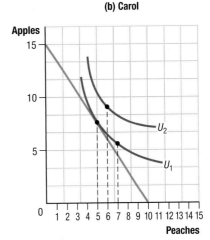

(c) Ted

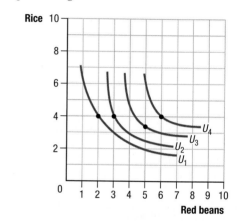

a. Suppose that the price of peaches falls to $2. Draw a new budget line for each consumer and find the new optimal bundle of apples and peaches each would buy. How does the new quantity of peaches compare to the original quantity? Indicate the change in the first column of the table below (an increase of one unit might be denoted as a +1).

b. For each consumer, determine the substitution effect of the price change by drawing a hypothetical budget line with the same slope as your new budget line, but just tangent to the consumer's original indifference curve. How much of a change in peach consumption does the substitution effect account for? Indicate that change in the first column of the table below.

c. Now, add in the income effect. Compare each consumer's peach consumption in (b) to his or her final peach consumption in (a). Indicate the difference in column 3 of the table below. Double-check your work to ensure that the last two columns add up to the number in the first column.

d. Do Bob, Carol, and Ted consider peaches normal, inferior, or income-inelastic?

	Total Effect of Price Change	Substitution Effect of Price Change	Income Effect of Price Change
Bob			
Carol			
Ted			

13. Carmen's preferences are such that she is always indifferent between watching two movies or seeing one basketball game.
    a. What must Carmen's indifference curves look like?
    b. Suppose that Carmen has an income of $90. If a movie costs $10 and a basketball game costs $18, what will Carmen's optimal consumption bundle be?

14. Consider the following diagram, which illustrates Gaston's preferences for red beans and rice. Gaston has an income of $20. Rice costs $2 per serving.

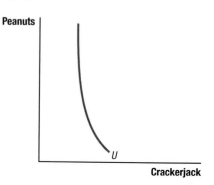

a. Derive Gaston's demand for red beans. Use prices of $2 and $4 in your analysis. Graph your results, and connect the points you plotted to yield Gaston's demand for red beans.
b. Suppose that the price of rice increases to $3. Again, derive Gaston's demand for red beans using the same prices you used in part (a).
c. Does Gaston's demand for red beans increase or decrease as a result of the increase in the price of rice?
d. Does your answer to (c) indicate that red beans and rice are substitutes or complements?

15. Consider Harry's indifference curve indicated in the graph below:

a. True or False (and explain): Peanuts and Crackerjack are clearly complements.

b. True or False (and explain): Peanuts and Crackerjack are clearly both normal goods.

16. True or False: If pizza and calzones are substitutes, then the substitution effect of a price change will be in a different direction than if pizza and calzones are complements. Explain, using a diagram.

17. Armen lives in Washington State, where grapes are grown. Armen's twin Allen lives in New York, where grapes must be trucked in from Washington at a fixed cost of $0.20 per pound of grapes. Armen and Allen have identical tastes, but Armen tends to purchase lower-quality grapes and Allen tends to purchase higher quality grapes. Use indifference curve analysis to explain this oddity.

18. Mitch cares only about how much he can write. Because a pen will write 7 miles of text and a pencil will write 35 miles of text, Mitch considers them perfect 5-to-1 substitutes. If the price of pens is given by P_{pen} and the price of pencils is given by P_{pencil}, and if Mitch's income is given by Y, use indifference curve analysis to *derive* the demand curve for pencils.

19. Brady, who has ordinary-shaped indifference curves, buys 16 ounces of salt each year. Even when the price of salt doubles, Brady continues to purchase exactly 16 ounces.

a. True or False (and explain): Salt is neither inferior nor normal to Brady.

b. What is Brady's price elasticity of demand for salt?

c. What is Brady's income elasticity of demand for salt?

d. What can we say about the substitution and income effects of a change in the price of salt?

20. At a price of $3 per gallon, Yoshi (an average buyer) purchases 200 gallons of gasoline each year. The government proposes imposing a $0.50 tax on each gallon of gas, and then compensating consumers for the price increase by mailing each taxpayer a check for $100.

a. What will happen to Yoshi's consumption of gas? Show, using an indifference curve diagram with gasoline on the horizontal axis and a composite good (price = $1) on the vertical axis.

b. Will Yoshi be better off, worse off, or indifferent to the change? Explain, using your diagram.

c. In terms of revenue, will the government be better off, worse off, or indifferent to the proposal? Explain.